By His Own Words

Robert Lathan, Jr.
Renowned Editor and Gentleman

by S. Robert Lathan, Jr. MD

Published by
WINGS PUBLISHERS, LLC
Boca Grande, Florida

Text ©2021 by S.Robert Lathan, Jr. MD
Publisher and Editor Ginger Watkins
Design and Layout by Nicola Simmonds Carmack

All right reserved. No part of this publication may be reproduced, stored in a retrieval system, or transmitted in any form or by any means – except for brief quotations in previews and reviews, without permission of the author.

Manufactured in the United States of America

10 9 8 7 6 5 4 3 2 1
First Edition

ISBN
978-1-930897-28-1

Dedication

To the newspaper editors and writers who daily

"Uniformly recognized their responsibility to the public"

Robert Lathan, Jr.
Newspaper Editor for over 30 years

Acknowledgements

I want to thank the librarians and archivists who have graciously answered my questions and searched for materials to enhance the knowledge of the Lathan family.

I thank my publisher, Ginger Watkins who patiently waded through all the materials, organized them, and assisted in editing my thoughts into this story of Robert Lathan, Jr. as she has done previously on four other books. I have certainly received her extraordinary service for many years.

I thank John Rivers of Charleston, SC who helped me on my first book, History of South Carolina and on this book by sending me the book Outspoken, 150 years of News and Courier to assist me in my research on Robert Lathan, Jr.

I thank my wife Millie who has most of all patiently stood by my side for over 56 years and has encouraged all of my endeavors. Her great skill, judgment, creativity, and tact has served me all of this time.

Preface

The saga of the Lathans started between the 17th and 18th centuries when many people of Scotland took refuge in Northern Ireland. Among those were the Lathans, then called "Leathen." The earliest known ancestral Lathan to migrate from Melrose, Scotland to Ballymena in County Antrim of Northern Ireland was James Lathan. He married Peggy Waugh and had five sons and two daughters.

In 1788, three of James' sons, emigrated from Ireland to the United States. Robert Lathan and his wife Nancy Martin and their five children arrived in Charleston, SC and later settled in Fairfield County. Not long after arriving, he purchased land from the county and sold 188 acres to each of his three sons.

Robert Lathan's son Samuel Martin Lathan, born in 1797, owned land between Blackstock, SC and White Oak, SC on the Big Wateree Creek flowing into the Catawba River. He purchased another 188 acres from his father for $500, and later bought the adjacent acreage from his two brothers. Samuel and his wife had eleven children.

One of Samuel Martin Lathan's sons was Robert, a Presbyterian minister and an educator at Erskine College who wrote several books. Another younger son, Samuel Boston Lathan, was a Confederate soldier and my grandfather (this book's author, S. Robert Lathan, MD). The Reverend Robert Lathan, DD was the father of Robert Lathan, Jr., the newspaper editor and the subject of this book.

The Lathan brothers, the Reverend and the soldier, were both writers and historians, affectionately called "scribblers." Reverend Robert Lathan wrote over a hundred newspaper articles around 1876 that were published in the *Yorkville Enquirer* describing the early settlements of South Carolina and the Revolutionary War battles in the state. These writing ledgers were found in my bookshelf by my brother-in-law, John Rivers, and in 2002 published by me as The History of South Carolina, my first book. It is still sold frequently in the Kings Mountain National Military Park.

My grandfather Samuel Boston Lathan told all of his Civil War soldier reminiscences and many other stories and speeches from his home in Chester, SC through written articles that were collected and published by me in a book Grand Old Man in 2012. I have collected many other "sketches" written by both brothers from newspaper archives.

Over the last twenty years, I have been very interested in researching the life of the editor Robert Lathan, Jr., the youngest son of the Reverend Robert Lathan DD. I was influenced again by John Rivers of Charleston, who gave me a biography of Robert Lathan, Jr. as editor of the *News and Courier*. Lathan won the Pulitzer Prize for best newspaper editorial in 1924. The book given to me was Outspoken 150 Years of the News and Courier, which was published by Herbert Sass in 1953.

Robert Lathan, Jr. was born in 1881 in Yorkville, SC. He was my first cousin once removed and later died one year before I was born. In a speech he wrote in 1937, he refers to his "earliest and certainly my continuous recollections as bound up with the newspapers of South Carolina. I could not have been more than four or five when I went with my father to the offices of the Yorkville Enquirer."

From his early age, newspapers became his life's work. He started his first job as assistant and secretary to the editor of *The State* newspaper in 1900. Also, it might have been a coincidence that his mother's first cousin was the wife of the editor, NG Gonzales.

Lathan's newspaper work covered from Columbia, Charleston and Asheville, NC through WWI, the 1918 pandemic, and the Great Depression. His devotion to informing the public is captured in his quote: "The fact that from the earliest times the men who conducted newspapers have uniformly recognized their responsibilities to the public."

From James Lathan through his son Robert Lathan, these Lathan descendants have achieved much to our society. Those of us who share the Lathan name are proud of our heritage and of the legacy we leave to our descendants.

S. Robert Lathan, Jr. MD

Contents

Chapter One — A Thought Provoking Editor

Chapter Two — A Renowned Editor Mourned

Chapter Three — Born to Be an Editor

Chapter Four — An Eager Student of the News

Chapter Five — A Devoted Newspaperman

Chapter Six — A Discerning Editor

Chapter Seven — An Editor of Expansive Horizons

Chapter Eight — The Best Writer For "A Good Year and a Goodly Land"

Chapter Nine — A Gentleman in the Highest and Best Sense of the Term

References

Speeches

Introduction

The author, S. Robert Lathan, Jr. MD has researched the biography of Robert Lathan, Jr, his cousin, the Editor who spent most of his adult life working for newspapers in South Carolina and North Carolina. Dr. Lathan has gathered many of Editor Lathan's important and thought provoking words in the following pages.

The exact words of Editor Lathan, found in editorial columns, speeches, and letters are highlighted in this book by the use of an old style newspaper font, an example is the beginning line of the Pulitzer Prize winning column.

This article is being written on election day.

The book title, chapter and section titles highlight an Old English font similar to the font chosen by Editor Lathan for his business card and materials.

viii

Chapter One

Robert Lathan, Jr.
A Thought
Provoking Editor

Who is to speak for the South?
How many of her citizens are prepared
to help formulate her replies?

RL 1924

Pulitzer Prize Winner for Editorial Journalism for 1924

Mr. Lathan wrote the editorial on election day, when the voters were going to the polls to elect a Republican President, Calvin Coolidge. As Mr. Lathan pointed out in the article, he did not know whether the Republicans or the Democrats would win the election.

But regardless of the outcome, he said, the South lacked political leaders of stature and a positive program.

> The root of the South's present plight lies in the fact that it has today virtually no national leadership. With Labor organized and militant, with radicalism organized and in deadly earnest, with conservatism organized and drawing the lines sharply, what is the South to do, what course shall she take, where do her interests lie, what is due to happen to her?

Herbert Ravenal Sass, Lathan's good friend and prolific writer described the setting of the composing of the editorial in the offices of The News and Courier on November 4, 1924.

"When Mr. Lathan had finished hammering out the editorial-at the big desk used by his distinguished predecessors, Dawson and Hemphill-he walked from his office to the newsroom and read it to one of the members of his staff.

'Well, what do you think of it' the editor asked, when he had finished reading the article aloud.

'Powerful,' replied the staff member, really meaning it.

Mr. Lathan never liked to be 'yessed,' and his staff member knew that the editor had read the piece not for commendation but for criticism. The staff member could not think of anything which might improve the editorial, and Mr. Lathan sent it to the composing room. But neither the staff member, nor Mr. Lathan had any idea that the 'powerful' article was destined to win the Pulitzer Prize." Outspoken, 1958

Column beginning as appeared on November 5, 1924

WEDNESDAY, NOVEMBER 5, 1924

The Plight of the South

This article is being written on election day but before the result of the voting can possibly be known. No matter. The suggestions it contains will still be pertinent, whatever the story told by the first page this morning. It makes very little difference what any of us think about the outcome of yesterday's balloting. It makes a considerable difference whether or not the people of the South realize the precarious situation which this section has come to occupy politically.

THE PLIGHT OF THE SOUTH
The News And Courier, Charleston SC

Robert Lathan, Editor
November 5, 1924

This article is being written on election day but before the result of the voting can possibly be known. No matter. The suggestions it contains will still be pertinent whatever the story told by the first page this morning. It makes very little difference what any of us think about the outcome of yesterday's balloting. It makes a considerable difference whether or not the people of the South realize the precarious situation which this section has come to occupy politically.

As yet we doubt if very many of them do realize this; and yet it is, we think, the outstanding political development of the time so far as we are concerned. Look at the facts. They are not pleasant to contemplate but they cannot be ignored longer. We are in a sad fix politically in this part of the country and if we are to find a remedy for our troubles, we must first of all determine what they are. That will take considerable discussion and all we can hope to do now is to help start the ball of this discussion rolling. If that can be accomplished, we may achieve the new program and the new leadership which we so much need.

For at the root of the South's present plight lies the fact that it has today virtually no national program and virtually no national leadership. Is it strange that it should be treated by the rest of the country as such a negligible factor? What is it contributing today in the way of political thought? What political leaders has it who possess weight or authority beyond their own States? What constructive policies are its people ready to fight for with the brains and zeal that made them a power in the old days?

The plight of the South in these respects would be perilous at any time. In a period when political currents are deeper and swifter than ever before, with more violent whirlpools, more dangerous rocks and shoals, ours is truly a perilous position. Changes which used to be decades in the making now sweep over us almost before we know they are in contemplation. It is true everywhere. In all the countries of Europe the pendulum is swinging now far to the left, now far to the right. And the South has belonged to the school politically which sought as a rule the middle of the road, eschewing ultra-conservatism on the one hand and radicalism on the other. With Labor organized and militant, with radicalism organized and in deadly earnest, with conservatism organized and drawing the lines sharply, what is the South to do, what course shall she take, where do her interests lie, what is due to happen to her?

These are questions which already begin to press for answers. Who is to speak for the South? How many of her citizens are prepared to help formulate her replies?

Chapter One

The News and Courier

COMPLETE ASSOCIATED PRESS SERVICE

THE WEATHER
South Carolina: Fair Wednesday and Thursday; gentle winds, mostly southwest.

ESTABLISHED IN 1803   CHARLESTON, S. C., WEDNESDAY MORNING, NOVEMBER 5, 1924   PRICE 5 CENTS

COOLIDGE AND GEN. DAWES SEEM TO HAVE WON; TEN MILLION DOLLAR BOND ISSUE DEFEATED

PRESIDENT WINS EAST AND THE MIDDLE WEST
Has Also Established Leads Beyond Mississippi and May Get 300 Electoral Votes

"Remember 1916," Say Democrats
Washington, Nov. 4.—"Remember 1916," said D. C. Hodgkin, assistant to Chairman Shaver of the Democratic national committee tonight, when informed that several prominent Eastern newspapers supporting John W. Davis, had conceded the election of President Coolidge. Committee officials in Washington, he added, "await confidently" the returns from Western and border States.

COOLIDGE NOT RUFFLED BY ELECTION DAY
Spends Day Just as He Would Any Other—Semiweekly Cabinet Meeting Is Cancelled

M'DONALD OUT: BALDWIN WILL FORM CABINET
Labor Premier Resigns and King Calls Upon Baldwin to Organize New Government

Polk Says Davis Believes Election Going to House
Candidate's Friend Says Former Feels West Will Decide Issue—Thinks La Follette Will Get Six States

AMENDMENTS NOT CERTAIN OF PASSAGE
Overwhelming Vote Against Bond Issue Seems Likely, According to Early Scattering Returns

Nominee	Calvin Coolidge	John W. Davis	Robert M. La Follette
Party	Republican	Democratic	Progressive
Alliance			
Home state	Massachusetts	West Virginia	Wisconsin
Running mate	Charles G. Dawes	Charles G. Dawes	Burton K. wheeler
Electoral vote	382	136	13
States carried	35	12	1
Popular vote	15,723,789	8,386,242	4,831,706
Percentage	54.0%	28.8%	16.6%

As the election results declaring Calvin Coolidge the 32nd President of the United States were tabulated, editor Lathan's "Plight of the South" column was reprinted in other newspapers, across the South, inspiring many in the journalistic world to appreciate the wisdom of its author.

In December 1924, Lathan sent a copy of the editorial to Nicholas Murray Butler, President of Columbia University in New York. Mr. Butler commented that the editorial "seemed to me so striking and so candid a presentation of important political and social facts that nationwide attention should be given to it."

As the importance and truth of the editorial "Plight of the South" circulated across the South, it also began to be recognized and re-printed in other prominent journalist circles of the United States.

In January 1925, Lathan's November 4th editorial was submitted to the Carnegie Foundation at Columbia University, which administers the selection process and awarding of the Pulitzer Prize for Journalism.

Requests to Lathan for Submission

Columbia University
in the City of New York
SCHOOL OF JOURNALISM

November 18, 1924

Editor Charleston News and Courier
Charleston
South Carolina

Dear Sir:

    I am informed that a few days after the Presidential election you published an editorial under the title of "The Negligible South" which might be worthy of consideration for one of the Pulitzer prizes in Journalism. Will you be good enough to let me have a copy of it so that I may submit it for the consideration of the jury?

Yours faithfully,

J. W. Cunliffe

For the best editorial article written during the year, the test of excellence being clearness of style, moral purpose, sound reasoning and power to influence public opinion in the right direction, due account being taken of the whole volume of the writer's editorial work during the year, $500.

Butler's Encouragement

NICHOLAS MURRAY BUTLER
BROADWAY AT 116TH STREET
NEW YORK CITY

December 15, 1924

Robert Lathan, Esq.
    The News and Courier
        19 Broad Street
            Charleston, S. C.

Dear Mr. Lathan

      I thank you for your cordial note of the 12th and its very interesting sendings. I had spoken to several friends in this part of the country about the editorial entitled "The Plight of the South" which appeared in the News and Courier on the day following election. It seemed to me so striking and so candid a presentation of important political and social facts that nation wide attention should be given to it. I have spoken of it to Frank Munsey and have asked him to reprint it in the New York Sun at an early date.

      I am very much obliged to you for your kindly personal reference in your editorial of the 12th on the subject of the miscalled Child Labor Amendment. On the editorial page of the New York Herald Tribune for Friday last, the 12th, you will find another letter from me on the same subject.

      I wish you might read and comment on the very extraordinary discussion of this Amendment written by John Spargo, former Socialist, which appears in the Evening Banner of Bennington, Vermont, for December 12th. He promises a second article on the same subject, to appear in that same

-2-

paper tomorrow, the 16th.

I take pleasure in sending you with my compliments, under separate cover, a copy of a new book which the Scribner's have just published for me.

I deeply regretted not being able to accept the invitation to go to Charleston for the New England Society's dinner some years ago, but apart from my stated trip to Augusta, Georgia, in March of each year, I find it difficult to get away from my desk during the winter.

With cordial regards, I am

Faithfully yours

D

Columbia University
in the City of New York
SECRETARY OF THE UNIVERSITY

April 21, 1925

[Confidential]

Mr. Robert Lathan
   Charleston News and Courier
     Charleston, S. C.

My dear Mr. Lathan

    I take very great pleasure in notifying you, in confidence, that the prize of $500. established by the will of the late Joseph Pulitzer, for the best editorial article written during the year, the test of excellence being clearness of style, moral purpose, sound reasoning and power to influence public opinion in the right direction, has been awarded to the Charleston (S.C.) News and Courier, for the editorial entitled "The Plight of the South," published November 5, 1924.

    Public announcement of this prize will not be made until next Monday, the 27th, and in due course a check covering the amount of the prize will be sent to you.

                          Very truly yours

                          Frank D. Fackenthal

D

April 28, 1925.

Mr. Frank D. Wackenthal,
    Secretary of the University,
        Columbia University,
           New York City.

My Dear Mr. Wackenthal:

        I want to thank you very much, indeed, for your letter of April 27 which I got yesterday afternoon upon my return from New York and Washington where I have been for the past week. Of course I appreciate more than I can say the very great compliment which has been paid me in the matter of the Pulitzer award. It is a thing of which I am and must always be very proud.

        Very sincerely yours,

        Robert Lathan

Submission Form

Columbia University
in the City of New York

APPLICATION FOR A PULITZER PRIZE
IN JOURNALISM OR LETTERS

To be filed with the Secretary of the University on or before February 1

APPLICATION OF

In accordance with the provisions of the will of the late Joseph Pulitzer, the Pulitzer Prizes in Journalism and in Letters, and the Pulitzer Traveling Scholarships, open alike to men and women, will be awarded at Commencement, 1917, and each successive year thereafter.

Nominations of candidates for any one of the Pulitzer Prizes must be made in writing on or before February 1 of each year, addressed to the Secretary of Columbia University, New York, on forms that may be obtained on application to the Secretary of the University.

Each nomination for a prize must be accompanied by a copy of any book, manuscript, editorial, article, or other material submitted by any competitor for a prize, or on his behalf, which must be delivered at the time of nomination to the Secretary of Columbia University, New York, for preservation in the Library of the University. Competition for a prize will be limited to work done during the calendar year ending December 31 next preceding; in the case of the drama prize, the time runs over to February 1 of the succeeding calander year. Nomination of a play should be made during its performance.

In the case of the prizes in journalism, competition will be limited to those candidates who are proposed or endorsed for consideration by a member of the Advisory Board of the School of Journalism. The award of these prizes will be made as required by the provisions of the following subdivisions of these regulations and on the recommendation of the Advisory Board of the School of Journalism.

PRIZES IN JOURNALISM

The following awards will be made annually as Prizes in Journalism, after nomination by a jury or juries chosen from the members of the Administrative Board of the School of Journalism and from the teaching staff of the School:

(1) For the most disinterested and meritorious public service rendered by any American newspaper during the year, a gold medal costing Five hundred dollars ($500).

(2) For the best history of the services rendered to the public by the American press during the preceding year, One thousand dollars ($1,000).

(3) For the best editorial article written during the year, the test of excellence being clearness of style, moral purpose, sound reasoning and power to influence public opinion in the right direction, Five hundred dollars ($500).

(4) For the best example of a reporter's work during the year; the test being strict accuracy, terseness, the accomplishment of some public good commanding public attention and respect, One thousand dollars ($1,000).

(5) For the best cartoon published in any American newspaper during the year, the determining qualities being that the cartoon shall embody an idea made clearly apparent, shall show good drawing and striking pictorial effect, and shall be helpful to some commendable cause of public importance, Five hundred dollars ($500).

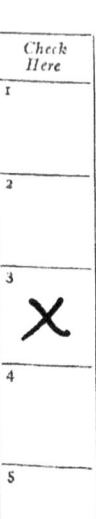

The Pulitzer Prize

Prior to his death Mr. Pulitzer had offered Columbia University the funds to create a journalism school. After his death his wish was fulfilled under the Presidency of Nicholas Butler Murray as well as a $2,000,000 gift for the Pulitzer Prize.

In writing his 1904 will, provisions for the establishment of the Pulitzer Prizes as incentives to excellence, Pulitzer specified solely four awards in journalism, four in letters and drama, one for education, and five traveling scholarships. In 1917, Columbia created the procedures and categories for the awarding of the annual Pulitzer Prizes.

Through the years the awards have been expanded into literature, history, and music. Each award is chosen by a juried committee and awarded in the month of April to include a cash prize as well as the honor.

Editor Lathan received notification of his award on April 25, 1925 at his office in Charleston. The announcement of the awarding of the honor was sent by the Pulitzer Committee to newspapers throughout the United States and internationally.

Newspapers Congratulate

The Pulitzer Award

The prize for the best editorial of 1924 goes to the *Charleston News and Courier* for an article entitled, "The Plight of the South" published on the morning of November 4. This is the first time in recent years that a southern newspaper has been so honored, although the *News and Courier* has long been noted throughout the country for the strength and clarity of its editorial utterances. It is a source of gratification to the people of the south, particularly those of the Carolinas, to know that the efforts of a home newspaper are thus singled out as models.

The *Star* extends its congratulations to *The News and Courier* and its editor, Mr. Robert Lathan, for the signal success they have attained. It is upon such leadership and sane thought that the south must depend during the coming year when her economic development will have reached the highest peak in history.

"It is upon such leadership and sane thought that the South must depend during the coming year when her economic development will have reached the highest peak in history."
Morning Star, Wilmington, NC

CLIPPING DEPARTMENT

NORTH AND SOUTH CAROLINA PUBLIC
UTILITY INFORMATION BUREAU

Newspaper Index-Journal

City Greenwood SC

Date April 27th, 1925

A High Honor

Editor Robert Lathan, of the *News and Courier*, has been awarded the Pulitzer prize for the best editorial written in 1924. The award carries with a medal a prize of five hundred dollars. It was won last year by William Allen White, of the Emporia Gazette, Emporia, Kansas.

Mr. Lathan's editorial was published the day after the general election in November and was entitled *The Plight of the South*. It attracted wide attention at the time and was copied and commented on extensively. It was timely, thought provoking and forcibly written.

Mr. Lathan's friends in South Carolina and they are legion, were delighted to hear of this recognition of his ability. They extended congratulations and wished him many years of the same high and patriotic service which marked the record thus far made.

Throughout this section of the state there will be especial pleasure because of the very high regard in which his father, the late Dr. Robert Lathan, author of Lathan's *History of South Carolina* was held. Dr. Lathan was for some years pastor of the historic Cedar Springs A.R.P. Church, just over the line in Abbeville County.

CLIPPING DEPARTMENT

NORTH AND SOUTH CAROLINA PUBLIC
UTILITY INFORMATION BUREAU

Newspaper The Observer

City Charlotte NC

Date April 28th, 1925

A WINNING EDITORIAL.

Robert Lathan, editor of The News and Courier, Charleston, S. C., has been awarded the Pulitzer prize of $500 for the best editorial which appeared in a newspaper in the United States last year. Mr. Lathan was made editor of the Charleston paper in 1910, and was said at the time to be the youngest man in the country to become editor of a recognized daily newspaper. The editorial, which appeared in his paper November 6, 1924, follows:

"Mr. Lathan was made editor of the Charleston paper in 1910 and was said at the time to be the youngest man in the country to become editor of a recognized daily newspaper."
    The Observer, Charlotte, NC

Congratulations from Friends

> **The News and Courier**
> 19 BROAD ST.
> CHARLESTON, S. C.
>
> EDITORIAL ROOMS
>
> I wanted to be one of the first to congratulate you but was out of town when the news came. It's great, but I'm not surprised in the least. That was <u>an</u> Editorial. It <u>had</u> to win.
>
> H. R. S.

Recognition of Lathan's "thought provoking work" was given by friends and associates as well as nationally recognized authors.
                      Herbert Ravenal Sass "HOBO"

Chapter One

> RICHARD I. MANNING
> 1600 PENDLETON ST.
> COLUMBIA, S. C.
>
> May 4, 1925.
>
> Mr. Robert Lathan,
> C% News & Courier,
> Charleston, S.C.
>
> My dear Lathan:-
>
> I want to congratulate you on winning the prize on the "Plight of the South".
>
> I was tempted to write you last fall about this editorial because I was in a meeting in New York at which were present a number of very prominent Republicans, one among them being Dr. Nicholas Murray Butler. Your editorial had just appeared and was the subject of considerable discussion and very commendatory comment.
>
> I hope I may have the opportunity of seeing you some time this spring so that we can talk over some of these matters which are of such vital interest to us.
>
> With all good wishes, I am,
>
> Very sincerely,
>
> RIM-MJE.
>
> Rich. I. Manning

Richard Manning, a friend and prominent South Carolinian

Columbia University, New York,
April 28, 1925

Editor, the News & Courier,
Charleston, S.C.

Dear Sir:

Allow me to congratulate you & your paper upon the receipt of the Pulitzer Prize for the best editorial. It is a fine and well deserved recognition.

Even in New York of mss's the trenchant comments of your editorial column with its excellent English and real literary flavor. This is a real honor for Charleston and the city should be proud of you.

Sincerely yours —

Hervey Allen
Hervey Allen

Chapter One

*Robert Lathan, Julia Peterkin, William E. Gonzales
at the South Carolina Press Association Banquet
honoring Pulitzer Prize Winners
Columbia, SC, January 15th, 1937*

Through the years that followed, Editor Lathan continued to provide leadership, not only to the field of journalism through column editorials, but also to his beloved communities. In January 1937, he was again recognized by his peers for his Pulitzer prize along with the only other Pulitzer winner from South Carolina, Julia Peterkin.

> (Continued on Page 13: Column 5.)
>
> **PULITZER PRIZE WINNERS GUESTS PRESS INSTITUTE**
>
> *Julia Peterkin and Robert Lathan to Speak on Program January 15.*
>
> Two South Carolinians, winners in previous years of the Pulitzer prize for writing, will be special guests of the South Carolina Press association as it midwinter institute in Columbia January 15, according to announcement made yesterday by William E. Gonzales of The State, president of the association. They are Julia Peterkin, whose "Scarlet Sister Mary" won for her the prize for the best novel, and Robert Lathan of Asheville, whose comment the morning after the 1924 presidential election won for him the prize for the best editorial of the year. He was then editor of The News and Courier of Charleston; now he is with the Asheville Citizen. Both Mr. Peterkin and
>
> (Continued on Page 5: Column 4.)

The two South Carolinians, winners of the Pulitzer Prize for writing were guests of the South Carolina Press Association on January 15, 1937. William E. Gonzales, editor of the State was president of the press association.

Julia Peterkin (1880-1961) was born in Laurens County, SC. In 1929, she won the Pulitzer Prize for her novel *Scarlet Sister Mary*. She wrote several novels about plantation life in the South, especially the Gullah people of the Low Country in South Carolina. The jury that year was divided as to her prize resulting in her win and the resignation of a member. Later in her career she was asked for assistance by another southern author to whom she recommended her publisher. *Lamb in her Bosom* won the prize in 1934.

As the program for the event of the South Carolina Press Institute in Columbia, SC, Robert Lathan was asked to address the health and future of the newspapers in South Carolina. His full address was published in the The State by William Gonzales, Saturday, January 16, 1937.

Through his presentation Lathan discussed many of the large consequential changes that has occurred in the United States and South Carolina, including the recovery and changes occurring after the close of the Civil War, WWI, the administration of Woodrow Wilson, globalism, the Great Depression and Social Security. The presentation covered five full columns in the paper.

South Carolina, Past and Present

Address Delivered Yesterday Afternoon Before the South Carolina Press Institute in Columbia

Robert Lathan, Editor

It is not strange therefore that when I think of South Carolina it is primarily of its newspapers and of the men and women who have made and are making those newspapers. It is not strange that the invitation with which you have honored me is one which I value to the highest degree.

There are today those who maintain that a newspaper is merely a merchandiser of news – or of news plus entertainment. You and I know that that this is not true.

We know what more than once the press of South Carolina has done for South Carolina. We know that the press can be and should be a powerful instrumentality of public service: that its supreme responsibility is to fix public attention upon the things that are vital; to maintain and promote standards that will conserve the public weal; to arouse the public conscience to its obligations; to serve as sentiments against dangers and as heralds of opportunities ; to help guide the public intelligence to sound decisions; to hearten the spirits of the people when they droop.

Repeatedly the press of South Carolina has done all of these things. That is the great tradition which belongs to the press of South Carolina today. And my message to you is that your times and your problems , your opportunities and your responsibilities are more challenging than any the press of South Carolina has been called upon to face in the past.

Are changes evil? If this be true Mr. President, then is there cause indeed that we should rend our garments, cover us with sackcloth and ashes, give ourselves over to lamentation and despair. But it is true? Are all changes that have happened as evil as they are sometimes made to seem?

If there is one thing I wish to make clearer than anything else, it is that the changes in which we embark are fraught with perils as well as hopes. It will take more than wise leadership to bring the hopes that have been aroused to fulfillment.

Excerpts from the speech are included here. Complete speech can be found in references. South 1937

Joseph Pulitzer 1847–1911

Joseph Pulitzer was an Hungarian immigrant who grew up well educated in Mako and Pest before his father went bankrupt challenging Joseph to emigrate at seventeen to Boston. He became a soldier in Sheridan's Troopers as he was paid to enroll. After the Civil War he found his way to St. Louis assimilating into a large German community. Holding many jobs for short periods of time his mainstay was the Mercantile Library where he could spend extra time on his passion for reading. In 1867, he became a naturalized American citizen and in 1868 was admitted to the bar and took his first job as a reporter for the *Westliche Post*.

In 1872 he purchased his first shares of *Westliche Post*. Within a few years, he owned the *St. Louis Dispatch* and the *St. Louis Post*, which were merged and owned by the family until 1995. As a wealthy newspaper owner, Pulitzer moved to New York and purchased the *New York World*, emphasizing sensational stories of human interest, crime, disaster, and scandals.

Due to Pulitzer's deteriorating health, he resigned from the company in 1907, and died in 1911. While traveling to his winter home at the Jekyll Island Club in Georgia, Pulitzer had his yacht stop for six days in Charleston Harbor, South Carolina caused by hurricane warnings. At the time Robert Lathan was editor of the Charleston *News and Courier* and visited with Mr. Pulitzer on the yacht.

Soon after the visits on the Pulitzer yacht, Mr. Pulitzer unexpectedly died. Mr. Lathan wrote the Pulitzer obituary the next day in the *News and Courier*. The obituary was printed in many other southern newspapers, honoring the memory and positive influence of Mr. Pulitzer on the journalistic profession.

> SEVEN EAST SEVENTY-THIRD STREET
>
> My dear Mr Latham,
>
> Please accept my grateful thanks for your sympathy in my great sorrow & for the beautiful flowers you so kindly sent.
>
> Sincerely Yours
> Kate Davis Pulitzer
>
> November 5th /911

Chapter One

After the visit, Mr. Lathan wrote to Mr. Henry Sydney Harrison of Charleston, W. VA.

The stenographic record of the conversation with Mr. Pulitzer about the author, Mr. Harrison and his book *Queed*, is an example of editor Lathan's ability to capture both the spirit as well as the words of a conversation then complete the sharing process with others through his own written words.

Dear Mr. Harrison:

It has occurred to me that it might be gratifying to you to know of the pleasure which *Queed* gave to Mr. Joseph Pulitzer. During the week preceding Mr. Pulitzer's sudden and unexpected death, I visited him several times on board his yacht. I lunched with him on Friday and noticed a copy of *Queed* lying on the reading table in the library.

"Have you read *Queed*, Mr. Pulitzer?" I asked.

"I have," he answered, "and with the greatest enjoyment:" and he went on to say that your book was one of the few novels he had read in recent years the reading of which had afforded him genuine satisfaction.

Who was it wrote *Queed*? he asked. I told him.

"Is this his first book?"

"I believe so."

"Do you know anything about the author?"

"Not personally," I answered, "but he was for some years a newspaper man in Virginia and preceded Mr. Hemphill as editor of the Richmond Times-Dispatch."

"Indeed!" said Mr. Pulitzer with interest. "And what is he doing now?"

"I understand," I told him, "that he retired from journalism to devote himself to literary work."

"Has he written anything else?"

"Nothing that I have seen except a short story in one of the magazines."

"How old is he?"

"I really do not know." In some way, however, I have gotten the impression that he is about forty."

"A good age! You know the Germans say that a man should never be judged for what he is worth until he reaches forty. I would say that if Mr. Harrison is not too young and not too old, he is a man of very great promise. I would like to know him. I would like to help that young man."

You probably know that Mr. Pulitzer had perhaps read as widely as any man in this country, a large corps of secretaries having been employed by him for years, ever since his blindness came upon him, in reading to him for many hours each day. As one of the many who found *Queed* thoroughly delightful, I have felt it an obligation to pass onto you a friendly judgement to which I am sure you will attach more than ordinary value.

Yours very truly.
Robert Lathan

Chapter Two

Robert Lathan, Jr.
A Reknowned Editor Mourned

You can not hope to eclipse the (Editors) courage, their integrity, their brilliance, their vigor, their usefulness. It would not be possible to wish anything better than that you carry on in the spirit which they exemplified.

RL 1937

Chapter Two

1925 South Carolina Press Association Meeting
Henderson, NC
left to right all were associated with <u>News and Courier</u>
August Kohn 1889–1891
Robert Lathan Jr. 1907–1927
W. W. Ball 1927–1951
Major J. C. Hemphill 1880–1910

A Very Productive Year

In January 1937, Robert Lathan journeyed back to his journalistic beginnings in his beloved Columbia, SC, where he started his newspaper career with *The State* in 1900. He was invited to be honored by the South Carolina Press Institute for his achievement in winning the Pulitzer Prize for best editorial written in 1924. In his address to the members of the Institute he spoke of the work that had been done especially in the critical days of the past by editorial leaders, many of them his mentors and many of them now deceased.

> My pleasure today in looking at the faces that I see is tempered by my sorrow for the faces that I miss; faces that are absent not only here but from this earthly scene. RL Jan 1937

A short nine months later, Robert Lathan, Jr. Editor of the *Asheville Citizen* succumbed to a cerebral hemorrhage at age 56.

Lathan's last appearance was early in September at the Pen and Plate Club when he was asked to be the respondent to political comments by J. Fred Essary, chief of the Washington Bureau of the *Baltimore Sun*. The program, though not previously written and published received high praise as being informative and enlightening.

September 25th, 1937

He came to his Asheville newspaper office that day as usual to write the daily editorials.

In the afternoon he was not feeling well and said he had lost his glasses and could not see. Associates noted that he was not altogether well and called a taxi for him. The physician who was summoned to his home, knew immediately that his condition was critical. Physicians remained with him until his death at 10 pm. Lathan had just recently returned to Asheville from a vacation to rest for his health at a South Carolina beach, assuming that he was perfectly well.

The next morning, The *Asheville Citizen* announced his death, describing the tremendous gift to the newspaper and the community that had been the life of Robert Lathan, Jr. The full column space normally reserved for Lathan's editorials were filled with praise from the community.

The *Asheville Citizen's* Very Personal Obituary

"Robert Lathan who fell on sleep last night was a great editor. He was one of the most potent editorial personalities which the South has known in a full generation.

He loved Asheville and Western North Carolina and he kept steadily before him the controlling fact that he was writing for Asheville and Western North Carolina. But his influence was never confined to this section. It overspread the boundaries established by normal circulation of the Citizen and reached out into the South and into the nation. He gave new prestige and a wider area of usefulness to this paper.

Mr. Lathan was an editor of national stature before he came to Asheville. Fresh upon his brow were the laurels which he had won and which had made him the natural choice for the Pulitzer in 1924.

Here he heightened the stature and expanded the reputation which he had won in his own state. Quickly catching the spirit of this community and this section, he assumed a role of personal and editorial leadership which was at its very height when death came with her forewarning as he prepared today's editorials.

Many ingredients entered into the making of Robert Lathan the editor. Not the least of these was an unfailing sense of justice. He never wrote an editorial in personal spleen. He never distorted a fact or twisted a phrase to injure any man. If he had personal enmities, he never allowed them to darken his thinking or to shape his editorial course.

Some editors always write at the top of their voices. Robert Lathan was not of that type. He strove unceasingly for simplicity and lucidity of expression. He studiously avoided pompous phrases and cheap emotion. The happy consequence was that his editorials could be read with enjoyment and understanding alike by the most cultured and least literate readers.

The influence of Robert Lathan upon the life and thought of this community was not confined to the power that flowed from his written words. Sage in counsel, eloquent of speech and positive in action, he was one of Asheville's most useful citizens. Any cause that promised the well-being of the community attracted his interest and his energies. He loved books, therefore he served on the State Library Commission. He was interested in the material advancement of this community, therefore he was a director of the Chamber of Commerce. He appreciated as did few persons the communities' responsibility to its charitable and character building agencies, therefore he served as President of the Community Chest, a director of the YMCA, the Red Cross and other agencies. He coveted the best of educational advantages for the children of all the people, therefore he served as a trustee of the Western Carolina Teacher's College. He was a man of deep and unaffected piety, therefore he served as vestryman of Trinity Church. And so it was through the whole gamut of a community organizing and exacting life.

It is easy to believe now that he literally wore himself out in the service of his community. For he never spared himself. He was never content to accept honors and to avoid their accompanying responsibilities.

Of his death, however, can it be truly said that it impoverishes a whole community. He had enmeshed himself so inextricably in the social, religious, civic and business life of this city that his leave taking now leaves many voids. As we look back now, it seems as though a whole host of men rather than one man had died.

Robert Lathan was a great editor. But he was something finer than that. He was a great gentleman in the richest implications and ramifications of that overwrought phrase. He looked out upon life with eyes that were always sharpened by gentleness. He sought eternally the gentle aims of this martial existence with gentle means. His unfailing courtesy was the normal expression of a gentle soul to whom kindliness was as natural as the breath in his nostrils. He was utterly incapable of anything cheap, shabby, or dishonest. In short, he was a gentleman."

THE ASHEVILLE CITIZEN

The *Asheville Citizen* continued publishing tributes to Editor Lathan for several days.

Civic Leader

"Mr. Lathan was a member of the Asheville Civitan Club and the Pen and Plate Club. He served as president of the Community Chest here for one year, in 1932 and 1933 and headed the annual campaign that year for funds. His leadership in this drive, friends recalled last night, resulted in a generous response of contributions. He also was active in the Buncombe County Chapter of the American red Cross and took part in all affairs of the Chamber of Commerce, the YMCA and other civic and charitable organizations here.

At the time of his death he was serving as a member of the advisory board of the school of journalism of Columbia University. For several years he served on the vestry board of Trinity Episcopal church and at one time was president of the Men's Club of that church.

He also was a member of the board of trustees of Western Carolina Teachers college, a State-operated school at Cullowhee, NC. He was appointed to this post by Governor Clyde R. Hoey."

The *Asheville Citizen* published the comments by Governor of North Carolina, Clyde Hoey on September 27, 1937.

"Governor Clyde Hoey said today that the death of Robert Lathan, Jr. in Asheville last night removes one of the ablest editors from the service of the State press.

His brilliant career as a journalist is brought to an untimely end," the chief executive commented. The *Asheville Citizen* (of which Lathan was editor) and all western North Carolina have sustained a loss.

His inherent honesty, clear vision, broad knowledge, and facility of expression combined to make him an outstanding editor and a conspicuous figure in the professional, civic, and religious life of the commonwealth. I feel a personal loss in his passing and his host of friends will join me in expressing the deepest sympathy for his bereaved family and the management of *The Citizen*."

Newspapers in both South Carolina and North Carolina added the recognition of the achievements of Robert Lathan through editorial columns.

Newspapers Recognized Achievements

Chester Reporter

Robert Lathan

Southern journalism loses one of its exceptional figures in the death of Editor Robert Lathan, of The Asheville Citizen. And at a time when the South needs clear and virile thought in active expression more than at any time since the Reconstruction. The loss is one which will give cause for grief, for Robert Lathan was an editor of ability, of thoroughness, of recognized soundness of opinion and one who was doing an able part in guiding his region back to stability.

As a Pulitzer prize winner for his editorial in Charleston concerning the Southern political plight, as a specially selected Southern editor for the European tour for World Peace under the auspices of the Carnegie Foundation, as an editor who attained many honors along the course of his career, he was much publicized. These things made him known, but wherein he was chiefly valuable to his people was in a constant, consistent editorial pressure day by day, written in crystal clear, intellectual style, yet wholly in touch with actuality, looking to a greater, a brighter South. The South will miss him, perhaps more than it realizes.

Charleston *News and Courier*

PASSING OF A NOBLE EDITOR.

(From The Charleston News and Courier.)

The blood of strong and true men coursed in every vein of ROBERT LATHAN. He was of the Scots of Williamsburg and Clarendon and of the Scotch Irish of the Northern counties. Those who know their South Carolina will say that the "A. R. P." people (they used to be called "Seceders") are of the most reliable of its citizenry. ROBERT LATHAN'S father was a minister of that church, a close student, a man of cultivation. He wrote a history of York county, where he lived many years, where ROBERT, JR., was born.

ROBERT LATHAN always was a student. He was another of the numerous examples who prove that a diploma from a college is not essential to education and has not nearly so much relation to it as is popularly supposed. He was no "college man" but not many men were more roundly educated. For purity his style in writing has seldom been equalled in this part of the country; he was one of the too few who did not defile the mother tongue.

LATHAN won the Pulitzer prize for the "best editorial," that was distinction, but not, to our mind, his principal achievement. That lay in his strong, unswerving conduct of sound editorial policies and the illustration of high courage in critical times. If one will turn to the files of The Asheville Citizen of only a few years ago when that city's financial structure was tottering, its social structure involved with it, one will see the evidence of a firm hand and a clear head. They were sorely needed.

In the mountain country of North Carolina, Mr. LATHAN'S newspaper wielded a powerful influence and, on the better side always. Senator JOSIAH BAILEY was re-elected last year in great part by the votes of the free mountaineers, and LATHAN was a guide whom they trusted.

Now ROBERT LATHAN goes honored, clean-handed and clean-hearted to his honored fathers, leaving his old paper, The News and Courier, and his old friends, as well as his companions in North Carolina, to be proud of his life and sorrowing at his grave.

Chapter Two

Charleston *Evening Post*

Former Charleston Editor Passes Away in Asheville

The death of Mr. Robert Lathan, 56-year-old editor of the Asheville Citizen and one time editor of the News and Courier, occurred last night at his Asheville home. Death was caused by a cerebral homorrhage.

Funeral services will be held at Trinity Episcopal church tomorrow, conducted by the Rev. George Floyd Rogers, rector. The body will be sent to Darlington, former home of Mrs. Lathan, for interment Wednesday morning.

For twenty years a resident of Charleston, and for seventeen years in that period editor of the local newspaper, Mr. Lathan was widely known in this city, and by virtue of his high position in the journalistic field, over the two Carolinas. Prior to assuming the position of editor and general manager of the News and Courier he had served as city editor, telegraph editor and state news editor of the paper.

During his twenty years of service in Charleston Mr. Lathan took an active interest in community projects and civic activities, and through the columns of his paper an aggressive stand in politics. In 1924, he wrote the editorial "The Plight of the South Politically" which later was adjudged the best to have been written in the nation that year, and won a Pullitzer prize.

Three years later soon after assuming editorship of the Asheville Citizen, he was a member of a party of twenty-four newspaper editors from twenty-four states who toured Europe under the auspices of the Carnegie Endowment for International Peace. The trip had been arranged by Nicholas Murray Butler, of Columbia university and followed a similar visit to the United States by a group of British editors.

An eloquent public speaker, Mr. Lathan of recent years was much in demand in Asheville. Several years ago he gave a series of lectures on political subjects at Emory college and he also delivered several talks at the University of North Carolina on southern politics.

During the ten years he served as editor of the Asheville Citizen Mr. Lathan on several occasions visited Charleston and was always warmly welcomed by many of his old friends. On many of his visits he was accompanied by Mrs. Lathan, who survives.

Charlotte *Observer*

ROBERT LATHAN.

The death of ROBERT LATHAN, distinguished editor of The Asheville Citizen and for a decade in the front rank of commonwealth leadership, marks the end of the way of this useful and constructive citizen and talented literary light.

It cuts deeply into the life of Asheville where, for the ten years of his residence, he commanded a position of unique influence. No civic movement within that period nor community venture was undertaken until he was consulted and his interest and his approval procured.

It means a vast loss to the whole of the State.

MR. LATHAN was no provincialist. His interests and abounding enthusiasms could not be confined to Asheville. He was a state-character.

A man of superior good judgment, he was frequently sought out for consultation as to commonwealth undertakings. And once convicted and sure of his ground as to the wisdom and worth-whileness of undertakings designed to benefit the entire State, he launched with all the vigor of his great and resourceful mind and his intense energies into the support of these programs.

His death, too, removes the most honored and signally-recognized editor in North Carolina, and one regarded throughout the profession as among the ablest and most distinguished in the entire South.

MR. LATHAN was many-sided. And his versatility showed at its best at the editorial desk.

He was a good writer, but his journalistic genius lay in the wide reach of his knowledge and in his uncanny ability to diagnose a play in politics and economics and social trends and call the turn.

His daily contributions to the editorial page of The Asheville Citizen, as previously with the Charleston News and Courier, made up in vigor of expression for what it may have lacked in mere lurid and glamorous and showy, jazzy diction.

He belonged to the old school, although himself not old in years—the old school of journalists which paramounted smooth and simple phrasing of solid and provable and irrefutable facts.

The State

A fitting eulogy was published September 27, in the *The State* newspaper, Columbia, SC, Lathan's first journalistic work place in 1900 at nineteen years of age.

> **Robert Lathan, Editor.**
>
> No minister of religion respects his vocation for the priestly office more than Robert Lathan, late editor of the Asheville Citizen, respected his call to the practice of journalism. So regarding his profession, he served it with such devotion of all his talents that newspaper work was sensibly exalted thereby wherever his influence extended.
>
> Mr. Lathan believed his public was entitled to the best daily commentary upon the news that his abilities would yield. He was therefore at all times an arduous and enterprising student, informing himself in every way possible, and pondering his facts deeply. He would have adorned a university chair of political economy. His editorials were frequently distinguished for penetrating analysis. Always they were models of English writing, and consistently they were the unmistakable reflection of sound character and highminded thinking.
>
> For The State Mr. Lathan's career has had of course a special interest, for during three years he was on its staff.
>
> Robert Lathan deserves to be gratefully remembered, and he will be, in both Carolinas, as one of the finest and best public servants either state has given to the country.

"One of the best and finest public servants that either state has given to the country."

More Southern Newspapers

"He reached the heights in his chosen profession and Southern Journalism has lost one of its most brilliant representatives."
Index-Journal, Greenwood SC

"losing one of its most ablest and most widely known craftsmen."
Greensboro Daily News, Greensboro, NC

"...Lathan was a gentleman of exceptional personal charm..he liked people and understood them."
Wilmington Star, NC

"The loss is not only yours, but Southern Journalism"
Greensboro News Record

"Mr. Lathan's influence and leadership manifested in his ability as a speaker no less than in the effectiveness and inspiration of his pen."
Hendersonville Times-News

"Southern journalism has lost a bolstering and stabilizing pillar of journalism never more needed than now"
Durham Morning Herald (NC)

"A Carolina gentleman in the highest and best sense of the term."
Montgomery Advertiser (AL)

"A level headed man who kept both fett on the ground."
The Banner, Nashville, TN

New York Times

ROBERT LATHAN, 56, EDITOR IN ASHEVILLE

Newspaper Man of Carolinas 37 Years and a Pulitzer Prize Winner Is Dead

Special to The New York Times.
ASHEVILLE, N. C., Sept. 26.—Robert Lathan, editor of The Asheville Citizen, died at his home in Albermarle Park here tonight after a brief illness. His age was 56.

Mr. Lathan, who had served as editor of The Citizen since 1927, won the Pulitzer Prize for the best editorial in the United States in 1924. He was serving as editor of The Charleston (S. C.) News and Courier then. He also was a member of the advisory board of the Columbia School of Journalism. The prize winning editorial was on "The Plight of the South Politically."

He was a native of York, S. C. where he was born on May 5, 1881 the son of the Rev. Robert and Fanny Lathan. He was educated in the public and private schools of South Carolina. He taught in South Carolina from 1898 to 1899 and joined the editorial staff of The Columbia (S. C.) State in 1900 and worked there for three years.

From 1903 to 1906 Mr. Lathan was a court reporter and law student. From 1906 to 1907 he was news editor of The Charleston News and Courier. He remained there until 1927, and when he came to Asheville he was editor of the Charleston paper.

He was president of the South Carolina Press Association from 1925 to 1926 and in 1927 visited Europe with the Carnegie editorial party studying economics and politics.

His widow survives.

The *New York Times* recognized the passing of Pulitzer Prize award winning Editor, Lathan

Hundreds of condolence messages were sent by Western Union, by Postal Telegraph, by letter and handwritten notes pouring into the offices and home of Editor, Robert Lathan.

The tributes pointed to the exceptional qualities that had given Robert Lathan, Jr. the outstanding respect that he so well deserved. The overwhelming message was that Robert Lathan, the Editor, the community leader and the gentleman would be "sorely missed."

Many of the tributes that were archived in the South Carolina State Library are referenced here.

"genius as an editor and nobility of character"
Julian S. Miller

"Leader fearless in championing the public good"
K Foster Murray

"Sound and clear thinker, Man of character that can not be replaced"
Hugh Macrae

"His death a public calamity accomplished, honest and understood his time...cherish his memory and be better for his example"
NC Senator, Josiah Bailey

"Instinctive grasp of the implications of the whole problem and leading his readers in the in the paths of citizenship"
John Stewart Bryan, Richmond News

"Stood for the best things in our American tradition"
Frank P. Graham,
University of North Carolina

"a fine gentleman..one of the most distinguished members of our craft"
W. Orton Tewson, New York

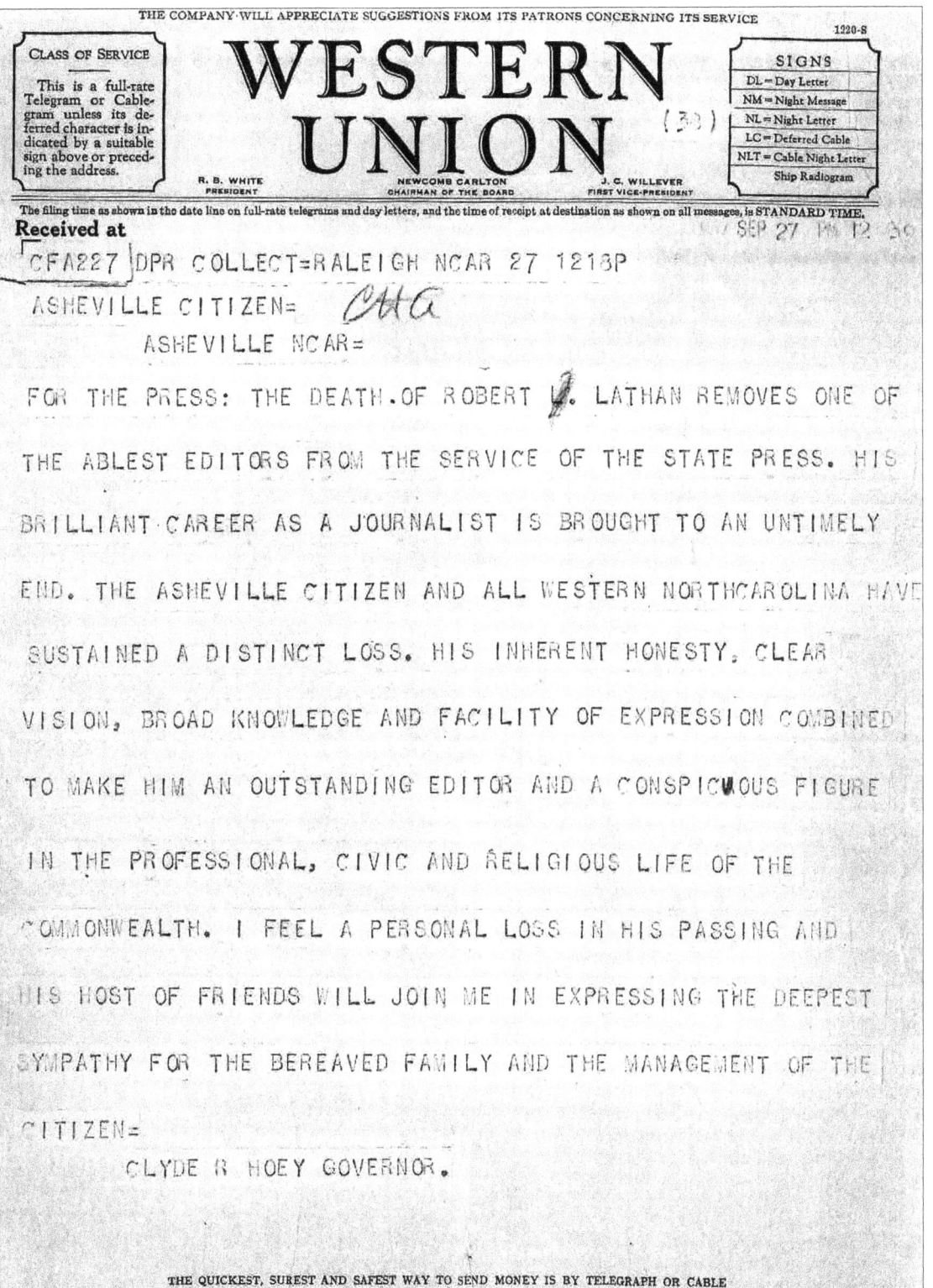

Death removes one of ablest editors of the state press.
Governor Clyde Hoey

Chapter Two

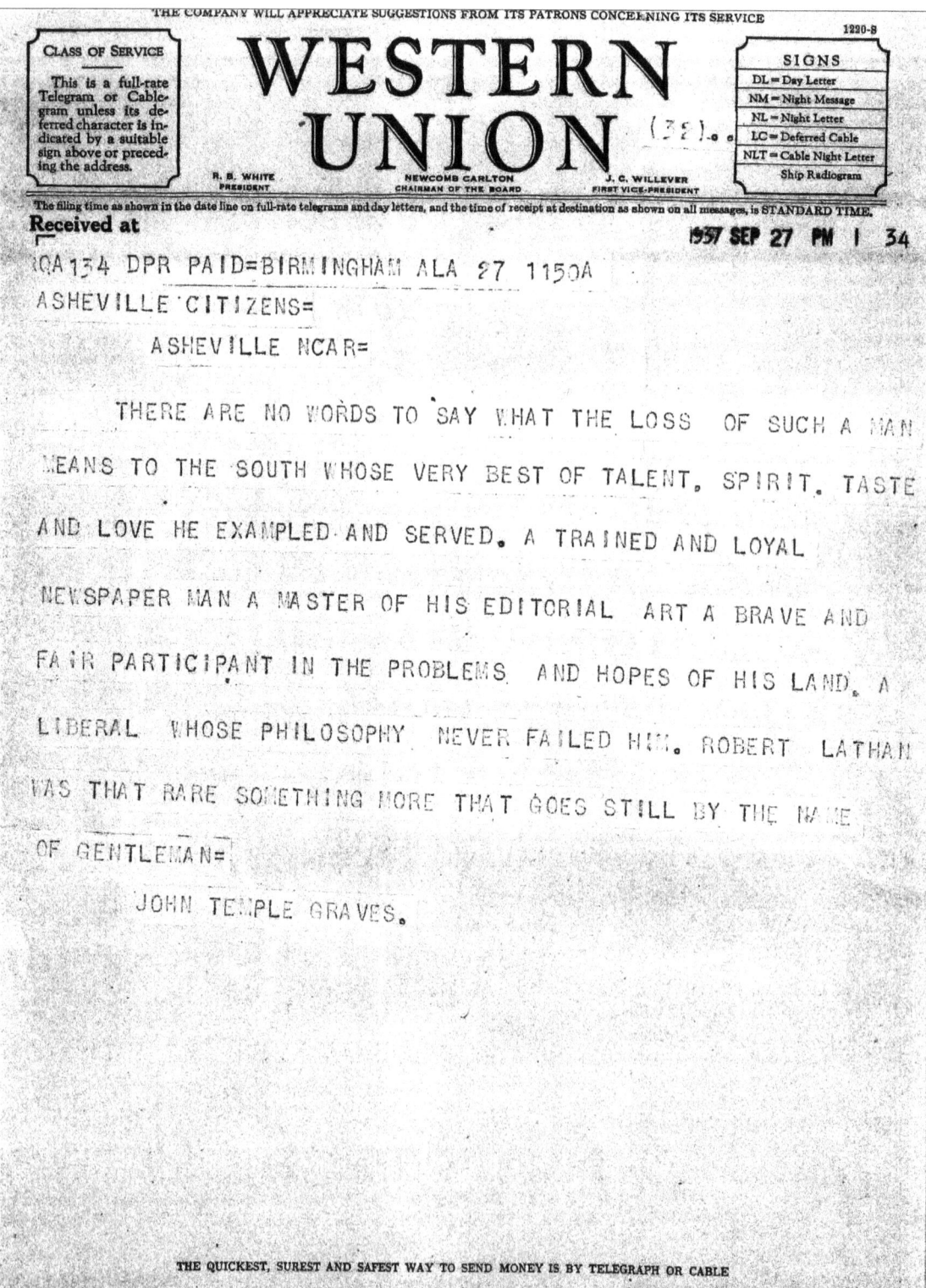

Very best of talent, spirit, taste and love
John Temple Graves

EDITOR MOURNED Services for Robert Lathan, editor of The Asheville Citizen for the last 10 years and winner of a Pulitzer prize in 1924, will be held in Asheville at 10 o'clock this morning. Burial will be Wednesday in Darlington, S. C. He died Sunday night after a cerebral hemorrhage.

Chapter Two

— THE — ASHEVILLE CITIZEN

EDITOR'S RITES SET FOR TODAY

Robert Lathan to Be Laid to Rest at Darlington.

MOURNED BY PRESS

Asheville Man Began His Newspaper Career on The State.

"Funeral services for Robert Lathan, 56, editor of the Asheville Citizen were conducted at 10 o'clock Tuesday morning at Trinity Episcopal Church in Asheville, NC. The Rev. George Floyd Rogers, rector officiated.

The body was taken to Darlington, SC for final rites at 11 o'clock Wednesday morning. Burial was in Grove Hill cemetery. The Rev. C. R. Cody conducted the services there.

Mr. Lathan was survived by his widow, the former Miss Bessie Agnes Early of Darlington, and one sister, Mrs. Oscar M. Lanier of Calhoun Falls."

Newspaper Staff Tributes

It was said that a railroad car full of floral tributes was brought to the graveside service. The especially poignant tribute from the staff of the Asheville Citizen was a wreath in the image of the red 30, which depicted the editing mark for END.

Community Resolution

Civitan Club of Asheville, NC

Resolved: That the Civitan Club desires to express its grateful appreciation for the influence which the life and work of Robert Lathan as had, and will continue to have, for the building of better citizens, and for the far-reaching good that will result therefrom.

Resolved, further: That the Members of this Club, collectively and individually, desire to record this expression of their warm personal friendship and admiration for Robert Lathan, as a man and a friend.

Burial Services

> "His life was gentle, and the elements so mixed in him
> That Nature might stand up and say to all the world,
> 'This was a man.'"

MANY ATTEND LATHAN BURIAL HERE YESTERDAY

Committal rites for Robert L. Lathan, fifty-six, editor of the Asheville Citizen, who died Sunday night at his home there, were held in Grove Hill Cemetery, Darlington, yesterday morning at 11 o'clock. The funeral services for the deceased were held in Asheville Tuesday morning at Trinity Episcopal Church, conducted by the Rev. George Floyd Rogers, rector.

The Rev. George Rogers, of Asheville, and the Rev. C. R. Cody, of Darlington, conducted the services at the grave here. The Rev. Mr. Rogers read the major portion of the impressive ritual of the Episcopal church, closing with "Crossing the Bar."

Pallbearers at the burial services here were G. E. Dargan, A. S. Dargan, L. W. Williamson, J. A. McLeod and Dr. O. A. Alexander, of Darlington, and Mason C. Brunson, of Florence.

Those who attended the funeral and burial services here from Asheville were newspaper associates of Mr. Lathan: Don S. Elias, vice president of the Asheville Citizen-Times Company; W. Randall Harris, assistant general manager, and Walter S. Adams, managing editor of The Citizen and The Times, and Charles K. Robinson, editor of The Times. The Rev. George Floyd Rogers, rector of Trinity Episcopal Church in Asheville, of which Mr. Lathan was an outstanding member, came with them.

Similar Unexpected Losses

Editor Robert Lathan died suddenly on September 26, 1937 at age 56. He came to his Asheville, NC office that day as usual to write the editorials for the Asheville Citizen. He became ill in the afternoon, went home in a taxi, collapsed soon thereafter and died in a few hours from a cerebral hemorrhage at the height of his career.

Similar to the circumstances of Lathan's sudden death were the circumstances of the death of President Franklin Roosevelt eight years later in 1945 at age 63. President Roosevelt had spent the afternoon reading his mail when he suddenly collapsed and became unconscious and died several hours later. Both men died of cerebral hemorrhage at the height of their careers.

Chapter Two

Condolences to Bessie Lathan

WASHINGTON, D. C.
MUNSEY BUILDING

LONDON, ENGLAND
DORLAND HOUSE

WHALEY-EATON SERVICE
The Standard Washington Authority
FOUNDED 1918

Dear, dear Mrs. Lathan:

    My heart pours itself out for you. Not until this morning did I learn, through Herbert Sass, that Bob had gone. He must have passed while I was on Edisto interring the ashes of Mrs. Whaley, who left us September 18. My own deep anguish can make me understand your own all the more, if that be possible. I wish that I could see you, for I might be able to say something to you that would be a real comfort, and I shall do so later. You two were so close. He was so fine.

    Your friends will all be wonderful - how much they want to help - but you have to make this fight in loneliness and prayer and courage and faith. The last is the most important of all - real faith, deep faith. There is a resurrection. This is not all. Believe that, believe it in the very depth of your soul, for it is true. Never doubt it.

    They will tell you how great and fine and good he was, but only you knew the true magnitude of his soul. That was the best of his virtues. He had a seeing heart as well as a seeing mind. There was nothing small or mean or restricted about him. That was why his service to the South was so priceless. No taint of selfishness was in his thought. He thought broadly and he served broadly.

    I always thought of him - and you - as among the dearest of my friends. Even though we saw each other very infrequently, the feeling of association was always there. Usually he would stop by on his visits, in the Spring, to New York, and I missed him this year, but I did not know at all that he was sick. He seemed to be so big and strong, so superior to mere physical things.

    I hope that later, when you have been able to readjust yourself, you will write. Tell me where you will be and what you are doing. I expect to go South more frequently. If you are going to be in Darlington I shall certainly stop by to see you on my next trip, whenever that is.

    From my heart

Oct. 8.

PHWhaley

I use the typewriter only that you may the better read.

Mrs. Bessie Lathan received this most movingly expressive letter a few weeks after the loss of her husband.

Chapter Three

Robert Lathan, Jr. Born To Be An Editor

I could not have been more than four or five years of age when I went with my father to the office of the *Yorkville Enquirer* and saw old Capt. Lewis Crist puttering about in his shirt sleeves. I remember him distinctly.

RL 1937

Chapter Three

The Lathan Family

James Leathen (Lathan) — Peggy Waugh
1730   1731

↓

Robert Lathan — Nancy Martin
1759-1842

1788   ↓   Arrived in
Three Brothers   South Carolina

Samuel Martin Lathan — Martha Patterson
1797-1890

↓   ↓

Rev. Robert Lathan, D.D.   Samuel Boston Lathan
1829-1896   1842-1939
"Scribbler"   "Scribbler"
Revolutionary War History   Civil War History

↓   ↓

Robert Lathan, Jr.   Samuel Robert Lathan
1881-1937   1880-1942
Editor

↓

S. Robert Lathan, Jr. M.D.
1938-
Author

↓

S. Robert Lathan III
1976-

↓

Eli Robert Lathan
2013-

Robert Lathan, Jr.
1881–1937

Robert Lathan, Jr. was born May 5, 1881 in Yorkville, York County, South Carolina. He was the son of Reverend Robert Lathan, DD and Frances (Fannie) Eleanor Barron. Both of his parents had long and storied family histories in South Carolina.

Father, Reverend Robert Lathan
December 27, 1829-June 15, 1896

Mother, Fannie Barron Lathan
May 30, 1838-November 4, 1899

Lathan Family History

The saga of this Lathan family started between the 17th and 18th century when many people of Scotland took refuge in Northern Ireland. Among those were the "Leathens," later becoming Lathan. The earliest known ancestral Lathan to migrate from Melrose, Scotland to Ballynena in County Antrim of Northern Ireland was James Lathan. He married Peggy Waugh, having five sons and two daughters.

In 1788, three of James' sons moved to the new American country. Robert Lathan and his wife Nancy Martin and five children arrived in Charleston, SC. After a year the family moved to Fairfield County where Lathan purchased 150 acres from the county for 50 pounds sterling. He later purchased more land and sold 188 acres to each of his three sons. In 1812 he petitioned for and received citizenship in the United States.

Robert Lathan's son Samuel Martin Lathan was born in 1797. He owned land between Blackstock, SC and White Oak, SC on the Big Wateree Creek flowing into the Catawba River. He purchased 188 acres from his father for $500 and later bought the adjacent acreage from his two brothers. Samuel and his wife had eleven children.

One of Samuel Lathan's sons was Robert born December 27, 1829 in Fairfield County, SC.

This son, the Reverend Robert Lathan, D.D. was a prominent ARP minister and noted historian who graduated from Erskine College, Due West, SC in 1855 and from Erskine Theological Seminary in 1858. He received an honorary Doctor of Divinity degree from Westminster College Pennsylvania in 1881. He was inducted posthumously into the Academic Hall of Fame at Erskine College in 2002.

Rev. Lathan lived in Yorkville, SC for 25 years, serving as an ARP pastor in both Yorkville and Tirzah, SC. While in Yorkville he taught in the schools and served as county commissioner of education as well as contributing articles to the *Yorkville Enquirer* newspaper. He was fondly known as a "scribbler" for his numerous written works.

The editor of the *Enquirer*, W.D. Grist described Dr. Lathan "as probably one of the most scholarly men ever to live in the state." He read the Old Testament from the original in Hebrew and the New Testament from the Greek and Latin, and in both cases as fluently as in English. He used his English Bible from the pulpit. He was recognized everywhere as a master of mathematics from arithmetic to calculus and also of astronomy.

If Dr. Lathan had any particular hobby, it was his love for history including original research. While professor at Erskine College, he published four books, the History of the Associate Reformed Synod of the South in 1882, and Historical Sketch of the Union Associated Reformed Presbyterian Church, Chester, SC in 1888 and History of Hopewell Associate Reformed and Its Pastors in 1878.

Dr. Lathan was especially interested in the history of South Carolina and prepared a history from the first settlements up to the close of the Revolutionary War, which was published in installments in the *Yorkville Enquirer* between 1874-1876. The newspaper columns were later the subject matter for a book titled, History of South Carolina which was published in 2002 by S. Robert Lathan, Jr. MD, his grand nephew. Rev. Lathan also wrote a sketch of his ancestor Robert Kilpatrick called a History of the Revolution, published in 1913.

Rev. Robert Lathan was married in 1859 to Fannie Barron, the daughter of Dr. Archibald Ingram Barron of Yorkville, SC. Lathan served as chaplain in the Confederate Army during the entire duration of the War Between the States. They had four daughters and three sons, the youngest was the Pulitzer Prize winner, Robert Lathan, Jr.

Reverend Lathan and Mrs. Fannie Lathan's seven children:

Samuel Boston Lathan 1862-1929
Anna (Annie) Isabelle Lathan 1865-1903
Mary Amelia (Melle) Lathan 1867-1933
Nannie B. Lathan 1869-1913
Archibald Ingram Lathan 1871 infant
Emma Martha Lathan 1875-1969
Robert Lathan Jr. 1881-1937

In 1884 when Robert Lathan, Jr. was three years old, he and the family moved from Yorkville to Due West, Abbeville County, SC where his father the Reverend Robert Lathan became a professor at Erskine Theological Seminary. Robert Lathan, Jr. featured the early influence of newspapers in a speech to the Press Club in 1937.

> One of the things that stands out in my memory of my first trip to Abbeville is eating dinner in the editorial office of the *Press and Banner* with my father and Mr. Hugh Wilson. If I had the ability to draw, I could, I think, a picture of him now, coming across the square with his close-cropped reddish beard and high silk hat. RL 1937

In 1892, Robert Lathan, Jr. began as an eleven year old member of the Preparatory Department at Erskine College. There were twenty students with Professor J. L. Presley. The courses of study that each student were required to master were extensive. The tuition was paid in cash for $30 for two years. The pupil at the end of a two year course was prepared for the freshman class of Erskine College.

Catalog as Lathan Began School

ANNUAL CATALOGUE

—OF—

Erskine College,

DUE WEST, ABBEVILLE COUNTY

SOUTH CAROLINA.

COLLEGIATE YEAR 1892-93.

PRESBYTERIAN PUBLISHING COMPANY,
Due West, S. C.
1893.

Preparatory Department.

NAME.	RESIDENCE.
Devlin, W. T.	Verdery, S. C.
Devlin, O. E.	Verdery, S. C.
Devlin, J. O.	Verdery, S. C.
Dunn, A. F.	Level Land, S. C.
Ellis, E. D.	Due West, S. C.
Estill, J. H. Jr.	Savannah, Ga.
Estill, W.	Savannah, Ga.
Estill, M. W.	Savannah, Ga.
Giffen, B. J.	Due West, S. C.
Hunter, N. A.	Prosperity, S. C.
→ Lathan, R.	Due West, S. C.
McDavid, R.	Due West, S. C.
McGee, C. M.	Due West, S. C.
Nance, C. D.	Cross Hill, S. C.
Neil, D. P.	Lancaster, S. C.
Nickles, J. M.	Due West, S. C.
Nickles, W. J.	Due West, S. C.
Pratt, C. D.	Due West, S. C.
Pressly, D. L.	Due West, S. C.
Smith, M. B.	Due West, S. C.

knowledge of the development of our Literature. Text-books: Effingham Maynard's English Classic Series for Spenser and a number of other writers; Maxey's Hamlet; Kellogg's edition of any other plays of Shakspeare; Rolfe's Selections from Wordsworth; Rowe's edition of Tennyson's Coming and Passing of Arthur; Wallace's edition of Tennyson's Princess; Belfield's Selections from DeQuincey; Shaw's History of English Literature; and Bascom's Philosophy of English Literature.

The Professor gives informal lectures as the needs of the class suggest; and at different times throughout the session the students write essays on subjects connected with the course of study.

HISTORY.

Instruction in History will be given for the present by different Professors. During the past session the work was done mainly by the President. Most of the time was taken up in the study of certain periods, the Elizabethan Age and the Age of the Puritan Revolution, but a general account of the Middle Ages also was given.

The work of the next session will be similar in character to that of the last, but the course will be somewhat fuller, as it will include Freeman's General Sketch of History, which will be studied by the Freshman Class.

HEBREW.

By action of the Board of Trustees, any one who so desires may take Hebrew instead of one of the Modern Languages. This arrangement was made especially for the benefit of those looking forward to a theological course; but instruction will be given, without extra charge, to any one who may wish to study Hebrew. Dr. W. L. Pressly, of the Seminary, has charge of this Department.

PREPARATORY DEPARTMENT.
Professor, J. L. Pressly.

The course of instruction in this Department is so arranged and graded that the pupil at the end of a two years' course will, in most cases, be prepared for the Freshman Class.

Prof. Pressly gives his whole time to the Department. The Faculty exercise a general supervision over it. The tuition in this Department is paid, not by scholarship, but in cash; and the amount is $15 per term in advance, or $30 for the whole session.

The course of study is as follows:

First Grade—English Grammar; Arithmetic—Wentworth and Hill; Progressive Intellectual Arithmetic—Wentworth; Histories of Greece and the United States—Goodrich and Barnes; Introductory Latin Composition—Leighton.

Second Grade—Introduction to Latin Composition—Leighton; Latin Grammar—Allen and Greenough, in connection with Cæsar; Progressive Practical Arithmetic—Wentworth; Shorter Course in Algebra—Wentworth; Greek—White's First Lessons; and two books of the Anabasis.

Special attention paid to writing and spelling.

Expenses

These include Tuition, Board, Washing, Lights, Fuel, Books, College and Society Fees, as follows:

Tuition—by Scholarship	$ 20 00
Board in families—from $10 to $12 per month—say	100 00
Washing—$1 per month	9 00
Lights and fuel	10 00
Books	10 00
College and Society Fees, per year, about	15 00
Aggregating, with board	$164 00

It should be stated that the Board of Trustees has fixed the rate of Tuition in the Preparatory Department at Thirty Dollars.

The above may be sufficient to satisfy inquiries which are frequently made in respect to the necessary expenses of a student.

Every one knows that clothing, pocket money and all matters of this sort depend entirely on the indulgence of parents and the habits of their sons.

The Contingent Fee of Ten Dollars must be paid in full within six weeks after entrance.

Chapter Three

Lathan Requested Information from Business School

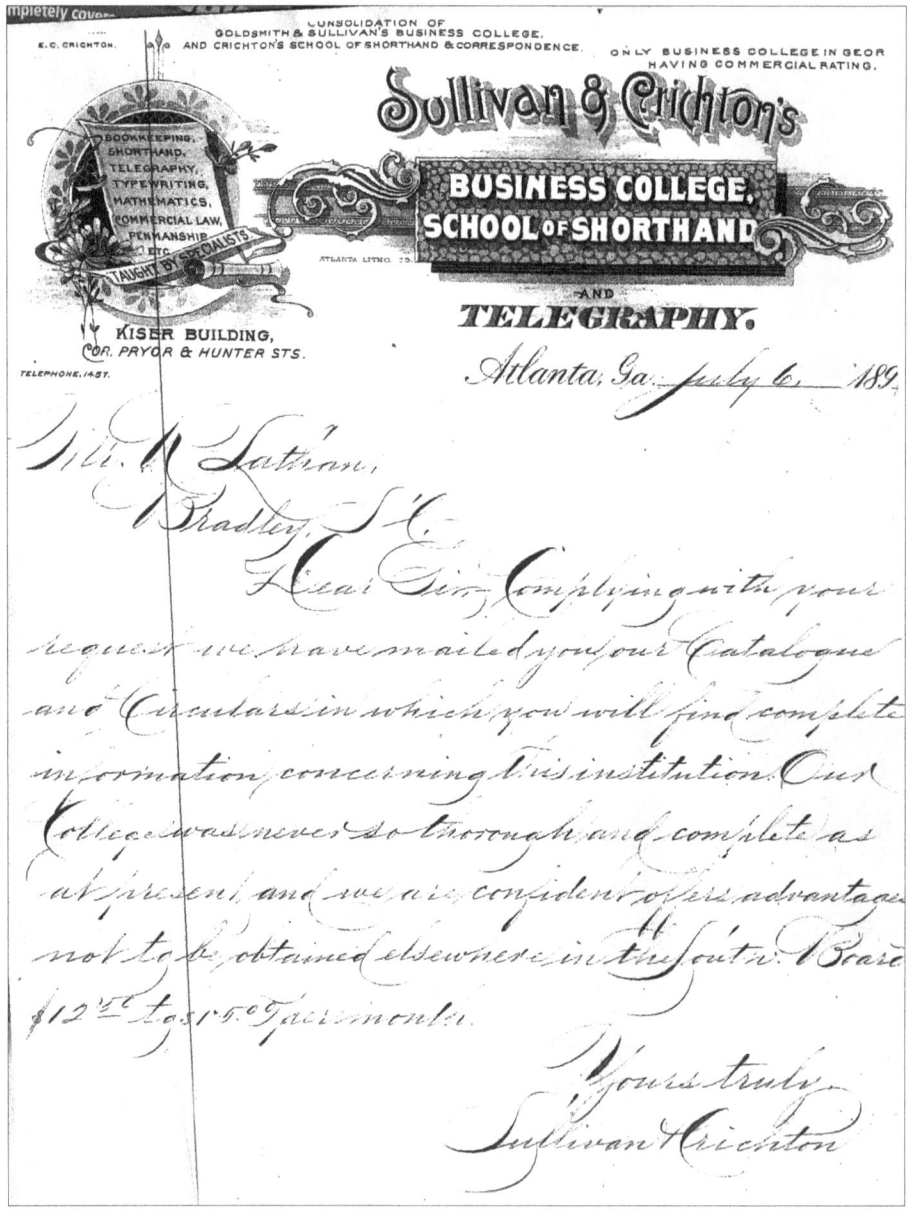

After only a few short years of living in Due West and mastering his studies at the preparatory school, Lathan's father, the Reverend Robert died.

Robert Lathan, Jr. continued his education through books, catalogues and personal studies, much under the guidance of his older brother Samuel Boston Lathan.

His father died in July of 1896. Robert Lathan, Jr. at fifteen years old requested a catalog from the Sullivan & Crichton's Business School and School of Shorthand in Atlanta, GA. The letter shows his interest in business at this early age. Only ten days later, in July 1896, he requested information from the Maryland Business School in Baltimore, MD and three months later, he received more information from a business school in accounting and penmanship in Burlington, Iowa.

Lathan's Teachers Certificate

STATE OF SOUTH CAROLINA,
DEPARTMENT OF EDUCATION.

Teacher's County Certificate of Qualification, No. 38

Experience in Teaching ...... years.   Attendance on Teachers' Institutes, ... years.   *First* Grade, Class

THIS CERTIFIES, That *Mr. Robert Lathan* having furnished sufficient evidence of good moral character, and having passed a satisfactory examination in the following named Branches, with the annexed results, is recommended and authorized to teach in the Free Public Schools of this County:

Subject	Per Cent	Subject	Per Cent	Subject	Per Cent	Subject	Per Cent	Subject	Per Cent
Orthography	100	Geography	80	Elementary Algebra	50	Elementary Vocal Music		Theory and Practice	
Reading		English Grammar	78	Elementary Science		Elementary Drawing			
Writing	96	U. S. History	83	Elementary Eng. Literature		Civics and Ethics			
Arithmetic	80	S. C. History		Elementary Agriculture		Physiology and Hygiene	85		

GENERAL AVERAGE 81½

THIS CERTIFICATE to continue valid for the term of TWO YEARS from the date hereof, unless sooner revoked.

Given under our Hands and Seals at *Abbeville*, on the 18th day of *February*, A. D., 1898

W. T. Milford [L.S.]
S. P. McElroy [L.S.]
R. F. Gilliam [L.S.]

County Board of Education for *Abbeville* County.

In pursuit of both an income and an opportunity to further his education, Lathan stood for the required testing of candidates for teaching positions in South Carolina. On February 18, 1898, Lathan received a teacher's certificate of qualification from the State of South Carolina School of Education, Abbeville County, which was valid for two years.

On June 4, 1898, Mr. J. J. Baker of Anderson, SC sent a letter to Robert Lathan reporting that his son, George Baker, had resigned his position as a teacher in the Trinity School to enlist in the Cuban War. Mr. Baker suggested that if Lathan was interested, he should apply as a teacher and correspond with Mr. P. H. Brown, an influential member of the board in Waco, SC.

Chapter Three

Recommendation to Change Teaching Position

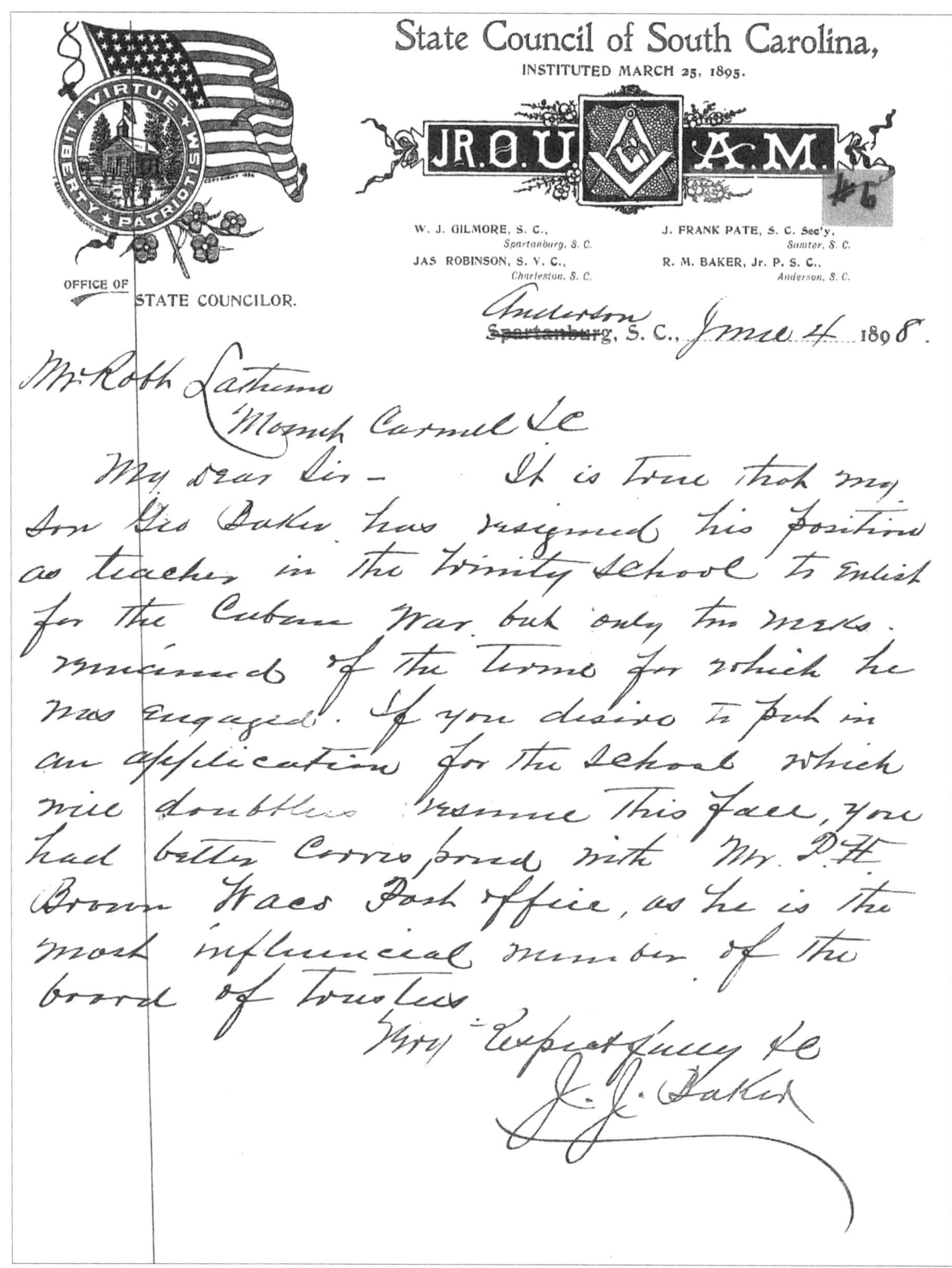

State Council of South Carolina,
INSTITUTED MARCH 25, 1895.
JR. O. U. A. M.

W. J. GILMORE, S. C., Spartanburg, S. C.
JAS ROBINSON, S. V. C., Charleston, S. C.
J. FRANK PATE, S. C. Sec'y, Sumter, S. C.
R. M. BAKER, Jr. P. S. C., Anderson, S. C.

OFFICE OF STATE COUNCILOR.

Anderson, S. C., June 4 1898.

Mr Roth Latimer
Mount Carmel S.C.

My Dear Sir — It is true that my son Geo Baker has resigned his position as teacher in the Trinity School to enlist for the Cuban War, but only two weeks remained of the terms for which he was engaged. If you desire to put in an application for the school which will doubtless resume this fall, you had better correspond with Mr. D.H. Brown Waco Post office, as he is the most influencial member of the board of trustees.

Very respectfully &c
J. J. Baker

Teacher in South Carolina Schools 1898-1900

On June 28, 1898, Mr. G. C. Grand, from Latimer, SC sent a letter to Lathan in Mt. Carmel, SC stating that Lathan had been elected as a teacher for the Latimer School. The salary was to be $30 per month, not including board.

A few months later, Lathan received a letter from Waco, SC reporting that the school term would begin around November 15 and continue for six to seven months, paying $35-40 a month. In the fall of 1898 the seventeen year old Robert Lathan, Jr. began as a teacher in the school in Latimer, Abbeville County, SC continuing to teach in the county for three years until 1900.

In 1899, teacher Lathan of Latimer, SC. requested of the Carolina Teachers' Agency the purchase of school furniture, and books. In May 1899, Lathan received a letter from F.M. Sheridan, Manager of the teacher's agency in Greenwood, SC. stating.... "We are pleased to quote you the following prices on school desks..of very low prices and we feel sure you cannot get any other first class desks any cheaper." Desks were approximately $1.50 each. Another letter was received confirming the quote and enclosing a statement of the order for $88.30 for desks including the freight.

Teacher Lathan Requests Supplies

F. M. SHERIDAN, Manager.　　　　　　　　　　　　　　　　　GEO. W. HART, Secretary.

Carolina Teachers' Agency,
GREENWOOD, S. C.

SUPPLIES SCHOOLS, COLLEGES AND UNIVERSITIES, WITH THOROUGHLY COMPETENT INSTRUCTORS.

OUR TERRITORY COVERS THE ENTIRE SOUTHEAST.

SCHOOL FURNITURE, SCHOOL BOOKS, SCHOOL LIBRARIES.

May 6, 1899.

Mr. R. Lathan,
　　Latimer, S. C.

Dear Sir:-

Yours of the 5th inst. received. We are pleased to quote you the following prices on school desks,- On the Celebrated New Rubberless Wabash Automatic School desks, f. o. b. factory Wabash, Ind.,-

	Singles	Doubles
Nos. 1&2	$1.80	$2.15
Nos. 3 & 4	$1.70	$2.05
Nos. 5 & 6	$1.60	$1.95
Rears, any size	$1.50	$1.90

These are very low prices and we feel sure that you can't get any ohter first class desks any cheaper. These desks are guaranteed by the factory for ten years and we feel sure that they will last twice that long if they are not too roughly used. They are no cheap desks, that is, in construction but they are cheap in price.

We have placed a number of them in the Graded Schools here and have placed a large number in the schools thoughout the State. They are all giving good satisfaction and we feel that the purchasers are all well pleased.

We would be glad to have you to give us your order and we know that you would be well pleased with the desks. They can be shipped promptly and can be gotten here in a short while.

While we believe that the above prices are as cheap as any you can get still we will make you the following offer,-we will take your order at 5¢ per desks less than you can buy any other first class desk. We have had some to take advantage of this offer.

The prices of desks has advanced during the last few days and we have been notified that a still further advance is expected soon. We inclose a a catalogue of school supplies and will give you a discount of 40% of list prices. We hope to receive your order. Very truly yours,

　　　　　　　　　　　　　　　　　　　　　　　　CAROLINA TEACHERS' AGENCY,
　　　　　　　　　　　　　　　　　　　　　　　　F. M. SHERIDAN, Manager.
　　　　　　　　　　　　　　　　　　　　　　　　GREENWOOD, S. C.

Recommendation for a Better Teaching Position

> Office of
> James M. Carlton,
> Physician.
> Mt. Carmel, S. C., May 11th 1895.
>
> M_____
>
> To Whom it may concern:
> This is to certify that I am personally acquainted with Mr. Robert Lathan; that he is a man of unusually bright intellect, high moral character, strictest integrity and deserves more than any young man of my acquaintance.
>
> J. M. Carlton.

In May of 1899, after Lathan had been the teacher in Latimer School for a year, several prominent community members wrote letters "To whom it May Concern," certifying that this young man was of strong character, accurate scholarship, good sober qualities, and always attentive of his duties. The recommendations of W. W. Bradley, John Morrah, William Gillen, George Gross an E.L. McAllister and Dr. Carlton, afforded Lathan the opportunity to accept a better teaching position during his second year.

Chapter Three

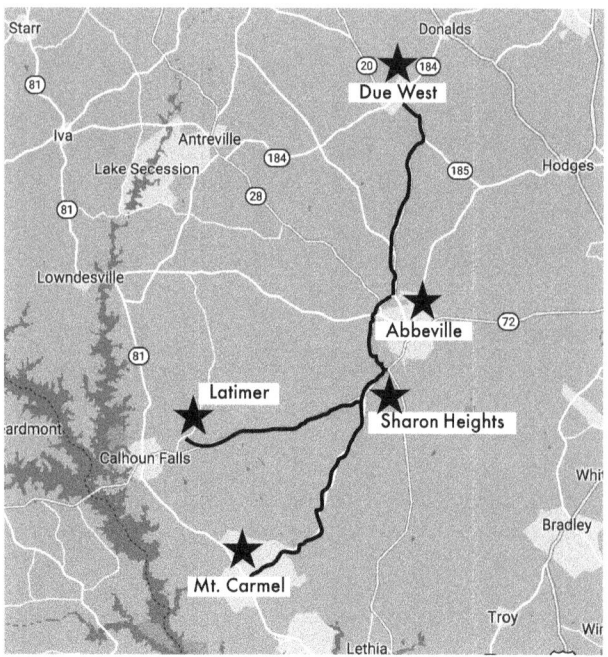

After successfully completing the 1898-1899 school year at Latimer, Robert Lathan took a position for the following school term at Sharon High School in Abbeville County, SC.

During his time in Abbeville, Lathan ordered more publishing supplies from a firm in Battle Creek, Michigan. They acknowledged receipt of his payment of $4.01 for the supplies and returned to him the excess of $.47 in postage stamps. Since he had ordered previously from this company, their question to him was "to inform us if you have left the public schools at Mt. Carmel?"

In his teaching role in Sharon High School in Abbeville, Lathan wrote a letter in January 1990 to Governor Roosevelt of New York. Within a month, Lathan received a return letter from the State Historian that "his esteemed letter" had been forwarded to the New York Historical Society.

During Lathan's time as a young teacher, the older brother, Samuel Boston Lathan continued to correspond with his younger brother. Their nineteen year age difference made him a father figure and counselor to Robert Lathan.

The correspondence and counseling between brothers went both ways as the older Lathan wrote in early January 1900 that he wanted "to acquaint you with an offer I received today, and to ask you what you think of it." The offer consisted of the senior Lathan buying a one half interest in a business college in Spartanburg, SC. from Miss Neel and becoming its manager. With beautiful flourishing script, he described to Robert the predictions of Miss Neel of 100 students per year taking $35.00 courses with a probability of his making $11,500 per year profit from the school. He would be forming the organization of the school and teaching stenography and typing to many students including those from Wofford and Converse Colleges.

In a second letter he asked for Rob to travel to Mt. Carmel for a weekend to discuss the business proposition and to bring writing papers plus the letter of samples of the art school in Columbus, Ohio. He believed that Robert had access to these materials. The senior Lathan reported that he was traveling to Mt. Carmel, SC in a few days to begin teaching writing at the Shorthand and Typing School and would need the supplies.

Letter from Samuel B. Lathan, Robert Lathan's Oldest Brother

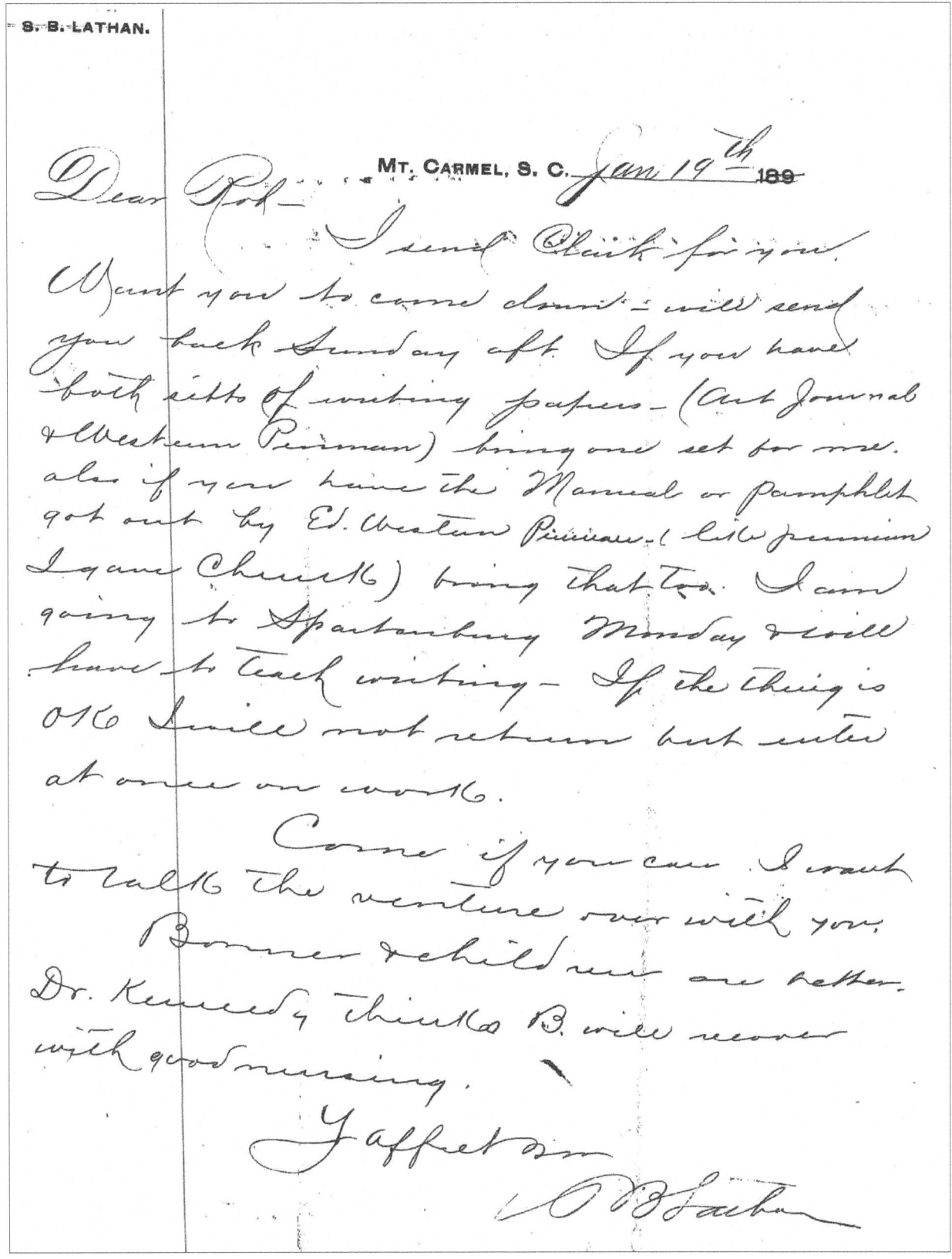

Lathan Orders Supplies to Prepare for New Tasks

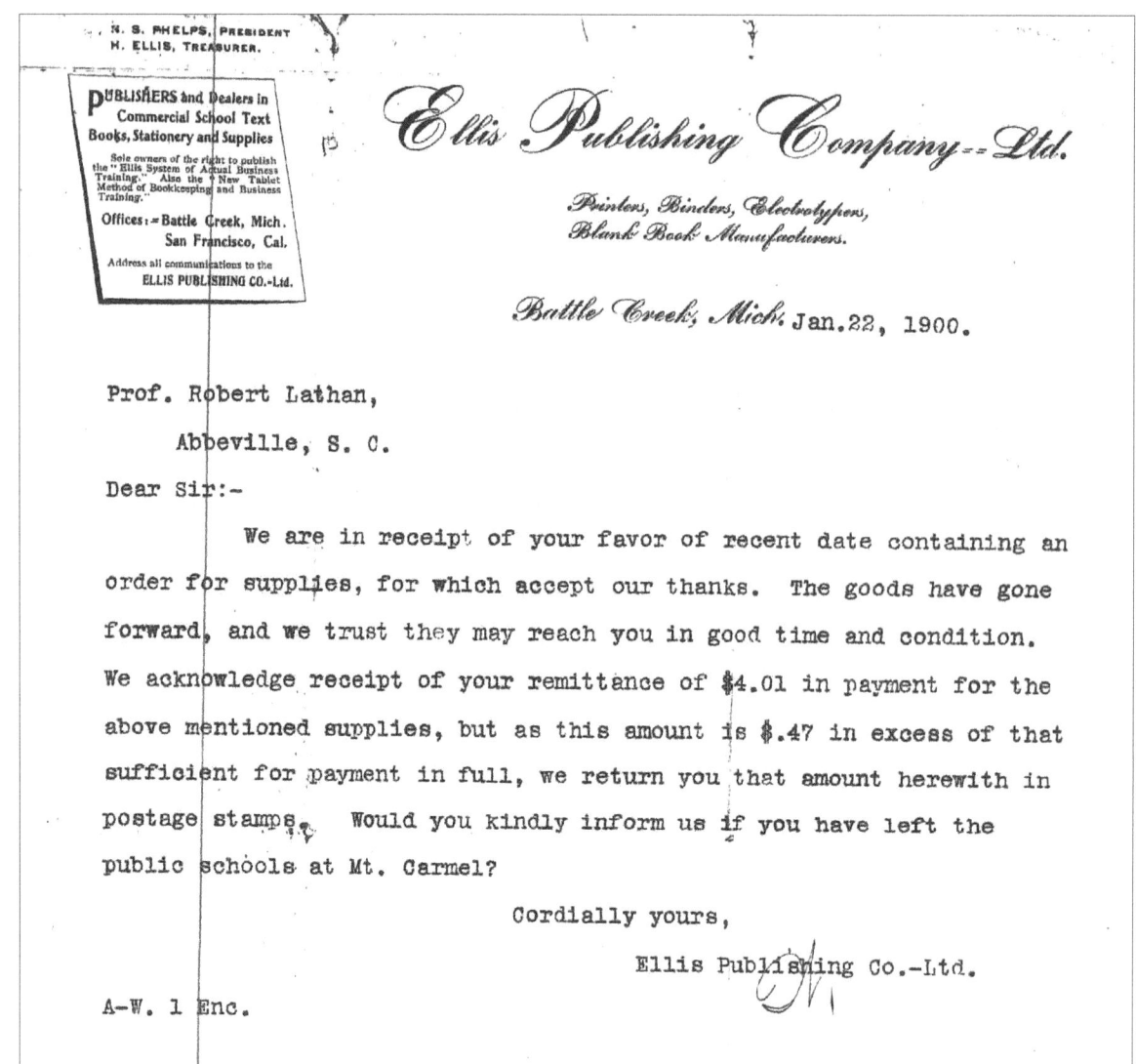

In February, 1900, SB Lathan was now working in Spartanburg, SC. His letters to his brother showed the new letterhead of the Spartanburg Business College with Mr. L. B. Vernon, President and S.B. Lathan, Business Manager. His first letter started "Dear Rob, I am here and my work is well. I am teaching Commercial Law, Business Forms, and Correspondence, as well as looking after the business management of the entire school." He admonishes his brother to keep on the lookout for possible pupils for the school, especially in the Abbeville boys.

In March, S. B. Lathan's letter to his brother showed even more skill at penmanship, but less progress at making a profit at the school as the tuition gathered has not yet covered the expenses. He reports that he "has reorganized the school, brought it into some form and the thing is now showing life and enthusiasm. I feel sure that in a few months time it will be paying handsomely." In the meantime he did appreciate the loan sent to him by his brother. S.B.Lathan stressed that his financial plans for the school were not being achieved and felt that providing a summer course in typing and shorthand to his nephew free of tuition in exchange for his nephew teaching the same course in the night school would add to the finances of the school. He also described a new project of renting a home for his family and taking in boarders from the school. He felt he could cover all of the household expenses.

By the end of April and several letters later, SB Lathan admits that many problems had not been satisfactorily handled, like the shorthand and typing department.

He also advised that he was working in the Bookkeeping Department and everything was "topsy turvey."

S.B. Lathan's Description of Business College Duties

L. B. VERNON, President   Spartanburg Business College   S. B. LATHAN, Business Manager

BOOK-KEEPING
PENMANSHIP
BUSINESS LAW
BUSINESS FORMS
ENGLISH
CORRESPONDENCE

SHORTHAND
TYPEWRITING
COURT REPORTING
SPELLING
RAPID CALCULATION
ARITHMETIC

Spartanburg, S. C., Mch 14th 1900

My dear Rob,—

I am not well this afternoon & unable to run around after students — so I'll write a short note. I have been threatened with cholera morbus all day. Ate heartily of fresh pork yesterday and am now paying the piper.

I am more than obliged to you for the loan. I did not want to go to Miss Neel if I could help it — as I believed — and still believe — that it would make a much better impression if I could make our tuition fees meet all expenses, which at this time are abnormally heavy. Two more pupils will put me "on velvet" and over — and I will have them next week.

Up to date I have brought in $145.00 into the treasury. For my first 5 week's work — a stranger to every one — I am very well satisfied. What is still

S.B. Lathan Encourages Lathan to Join his Business College

> **Spartanburg Business College**
> L. B. Vernon, President — S. B. Lathan, Business Manager
>
> BOOK-KEEPING, PENMANSHIP, BUSINESS LAW, BUSINESS FORMS, ENGLISH, CORRESPONDENCE
>
> SHORTHAND, TYPEWRITING, COURT REPORTING, SPELLING, RAPID CALCULATION, ARITHMETIC
>
> Spartanburg, S.C. April 20, 1900
>
> My dear Rob,—
>
> I hardly know where to direct this but I suppose the Post Master will forward it if not called for.
>
> Mrs. Vernon is anxious for you to come on at once and begin work. She wants you to take up Short hand, and feels sure that you will after a months work in the day classes, be able to teach the night pupils short hand & keep well ahead of them. I believe you can. Besides this you can spend your spare time in day, working up the night school — a thing I have never been able to do. She thinks you can easily build it up to a paying thing, and I believe you can. You will get your short hand course free, of course. If you decide to come on at once let me know, so I can meet you here. I think the sooner you get at the Short hand the better, for now the classes have hardly begun, and as they are boys of no prior mental training

In April of 1900, Robert Lathan received a letter from his brother stating that "Mrs. Vernon is anxious for you to come on at once and begin work. She wants you to take up short hand and feels sure that you will after a month work in the day classes." He reports that Robert Lathan will be able to outstrip the ability of the boys that he will be instructing. He also suggests that his young brother might be able to enter classes at nearby Wofford College. The older brother seems very anxious for the younger brother to come and work in Spartanburg just as soon as school is closed in Abbeville. He also wrote that it was his desire to change Robert Lathan from a school teacher to a businessman.

Chapter Three

Lathan Completes his Obligation to Business College

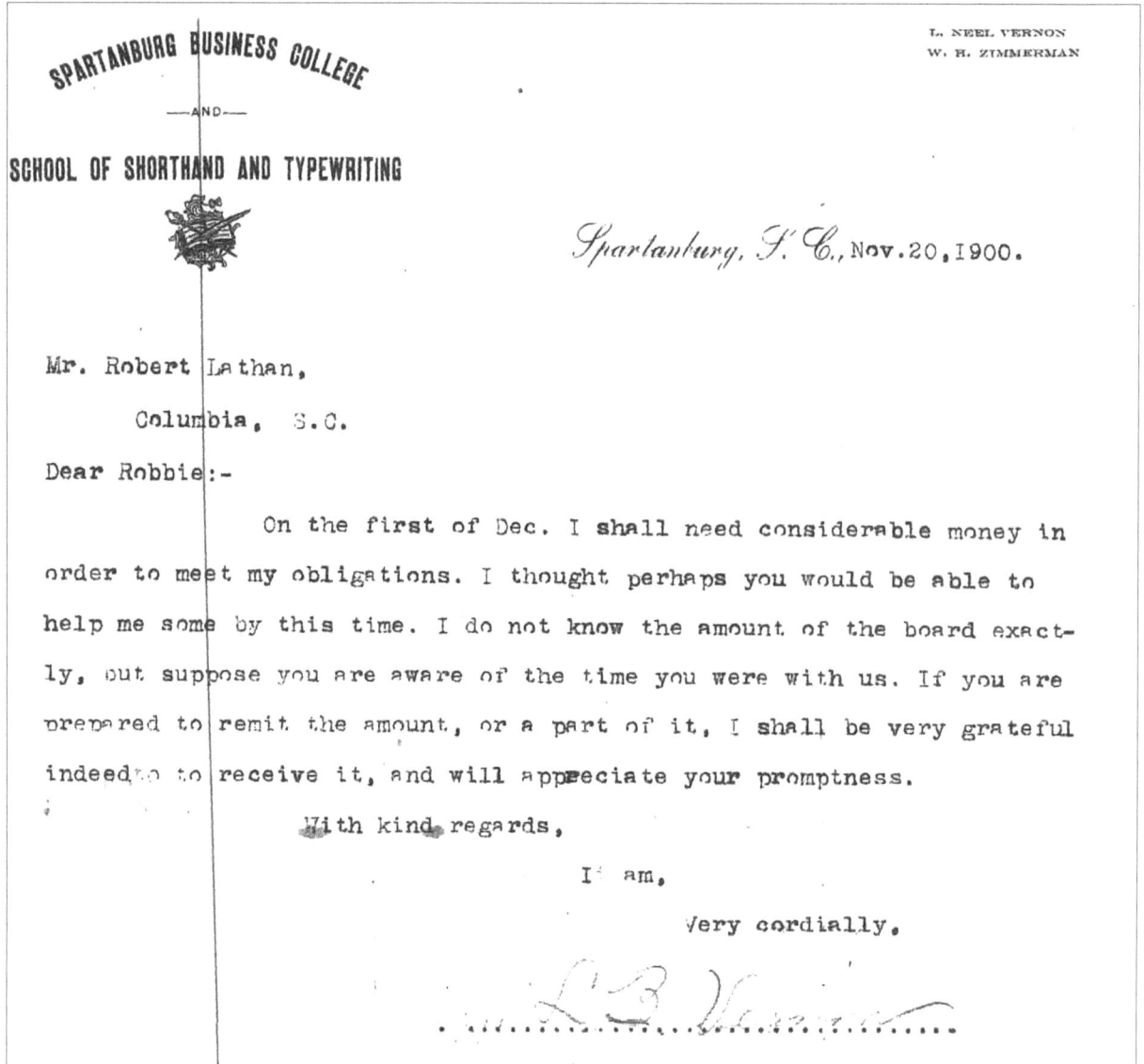

Robert Lathan, Jr. did arrive at the Spartanburg Business School taking shorthand and typing courses while teaching the same. While his tuition was free, his board was not as he subsequently at the end of the term received a payment request from LB Vernon.

In a letter dated November 1990 from Mr. L B. Vernon, President of School of Shorthand and Typing, Spartanburg, SC, Vernon requested money to reimburse the school for Robert Lathan's board expenses. "On the first of December I should need considerable money....If you are prepared to remit the amount of board expense..I shall be very grateful indeed.

Lathan did reimburse the school for his expenses as he decided to change focus from school to newspapers.

Chapter Four

Robert Lathan, Jr.
An Eager Student of the News

I had just turned 19 when one of my duties under N. G. Gonzales was that of clipping for him anything I saw in *The State* papers that I thought would interest him.

RL 1937

Chapter Four

Eager Student
1900–1903

The 🌴 State

The *State* Newspaper was founded in 1891 by two Gonzales brothers, NG and Ambrose in Columbia, SC. The brothers believed strongly and practiced successfully covering all of the news surrounding the political actions and climate of the government in South Carolina.

In the late summer of 1900, correspondence shows that Robert Lathan, Jr. became interested in applying for a position in journalism with *The State* newspaper in Columbia, SC. He wrote to the editor, Mr. NG Gonzalez expressing his interest. During the prior year, Lathan had been taking courses as well as teaching shorthand and typing at the Spartanburg Business College where his brother S. B. Lathan was business manager. His handwriting demonstrates the training that he had in communication skills.

Within a short period of time, Mr. NG Gonzales, Editor of the *The State* answered that Lathan was "strongly recommended to me, and there is a good opening here for a bright, educated young man willing to start at the bottom and work up. At first the work will be stenography, typewriting and clipping" skills that Lathan had been perfecting at the Spartanburg Business School.

Mr. Gonzales admonishes his possible new empolyee on several very important requirements, "anyone who works for us must be faithful, devoted to the interests of the paper and ready to put his hand to anything." Also, "whether you wish to make journalism a profession…but we don't want mere transient scholars."

Lathan's Letter of Acceptance to The State

SPARTANBURG BUSINESS COLLEGE

SCHOOL OF SHORTHAND AND TYPEWRITING

L. B. VERNON, President
S. B. LATHAN, Business Manager

Spartanburg, S.C., Aug 18, 1900.

Mr. N. G. Gonzales
Columbia, S.C.

Dear Sir:—

I have just learned through Miss Thomason of your city, that the position about which I a short time since had some correspondence with you through Mr Macfeat, is still vacant. As I beleive that I am now prepared to fill this place to your satisfaction, I would respectfully offer myself for it.

Trusting to hear from you in regard to the matter, I am

Yours very respectfully
Robert Lathan

Letters to Lathan of Acceptance and Instruction

> **EDITORIAL ROOMS.**
> N. G. GONZALES, EDITOR.
>
> **The State.**
>
> COLUMBIA, S. C., Aug. 25 1900.
> 3 a.m.
>
> Dear Sir: I have been too busy to answer your note before now. You were strongly recommended to me, and there is a good opening here for a bright, educated young man willing to start at the bottom and work up. At first the work would be stenography, typewriting and clipping. Later it could be anything you proved yourself competent to do. Our force is small and future opportunities are large.
>
> We can afford to pay little at first as a stenographer is an innovation and luxury for the editorial department, so much will depend on what you are willing to work for. Please tell me this. Also how old you are, where you were educated and whether you wish to make journalism a profession. This is a good school but we don't want mere transient scholars.
>
> Yours sincerely, N. G. Gonzales

As a follow up on his first letter, Editor Gonzales wrote to Robert Lathan two weeks later to make sure he had not misled Lathan in his initial work offer. He explained that he had to consult with his brother who was president of the company about new hiring. *The State* would only consent to an engagement for three months, at the end of which time we will be able to know better whether we can continue the arrangement. The arrangement continued successfully for three years, until NG Gonzales was killed.

EDITORIAL ROOMS.
N. G. GONZALES,
EDITOR.

The State.

COLUMBIA, S. C., Sept. 6, 1900.

Dear Sir: I have delayed answering your letter because I had to consult my brother, who is president of the company. He will not consent to a positive engagement for more than three months; at the end of which time we will be able to know better whether we can continue the arrangement. Personally, I think we can and will; but I do not want to mislead you.

This year we are under heavy expense, paying debts and increasing our plant; and we cannot afford to take any risks until we see what the winter business will be.

If you can come at $8 a week to start with I shall be glad to have you. This is several dollars more than young lady stenographers can be had for, although it is small in comparison with what I hope to be able to pay some day.

I took my first work on The News and Courier in 1880 on the same condition — three months' trial. My advice to you is to come. You will learn much, the practice will perfect you and, if we should not be able to continue your services, you must be by the beginning of the year much better qualified to get a good job.

Let me know if you accept and when you can come and I will send you a pass.

Yours sincerely, N. G. Gonzales

Begins Newspaper Career

In September of 1900 Robert Lathan, Jr. began his four decade career in the newspaper world, at the *The State* newspaper in Columbia, SC. He was directly trained in journalism by the Editor, NG Gonzales, becoming his private secretary and assistant. As the nineteen year old, Lathan's long career in the field of journalism was just beginning. It continued through most newspaper roles including chief editor in two different states.

This first training job for Lathan was to be Mr. Gonzales' personal stenographer as well as covering routine news events occuring in and around Columbia. He fulfilled this sale successfully until the Editor, Gonzales died in January 1903.

Ambrose E. Gonzales   *NG Gonzales*   *William E. Gonzales*

Newspaper November 1902

WEDNESDAY, NOVEMBER 19, 1902.

Weather forecast for South Carolina: Fair Wednesday and Thursday; light variable winds, mostly easterly.

A Good Year and a Goodly Land.

The time has come, we think, to pronounce South Carolina finally "out of the woods"—industrially and financially out of the forest of gloom into which her people were plunged by war and reconstruction and, from which they have been slowly finding their way during the last two decades.

Lathan's responsibilities at the newspaper included composing the headlines of editorials written by and expressing important opinions of Editor NG Gonzales. Lathan spoke of one such time in 1902.

Excerpts from the speech are quoted here. Complete speech is in references.

South 1937

I think that I can definitely date the change. In the autumn of 1902, about the time of the State Fair, NG Gonzales wrote an editorial reviewing the improvement the year had recorded in South Carolina economically. I wrote the head for the article and his praise of the head the next day warmed my heart and fixed it in my mind. the heading was: "A Good Year and a Goodly Land."

Letter to Robert Lathan from Cousin SR Lathan

In September 1901, Robert Lathan received a letter from his cousin requesting information on a possible newspaper job.

The cousin who wrote the letter was a student at Erskine college and the father of this book's author Robert Lathan Jr., M.D.

On January 15, 1903, Lathan's boss and mentor, NG Gonzales was shot to death by Lt. Governor Jim Tillman in front of the State House in Columbia as he was walking from his office on Main Street in the middle of the day. He immediately was taken to Columbia Hospital where he died later.

The place (see arrow, right) where Mr. Gonzales was shot. He had just turned east from Main into Gervais, in front of the old street car transfer station. Across the way is the City Hall, which replaced the one at Main and Washington. It housed the Columbia Theater of hallowed memories, as well as the municipal offices. It is now the site of the Wade Hampton hotel.

During the time Gonzales was on his death bed, Lathan was called to capture his exact words for history. Present with him in his hospital room when he died was *News and Courier* correspondent, August Kohn and *The State* staff members, James Hoyt, Jr. and Robert Lathan. Dr. James Babcock was also present. Babcock and Lathan both recorded statements.

Robert Lathan's recorded statement was considered to be exactly the words uttered by NG Gonzales on his death bed.

Lathan Stenographic Record

Mr. Gonzales' Dying Statement
State of South Carolina
County of Richland.

Personally comes Robert Lathan, who says on oath that he was stenographer and secretary to the late NG Gonzales and occupied such a position at the time of the shooting of NG Gonzales. That on the afternoon of the said shooting, and just after the said NG had been brought into *The State* office on Main street, some fifty yards north of the point of the said shooting, said NG Gonzales told deponent that he, the said NG Gonzales, knew the result of such a shot as has he had received, and more than once while in said office, suffering from said wound, intimated in plain language that he knew his wound was mortal. That thereafter, and in a couple of hours thereafter, when said NG Gonzales had been conveyed to the Columbia hospital, to be there operated upon, he repeated said intimation of his wound to deponent. That while in this state of mind he made the following statement in words following, or of like import, to deponent, to-wit: "I started out from *The State* office walking, as usual, on the right hand side of the pavement going towards the State House, and I got close to the corner, the intersection of Main and Gervais Streets, where I had to turn to the left into Gervais Street on my may home, I observed Tillman. Two men were with him, Senator Talbird of Beaufort and another man, whose face I did not observe. Talbird was next to Tillman and this other man was on the inside. Tilman was on the outside. Knowing that if I kept straight on I would collide with him, because the three men were walking abreast and Tillman was the outside man, I also being on the outside, I cut diagonally to the left, intending to turn into Gervais street, as I could have done without touching the man of the three who was on the inside. As I got (I had just merely glanced at his face) on the turn, not more than two or three feet from the exact corner, Tillman suddenly pulled his pistol, or perhaps he had it in his hand or possibly up his sleeve, I did not notice, presented it and fired, making some exclamation which I have forgotten. The shock almost threw me off my feet. I swerved around and felt very weak. I threw my back against the pillar at the corner on the Main street side so as to support myself, and faced him. He had his pistol pointed at me, and I said to him: 'Fire, you coward! You have already killed me, and you know it. Shoot again.' Tillman said something about, 'You see, I took your advice,' then looked at my face, dropped his arm holding his pistol and sauntered out into the middle of the street." Replying to some questions. Mr. Gonzales continued, "I had no idea whatever of meeting him. I had seen him two days before in the lobby of the State House. He saw me and was talking to someone while I was walking around. He did not say anything. I did not say anything. The thing was finished as far as I was concerned." Mr. Gonzales was then asked whether Tillman said anything when he fired upon him. He replied that he did say something. Being further questioned whether he had sent Tillman any message, Mr. Gonzales answered: "Never sent him a word of message by any one." Then the question was asked, "Did you hear him say that you sent him a message by some one?" Mr. Gonzales answered, "No, he said something like, "'I have taken you at your word,' or something like that. I sent him no message, so help me God!" Mr. Gonzales further said that Tillman used the expression, 'I have taken you at your word' or something of similar import, after he fired.

On the first day of the present session of the General Assembly, or the day thereafter, I was in the lobby of the State House on the side next to the hall of the House of Representatives. While there I saw Mr. NG Gonzales standing just at the door of the committee room to the left as you enter the hall of the House of Representatives. He was talking to a gentleman. While he stood there, I saw James H. Tillman standing in the lobby within a few feet of the said Mr. NG Gonzales. He, the said Tillman, was speaking to someone when I saw him, and he passed on into the committee room opposite to that one near the door of which Mr. Gonzales was standing. Said James H. Tillman was obliged to have seen said NG Gonzales, as there was nothing interposing between them.

Robert Lathan   L.S.

Sworn before me this
Eleventh day of February, AD 1903.
C.M. Asbill L.S. N.P. of S.C

Chapter Four

> W. A. CLARK   WM. ELLIOTT, JR.
>
> **CLARK, ELLIOTT & CLARK**
> ATTORNEYS AT LAW
> 1233 WASHINGTON STREET
> COLUMBIA, S. C.   Sept. 26th, 1903.
>
> Robert Lathan, Esq.,
> Columbia, S.C.
>
> Dear Sir:-
>
>   The Tillman case is set for trial Monday, the 28th inst., in Lexington County. As you will be called early in the trial, it is necessary that you should be there on Monday, and at Solicitor Thurmand's direction, I write you. Trains leave Columbia for Lexington at 3:20 A.M., 1:45 P.M., and 4:30 P.M., over the Southern Railway.
>
>   Yours very truly,

Later, the verbatim stenographic record taken by Lathan was not introduced by the prosecution at the trial. Lathan had been prepared to appear at trial, but he was not called to testify nor his recorded account used.

The defense intimated that the superior Lathan version had been suppressed by the prosecutor because it probably contained material damaging to the prosecution's case, such as statements by Gonzales showing Tillman had good reason to fear him and act in self defense. The prosecution explained that it used Dr. Babcock's version because of his great reputation in the community and his lack of favoritism toward Gonzales, whereas it feared that Mr. Lathan's version would be dismissed as a biased document produced by Gonzales' secretary.

Stenographer for the Court 1903–1906

Even before the death of Gonzales and trial of Tillman, Lathan had made plans to further his education outside of *The State* and accepted the offer of Judge Purdy to become a court stenographer.

GONE TO HIS NEW DUTIES.

Mr. Robert Lathan Takes Charge as Third Circuit Stenographer.

Mr. Robert Lathan, the new official court stenographer of the third circuit, selected some time ago by Judge Purdy left yesterday afternoon to enter upon the discharge of his duties. Mr. Lathan has been connected with The State for several years and has made scores of friends in Columbia who sincerely regret to see him make his home elsewhere.

PURDY & REYNOLDS,
ATTORNEYS AT LAW,
SUMTER, S. C.

R. O. PURDY.
MARK REYNOLDS.

Decr, 20th, 1902

Mr Robert Lathan,
Care of "The State,"
Columbia, S.C.

Dear Sir:

I have decided to appoint you as Stenographer of the Third Circuit. There being only two applicants, and Mr Deal having been so very favorably commended to me, I have been somewhat embarrassed in making the choice; however, I have decided to appoint you, and you may call at the Capitol on Monday, and ascertain if you have to be Commissioned in a formal manner. I am so busy that I cannot look up the matter today. Your appointment will date from the 22" inst; you can commence the active duties of the Office later on, and when you have finished, or wound up, your personal matters. I assume that you will remove, or rather move to the 3" circuit — Soon? I trust that you may have a brilliant career as Stenographer, and that in the end, it may lead to something better.

Yrs truly,
R. O. Purdy

Judge Purdy's Invitation to Lathan

Circuit Court of South Carolina,

Third Circuit.

R. O. PURDY, Judge.

Sumter, S. C., Jany 2 1903

Mr. Robt Lathan,
Columbia

My dear Sir:

Yrs of the 28th inst. is before me. I will be away for quite awhile from Monday, and cannot name the day, but desire you to come over and spend the day and meet the members of the Bar and the officers of Court; and, as before stated, I desire to get acquainted with you. I will write you a day or so in advance.

Yrs truly,
R. O. Purdy

Lathan received another letter on Jan 2, 1903 from R O Purdy, who was now the Judge of the Circuit Court of South Carolina in Sumter, SC, explaining his personal absence from the area, but inviting Lathan to Sumter to meet the members of the Bar and officers of the court to become acquainted.

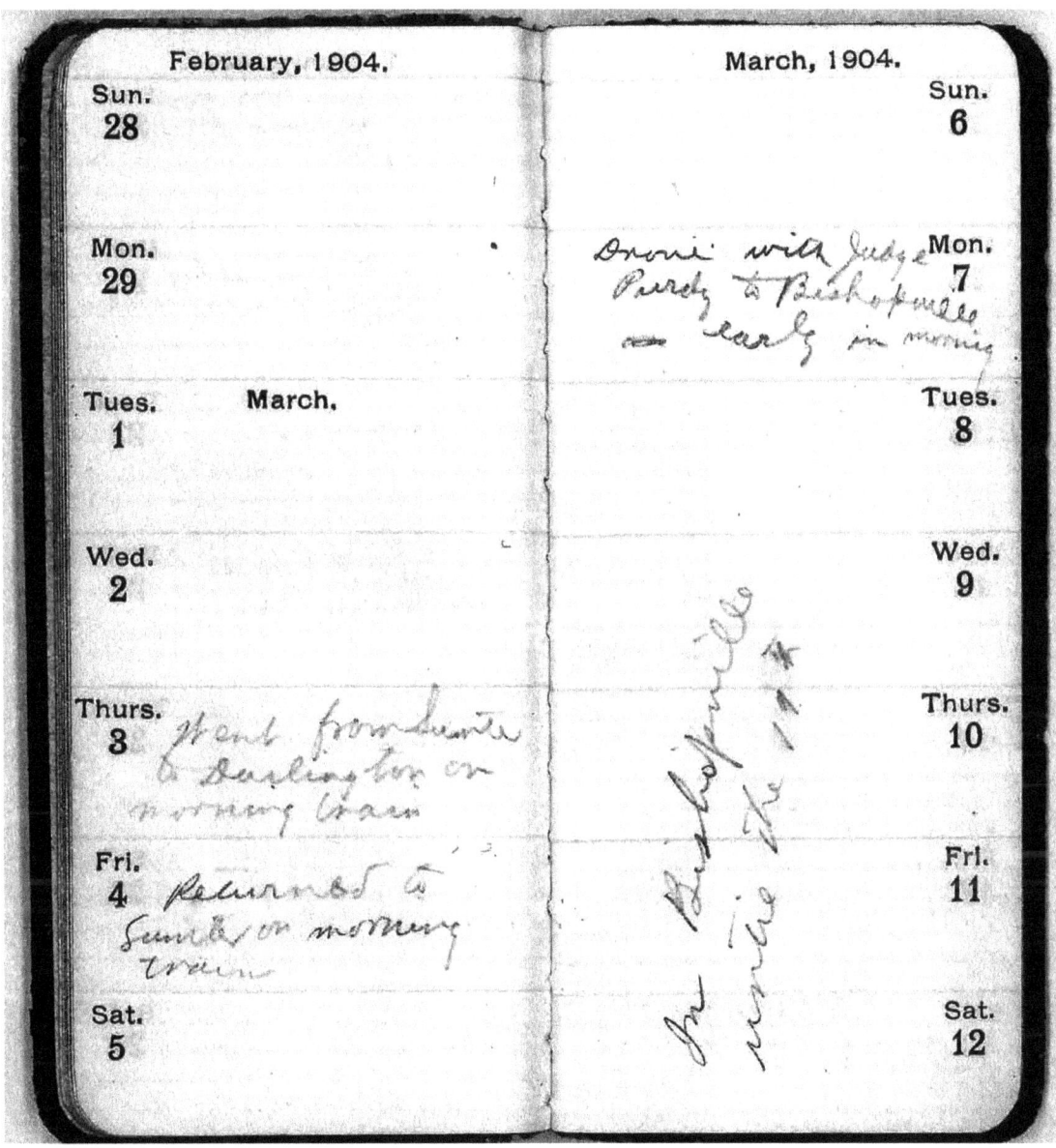

In the next three years, Lathan's ability to perform shorthand gave him success in his role of court stenographer while he also studied law. In the courthouse in Sumter, he developed a friendship with another court reporter, James F. Byrnes, which would continue for many years.

Lathan kept a pocket calendar of many of his personal and business trips in and out of Sumter. The calendar diary also included handwritten copies of poetry quotes interesting to him.

Chapter Four

Memoranda.

"I would so crucify him
With an innocent neglect
of what he can do,
A brave strong pious
scorn that I would
shake him."

"How cheerfully on
the false trail they cry!
O, this is counter, you
false Danish dogs."

"That which would
appear offense
in us,
His countenance, like
richest alchymy,
Will change to virtue."

"A perpetual feast
of nectar'd sweets,
Where no crude
surfeit reigns."

"Earth could not answer;
nor the Seas that mourn
In flowing purple, of their
Lord forlorn;
Nor rolling Heaven, with
all his Signs reveal'd
And hidden by the silence
of Night and Morn."

Memoranda.

"No sadder proof can
be given by a man of
his own littleness than
disbelief in great men." — Carlyle.

"Not warped by passion, awed
by rumor,
Not grave through pride,
or gay through folly;
An equal mixture of
good humor,
And sensible soft
melancholy."

And as Mr. Dooley says
to Mr. Hennessy, "an'
besides, Hinnissy, I'd
hate t' lose ye
as a sparrin' partner.
A man can only talk
good to his infeeryors, an' ye're
a great stimylant t'
conversation."

"Here's to the lying lips
we meet,
For truthful lips
are bores!
But lying lips are
very sweet,
When lying close to yours!"

The State.
DAILY, SUNDAY, SEMI-WEEKLY.

A. E. GONZALES,
Prest. and Gen'l Mgr.

COLUMBIA, S. C., Feb. 17th 1903.

I appreciate your letter my dear Lathan and shall, while I live, feel a deep interest in your welfare. My dear brother, was very fond of you and, although I saw you but seldom, I have, ever since, you have been connected with the office, valued your sterling qualities of heart and head. I want you to feel that you are still a member of The State's family and share the State's affections.

Yours sincerely
Ambrose E. Gonzales

Lathan's sincere attachment to the family of his deceased employer and mentor, NG Gonzales, continued even as he moved to Sumter, SC to serve as court recorder.

Relationships

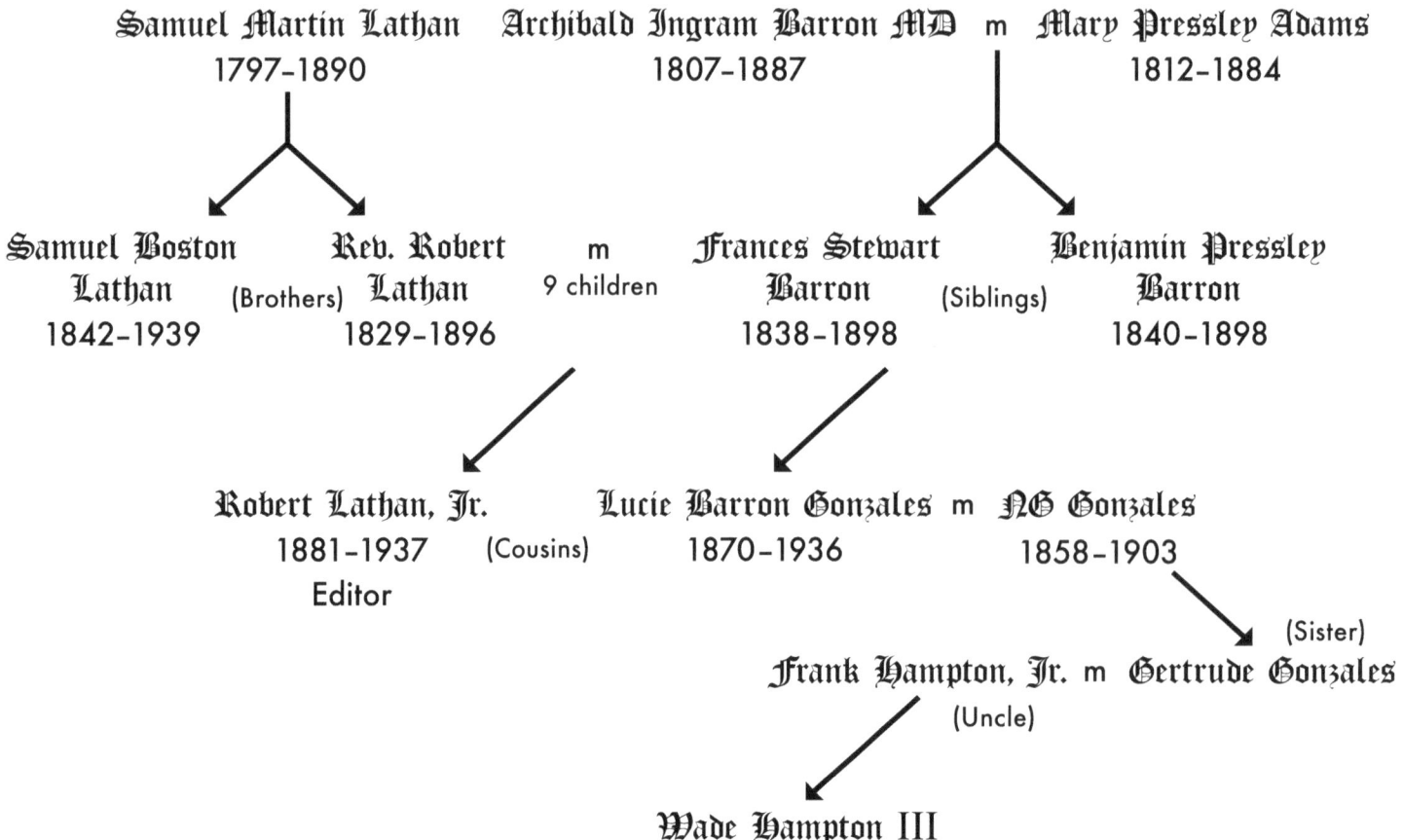

In February, 1903, he also received a letter from a cousin, Macie, in Manning, SC where Lucie Gonzales, the widow of NG Gonzales, had taken refuge in her grief.

"My dear Rob,
We read in *The State* that you had gone to Sumter and I have tried to reach you several times. I know you would do cousin Lucie so much good. She frequently speaks of how thoroughly you understood and appreciated her husband. She has not been well since his death and has not returned to Columbia. Show us how unselfish you can be and (travel) here to Manning. Yours affectionately, Macie."

Robert Lathan and Lucie Barron Gonzales shared the same grandparents and had affectionately referred to each other as "cousins."

Months after the death of Gonzales, Lucie Gonzales, his widow and the cousin of Robert Lathan wrote to Lathan on April 27, 1903.

Before Lucie's two year marriage to NG Gonzales she had been the state librarian. During her marriage, she was described as a "congenial companion of Mr. Gonzales with great nobleness of character" who withstood the tragedies of losing her only child and her husband in a short period of time.

She spent most of her life in Columbia being active in social, religious and civic life. She died in Columbia in April 1936 and was buried in the family cemetery there.

Personal Correspondence from Cousin Lucie

Columbia, S.C.
April 27th, 1903.

My dear Rob,

For some time I have wanted to write you and was only waiting to feel capable of giving you a readable letter. It looks to me as if that time is never to come and so I have decided not to wait longer.

I am thinking of you in Manning this week and at aunt Lou's, for I know it was their wish to have you with them Court week. I would so gladly be there with you, that is if you are not scary about mumps. I have a good case of them to-day but am not at all uneasy as I think them a very mild form.

ones and I want you and May to be with me just then.

Come to see me when you can. For your own and his dear sake you will always hold a very warm place in the heart of, Your loving & affectionate cousin,

Lucie Gonzales.

Chapter Four

Elizabeth (Bessie) Early Lathan
1882-1972

For the next three years, Lathan worked in Sumter as the court recorder, studying law and traveling by train the forty-five miles to Columbia and the forty miles to Darlington. His life now included the marriage to Bessie Agnes Early in 1904.

Robert Lathan, Bessie Early Lathan, Mabel West Early (sister in law of Bessie) and Edward A. Early (brother of Bessie)

Elizabeth (Bessie) Early was born on July 18, 1882 in Darlington, SC, a daughter of William Francis and Mary Parrot Early. She had one younger sister, Ella May, pictured here and a brother, Edward, pictured above.

From the collection of Darlington County Historical Commissioners Museum

Bessie Early Lathan

Mrs. Lathan grew up in a Queen Anne home in Darlington, which was one of several Victorian era residences that were attributed to Lawrence Reese. Mr. Reese was an African American master craftsman whose skills in architectural design and carpentry were self-taught.

This home was built in 1891 with ornate features such as Eastlake screen doors on the front entrance and Queen Anne colored glass borders. It was built for Bessie Early's parents, Mary Early and her cotton broker father, W.F. Early. The W. F. Early House is listed in the National Register as part of the West Broad Street Historic District.

Mr. Lathan and Mrs. Lathan visited her home in Darlington often. Many of the visits were noted in the local paper.

Editor News and Courier Here
Robert Lathan, editor of the Charleston News and Courier, spent several days in Darlington this week. Mr. Lathan is one of the best editorial writers in the South, and he has many friends here who are always glad to see him.

Mrs. Lathan was a member of St. Matthews Episcopal Church, Daughters of the Confederacy, and the Daughters of the American Revolution. Her full life resumed in Darlington after her husband's death in 1937. She died at age ninety and was buried in Grove Hill Cemetery in Darlington next to her husband, Robert Lathan. She was survived by one sister, Ella May Early.

Chapter Five

Robert Lathan, Jr.
A Devoted
Newspaper Man

I consider myself part of the *News and Courier* machine, ready to work wherever they put me, from reporting a dog fight to managing the property.

RL to Bessie

Chapter Five

South Carolina Circuit Court
Third Circuit
Robt. Lathan, Official Stenographer

Darlington, S. C. Feb. 10, 1906.

Major J.C. Hemphill,
　　The News and Courier,
　　　　Charleston, S.C.
My dear Sir:—

　　　　I spent yesterday in Sumter, with Judge Purdy, and after consulting with him in regard to my resignation as court stenographer I now write for the purpose of accepting the position you offer me on The News and Courier.

　　　　Judge Purdy has no one in mind whom he can put in my place, but he will at once begin to look out for some one and in this search he has commissioned me to assist him. You understand, of course, that it may take several weeks to find a man who is even reasonably well qualified to act as court stenographer and who is free to undertake the work; but I shall press the search with all diligence, and I trust that within a short time I shall be able to report a successful termination of it. I shall then be ready to report to you for duty.

　　　　And now, sir, I want you to understand how greatly I felicitate myself that, through the kindly representations of my friends, I should have found favor in your eyes. I earnestly hope that I shall justify their good opinion of me and that you may have no cause to regret having relied upon it.
　　　　　　　　Sincerely yours,
　　　　　　　　　　RL Lathan

To begin his return to the newspaper world, Lathan had to first resign his position with the circuit court and be accepted as an employee of J.C. Hemphill's staff in Charleston.

One of his attorney friends, E. F. Warren, from the court wrote to Lathan that he was

"...greatly surprised that you should have the nerve to desert the stenographic ranks... and not receive as much compensation in the new position."
　　　　　　　　　　E. F. Warren

Yet, to Lathan, working at a newspaper was his life's desire.

During his early years at the Charleston newspaper, he was described as young, handsome, energetic and hard working. His close friend, Herbert Sass, while working with him at the paper, is also quoted as commenting that Lathan's "impatience and temper had also to be mastered." <u>OUTSPOKEN</u>

Newspaper Man
1906–1927

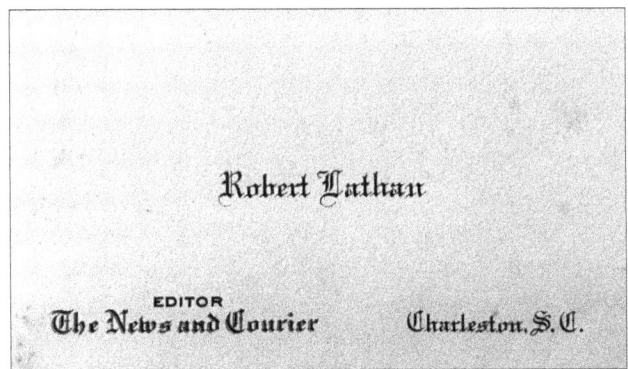

State News & City Editor
1906–1910

Chief Editor
1910–1927

In 1906, Robert and Bessie Lathan moved to Charleston where Lathan began his twenty-one year tenure with the oldest newspaper in South Carolina. As state news editor his responsibilities took him to the state capital in Columbia and anywhere else over the state geography where a story might be found, even if a dog fight, also known by many other names.

At age twenty-nine, Lathan replaced J. C. Hemphill as chief editor making him the youngest chief editor in the paper's history. His maturity, his keen insights and strong leadership had been recognized and rewarded.

As said by his friend, Douglas Jenkins of the American Consular Service

"You have won a great prize. In my humble judgment it is one of the most desirable positions in the newspaper world in our part of the country."

         D. Jenkins

Chapter Five

Letter from Robert to Bessie Describing His Job

The News and Courier
19 BROAD ST.
CHARLESTON, S. C.

Jan. 4, 1910

EDITORIAL ROOMS

My dearest Bessie:-

It is half past twelve o'clock and Frank West is waiting to go home with me for the night so I have only time for a note. I have been very busy today, as I had no help at all until tonight, all three of the reporters being away, as well as Mr. Hemphill. Baum is in bed sick and Dingle's sister is very ill.

When I got to the office this morning I found that Mr. Simons had been over to see me already and that he wanted to see me as soon as possible. I went to see him and had a confidential talk with him, or rather he had one with me, the upshot of the whole matter being that I can take charge of The News and Courier when Mr. Hemphill leaves if I want to do so. I haven't time to write you with any particularity, but he went over the whole situation and said that he had canvassed the matter thoroughly and was convinced that I was the man they wanted. Of course he was speaking for himself alone, but said that he knew that his recommendation would have great weight and would probably be accepted and acted upon. I told him the facts as to Mr. Hemphill having invited me to Richmond, and that I could not give him a definite answer until Mr. Hemphill came back and I knew just what they had to offer me there, but that in the meantime I considered myself of course a part of The News and Courier machine, ready to work wherever they put me, from reporting a dog fight to managing the property. iI am to talk the

The News and Courier
19 BROAD ST.
CHARLESTON, S. C.

EDITORIAL ROOMS

(2)

matter over with him Thursday as soon as Mr. Hemphill gets back, as they want to know as early as possible what they are to do, Mr. Simons not expecting Mr. Hemphill to remain here anyn longer new than is necessary for him to get his affairs straightened out on the paper. I think ~~hnahansum~~ he is wise in wishing to act promptly for I am ~~afmadumm~~ afraid that if he delayed his force here would be very much disorganized, Mr. Hemphill's announcement of his intended departure having upset the whole office.

Both ~~affors~~ places are most attractive to me, I confess, and both will undoubtedly be attended with difficulties. ~~HmanSimons~~ Of course I don't know yet just what the Richmond offer will amount to---financially, I mean, and of course I am obliged to consider that. Mr Simons seems to be genuinely anxious to have me stay here and I know that Mr. Hemphill wants me to go.

I would like to have written you with more detail but can't now. Will do so tomorrow if I can find time, but cannot promise.

Mr. Cooper is in very bad shape. I am afraid his condition is serious. He doesn't make any improvement, apparently and is in just about the same condition he was in before Christmas and suffers a great deal at times.

Give love to all and with many kisses believe me,

Always your own,

Robert

Chapter Five

Letters of Congratulations to Lathan

H. L. WATSON, PRESIDENT   **J S. BAILEY, SECTY & TREAS.**

The Index Publishing Company
(Incorporated)

Printers and Publishers

Lithographing, Engraving.
Notary Publics' Seals.

Greenwood, South Carolina,

Feb. 11, 1910

Mr. Robert Lathan,
    Charleston,
        S.C.

Dear Mr. Lathan:-

    I do not know of any item of news that has given me as much pleasure as the notice of your elevation to the editorship of the News & Courier. I have been watching with interest for the "news" to come out and hasten to congratulate you and the News & Courier.

    Although I retired from daily newspaper work at a young and "tender" or possibly fresh age, on account of health, and business somewhat, I have a keen interest in the life of the daily press of the State and especially in the work of the young men, being one of them you know, and whenever I see the ability of a young man like yourself properly recognized, naturally I am pleased.

    Take warning, --take care of your health. That's all the advice I want to give you. I wish you "mighty well."

                      Sincerely yours,

The last paragraph of the congratulatory note to Lathan was an unknowing prediction of the future.

State of South Carolina
Department of Agriculture, Commerce and Industries

E. J. WATSON, COMMISSIONER
J. D. DIAL, CLERK

Columbia, S. C., Feb. 12, 1910.

Mr. Robt. Lathan,
    News & Courier,
        Charleston, S. C.

My dear Bob:-

    I know that you are receiving many letters of hearty congratulations on the splendid recognition that has come to your fidelity and ability, but I cannot refrain from dropping you a line to say that personally I feel a great sense of pride in your success. I know of no man whose personal characteristics and ability better equip him for material service to the State in the sphere of active journalism, that moulds public sentiment for the upbuildung of the commonwealth. You deserve the recognition you have received at the hands of those you have been serving, and as I have said I feel proud of you.

    If at any time I can be of assistance or service to you you know you have only to call upon me.

                Most sincerely yours

                              E. J. Watson
                                Commissioner.

Chapter Five

A Variety of Newspaper Roles

The News and Courier
19 BROAD STREET
CHARLESTON, S. C.

EDITORIAL ROOMS

Oct. 8, 1908.

Miss Grace R. Hemphill,
Abbeville, S. C.

My Dear Miss Hemphill:

Mr. LaCoste tells me that for theatrical advertisements The News and Courier receives 15 cents per line Nonpareil. The theatrical notices are printed as a courtesy to the local management, and it is for printing these reading notices that newspapers like The News and Courier are given passes to the different attractions. The rates for carnivals and circuses vary so widely that it is impossible for me to give you any definite figures. A small "one-horse" affair is usually charged about 10 cents the line, but if a circus does two or three hundred dollars business with us, of course they are given a substantial reduction from this rate. The number of tickets varies, of course, according to the quality of the show and the amount of space we feel justified in giving them.

I thank you very much for having sent the cuts. Unfortunately, they did not reach here until ~~midnight~~ mid-day on Saturday and it was too late for us to use them last Sunday as the paper was very much crowded. I want to use one or two of them in the next two or three weeks. I will not use them at once as the news value of the story has, of course, vanished. I will see that they are returned to you just as soon as we have finished with them.

Yours very truly,

Robt. Lathan

Lathan's responsibilities included the scheduling of advertising submissions and notification of the prices for the different kinds of advertising.

Confrontations with John P. Grace

In 1911, the *News and Courier* became involved in several political campaigns featuring John P. Grace, who was then running for mayor of Charleston. Political warfare broke out between opposing factions in Charleston. Grace was of Irish descent, a Catholic, and a lawyer, who as a rousing speaker railed against the circle of old Charleston families who ran the city. The *News and Courier* consistently battled Grace.

To compensate, Grace started a rival newspaper, the *Charleston American*, which challenged the *News and Courier* for eight years. The low point occurred on May 2, 1914, when Grace accosted Lathan in the editorial offices at 19 Broad Street about 12:30 am and began verbally abusing the newspaper and its employees. Lathan later attempted to calm Mayor Grace and urged him to leave the building, but blows were exchanged with Grace and Lathan pummeling each other in the corridor until finally it was broken up by others.

The following year before the mayoral election, the Democratic Governor of South Carolina was asked to send the militia to Charleston to keep the peace during the election, using the assault by Grace on Lathan as the reason. Nonetheless, violence did break out in downtown Charleston with several shots being fired. An *Evening Post* reporter, Sidney Cohen was killed by a stray bullet.

Grace lost the 1915 election, but was elected in 1919. He continued to publish the *Charleston American*, competing with the *News and Courier* in circulation and in philosophy, such as support for the Allies in World War 1 by the *Courier* and support for the Germans in the *Charleston American*. Even with all of the controversies surrounding the elected tenure of Grace, one of the most traveled bridges in Charleston carries his name, the Grace Memorial Bridge.

The original Grace Memorial Bridge opened in 1927.

World War I

During the years of Lathan's editorial guidance of the *News and Courier* world events had a large impact on the newspaper audiences as well as the staff as they attempted to ensure full and accurate coverage.

Lathan himself had to register for the draft.

The United States participation in World War 1 was of major interest to newspaper readers. The newspaper solicited information from the military sources throughout the 1914-1918 period. After the War, Lathan continued to search for information on the achievements of the troops from North Carolina, South Carolina and Tennessee who served int the 30th Division, American Expeditionary Forces, brigaded with the British Army. The nickname of these forces was "Old Hickory."

Lathan continued to write to sources to provide documentation of the actions of the 30th Division, American Expeditionary Forces. The casualties as reported up to November 23, totalled 7623 of whom 1168 were deaths.

This 30th Division is credited with breaking Germany's Hindenberg Line in September-October 1918.

Editor Lathan's Correspondence

Letter to Edward Marshall Syndicate, c/o *The Sun*, NY. The syndicate accumulated news from war correspondents to be distributed to newspapers.

We have been unable thus far to secure any adequate story of the Thirtieth's achievements. It is known that its record is one of the most gallant and distinguished of any division. It was in the thick of fighting from midsummer until the end of the war. Some magnificent tributes have been paid by British officers but as yet we have no connected story of what it did and what it suffered. I am writing to ask if you could arrange to get us such a story. I believe that you would find in the record an epic narrative, one read eagerly with pride by all Americans.

During Lathan's tenure as editor, the *News and Courier* maintained correspondents in Columbia and Washington. During World War I correspondent, Warrington Dawson sent occasional reports from near the front. Dawson lived in Versailles and was the son of the former editor, Francis W. Dawson who died in 1889. Warrington sent many letters to Lathan and continued to write periodically for the newspaper until the 1950s.

Lathan Registered for Military Service

1918 Influenza Pandemic

A second major global tragedy was the 1918 Influenza Pandemic, the most severe pandemic of recent history. It was caused by an H1N1 virus with genes of avian history. In the United States it was first identified in an Army camp in early March 1918 in western Kansas. At this time very little was known about it. This time was at the height of World War I and the virus spread worldwide during 1918-1919.

Although it was frequently called the "Spanish Flu," Spain had only a few cases and Spain was neutral in World War I. It was called the" Spanish Flu" because only Spanish newspapers in Europe were publicizing accounts of the spread of the disease and were picked up in other countries.

In 1918, the world population was about 1.5 billion and the approximate 500 million cases were one third of the world's population who were attacked by this virus. As for statistics, it is impossible to state with accuracy the death toll. The statistics are estimates only.

In the United States in 1918, the population was 105 million with 675,000 deaths. Thus in the US in 1918, around .065% of the population died.

In Charleston, SC in 1918, the population was 60,000 with 5500 cases and 291 deaths.

In Atlanta, GA in 1918 the population was 200,000 with 800 deaths.

In ordinary influenza, the virus kills up to 650,000 per year in the world. In the US the numbers vary between 3000 to 50,000 per year depending on the virulence of the virus.

In the "Spanish Flu" the 20-40 year age group was very high, but very low in Covid-19 and in ordinary flu cases. In Covid-19 the group over 70 years old were much higher.

In the 1918 virus, its virulence was a unique feature and there was no vaccine or medical treatment to protect the people. With no vaccine to protect, control efforts worldwide were limited to non-pharmaceutical interventions such as isolation, quarantine, personal hygiene, masks, disinfection and social distance of public gatherings.

In Europe in WWI, initially, the new influenza across the battlefields was called the "three-day fever." By July in 1918, most thought the threat was over. But it was not. The second wave came in September, when over 1500 soldiers in Camp Devens in Massachusetts, near Boston were diagnosed in one day. Later in one day in Philadelphia 759 died.

Some victims died within hours of their first symptoms. Others succumbed after a few days when their lungs filled with fluid and they suffocated with death. This influenza did not discriminate. It was rampant in urban and rural areas to the remotest parts all over the world. The flu in 1918 afflicted over 25% of the US population. Between 2% and 3% of the world's population died. The death rate of ordinary influenza pandemics usually was around 0.1%. In October 1918, that month alone, 195,000 Americans died, making it the deadliest month in American history. Overall this severe pandemic lasted fifteen months.

The book *The Great Influenza* by John M. Berry, first published in 2005, has been powerful and extraordinary with its excellent medical history and featuring Dr. William Henry Welch as the single most powerful individual in the history of American medicine and the founder of Johns Hopkins Medical School.

Currently the United States population is approximately 330 million and world population is approximately 8 billion. In August 2021, the number of Covid-19 cases in the US has reached 42 million and approximately 501,000 deaths. In the world the number of cases is approximately 112 millions and 2.5 million deaths.

The case fatality (or mortality) rate is computed by dividing the number of deaths by the total number of confirmed cases. The fatality rates for influenza groups are approximate:

   1918 Pandemic 2-3 %
   Covid -19 Pandemic 1-2%
   Ordinary influenza 0.1%

1918 Influenza Pandemic

World
Population   1.5 billion
Deaths estimated   50 million

United States
Population   105 million
Deaths   675,000

2020 COVID-19 Pandemic
As of August 2021

World
Population   7.9 billion
Approximate cases   216.6 million
Deaths estimated   5.0 million

United States
Population   330 million
Approximate cases   39.6 million
Deaths   654,000

Lathan in Charleston

Lathan was a man of positive and pleasing personality. He had a multitude of friends throughout the country. Though an ardent Democrat, he believed that an editor should remain free of political alliances and cover all sides.

Living in Charleston for twenty-one years, provided Lathan with the ability to indulge in his favorite hobby of fishing in both salt and fresh water.

The *News and Courier* also found itself in continued opposition to Cole Blease, who was Tillman's successor as Governor and also elected US Senator. Lathan's strategy with Blease was to ignore him editorially when possible, though he may have had Blease in mind when he wrote his Pulitzer Prize winning editorial about the lack of responsible leadership in the South. Earlier, Lathan wrote of Blease.

I think there is nothing to be accomplished by continuing to harp upon the ignominy and disgrace which he has brought upon our state. RL

Yet under Lathan, the *News and Courier* continued to fight Blease whom they considered to be the "child of Tillmanism."

The Pulitzer Prize editorial, "The Plight of the South" appeared in the newspaper on November 5, 1924 and was adjudged the best editorial appearing in any newspaper during 1924. Lathan wrote the editorial on election day, when the voters were going to the polls to elect a Republican President Calvin Coolidge. As Lathan pointed out, he did not know which party would win the election, but regardless he said the South lacked political leadership. Many readers felt that the editorial was directed at politicians such as Blease.

In a speech covering current challenges to all newspapers emphasizing the sweeping changes taking place in the South, he asked what was the outlook for the future? He began the timeline during his Chief Editor tenure at the *News and Courier* beginning in January 1916 when the World War I had been raging, but America not involved.

Excerpts from the speech are included here. Full text is in reference section. Look 1926

..then it follows that all institutions newspapers should be constantly on guard lest they fall into a groove to the neglect of opportunities that are golden. And if this is true of newspapers in general, surely it is doubly true of the newspapers of the South at the present time. How then are the sweeping changes that are taking place in the South affecting the newspapers of this section? Is the press of the South adjusting itself adequately to the new conditions? What is the present status and what is the outlook for the future?

As slavery had cast its shadow over the whole destiny of the South in the years before 1860, so in the period that followed its ending the South's best thought had to be devoted for years following to working out a new modus vivendi. The political phases of this problem the South solved after a fashion in due course. But in 1916 it had not yet discovered how to build roads without money, and it neither had the money nor knew where to get it.

It had not learned how to make education accessible to all its population and was still apologizing for widespread illiteracy. Financially and economically its people continued to be in bondage to New York.

It is obvious when we stop to think that the changes the past ten years have made, striking as they have been, have in fact merely paved the way for further changes that in the very nature of things must be infinitely more striking. What will it mean when all of the people are educated, or at least have as much schooling as they are capable of taking? When agriculture has fully recovered from its troubles, most of which are accidental and temporary, and it again fully prosperous.

I can, however, venture a few suggestions as to what these changes that are taking place in the South mean to the press of the South. No matter what the future holds, already we are committed to changes that have moved so swiftly and cut so deep that as yet few of us appreciate the magnitude of the transformation that the South has experienced...What prophet of doom in January ten years ago would have dared to hint that any man or woman then living would live to see the day when it was the accepted thing on the part of great numbers of young girls, of respectable families, to drink the vilest corn liquor from hip flacks at public dances. And what pray would have been the fate of one so bold as to have foretold that before the decade was out one of the oldest and finest and proudest of Southern cities, famous for its mellow charm and dignity would be advertised on two continents by a dance banned by the police in many cities, frowned on by college faculties, and feared by apartment house owners as more dangerous than an earthquake.

Verily, verily, friends and brethren, in more ways than one the Grand Old South "ain't what she used to be!"

What I am trying to indicate is that difficult as were some of the problems with which newspapers were called upon to deal ten years ago, they were simple compared with those that confront us at the present time. ...Are the newspapers of the South competently manned for the extraordinary work ahead of them in these extraordinary times?

Since 1916 the newspapers of the South, generally speaking, have shared amazingly in the South's new growth...They offer their readers vastly more reading matter...but as yet they have not qualified for the new leadership that is required of them and in this respect they are vastly inferior to the newspapers of fifty years ago. In the average newspaper the editorial outweighed the business management. The newspaper was a public institution and took itself seriously as such...I want them to shift the interest back.

I want them to bear in mind that there is a vast difference between spending money on the reading matter of a newspaper and giving thought and study to how that money shall be spent.

Chapel Hill, 1926

In his seventeen years as editor he remade the *News and Courier* into a twentieth century newspaper. Its content was gradually modernized, using photographs, cartoons, crossword puzzles, and graphics. Coverage of sports increased and the sports section grew to a full page. A society column was added, and readers were given a full page of comics. Multi-column headlines were used for the most important stories of the day. The distinction between news and commentary was made clearer as all opinion was confined to the editorial page.

Under Lathan, the *News and Courier* opposed prohibition, endorsed state measures to improve public health in the counties, and urged more funding to support hurricane forecasting by the National Weather Service. The newspaper renewed its campaign against lynching.

The newspaper became a strong voice for conservation. One of their staff, city editor, Herbert Ravenel Sass, who would become a nationally known nature writer, provided frequent columns on conservation issues. He was joined in the coverage by Thomas P. Lesesne, a supporter of Low Country conservation as well as historic preservation. Alexander Sprunt, an ornithologist, wrote a regular column for the newspaper. The newspaper encouraged tourism to these areas and supported the building of better roads for access. Several of the writers published books of the subject covered in the columns.

Lathan was known throughout his newspaper career for encouraging the writing efforts of young and old in his community. One newspaper correspondent, the Reverend I. E. Lowery, AMDD took Lathan's words of encouragement and created his stories into a book published in 1911.

Three Published Authors

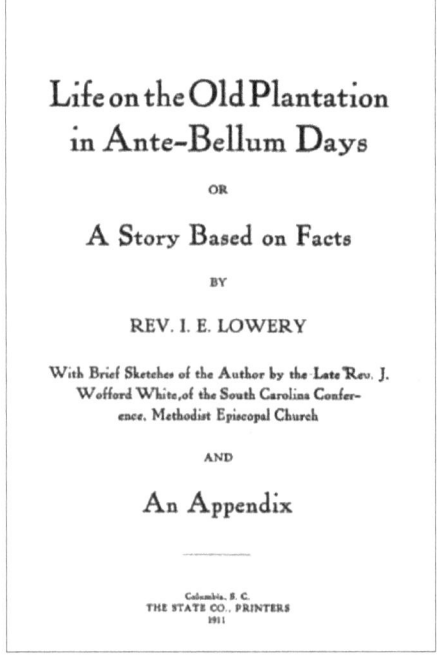

Letter Thanking Lathan for Assistance

Dear Sir:-

When I lived in Charleston, on one occasion I did some work for The News & Courier, and took the matter down to the editorial rooms at night, and while in your room you said to me: "Lowery, you write pretty well, why don't you try your hand at a story." I said in reply: "I never thought of such a thing." Then story has grown into a book of 186 pages, and I send you in this mail the first copy dropped from the press. Please do what you can to help me get it on the market.

I also enclose some notes, giving the names of some Charleston people - white and colored - mentioned in the book. Yours truly

I. E. Lowery

Poetry was also a regular feature of paper for many years, featuring poems of many prominent artists, including works of a contemporary poet, Robert Frost and long celebrated Alfred Lord Tennyson.

The newspaper promoted many sports including golf and gave "broadcast coverage" of major sporting events including the World Series games and the Jack Dempsey vs Gene Tunney heavyweight championship fight in 1926. As estimated 5000 sports fans closed Broad Street to gather around the newspaper office to hear a relay of the live "AP Flash" report of the event. Tunney's upset was the lead story the next day.

During his twenty-one year residence in Charleston Lathan was active in many community enterprises. His editorial policy was "keen and aggressive." He was president of the South Carolina Press Association in 1925-26. Lathan was also a member of the advisory board of the Pulitzer School of Journalism of Columbia University. In the summer of 1927, he traveled in Europe with a Carnegie editorial party of thirty newspaper editors from as many states. The group spent four months abroad under the auspices of the endowment for international peace. The tour was arranged by Nicholas M. Butler, president of Columbia University and followed by a similar visit to the US by a party of British editors.

Robert Lathan was an eloquent public speaker and was much in demand throughout the Carolinas. He spoke at various colleges, including Emory College in Atlanta and the University of North Carolina in Chapel Hill. His speaking themes included topics such as accepting the changes from agriculture in the South and the results of the emphasis on financial success in newspapers in opposition to good reading of different sections.

Lathan's Pulitzer Prize and his subsequent involvement with the Carnegie Endowment brought the *News and Courier* national prestige, but financially the newspaper was suffering. Following the death of its president, Rudolph Seigling, Jr. in 1926, the Seigling estate sold its controlling interest in the paper to James E. Rockwell of Duluth, Minnesota. Rockwell became president and publisher of the *News and Courier* with Lathan, who also held a stock interest, as its vice-president and editor.

In November 1926, Rockwell sold the newspaper to a group of Charlestonians including Julian Mitchell, Thomas A. Waring, Sr., Benjamin A. Hagood, and Robert S. Small. In the purchase, Mr. Waring, Sr. represented the ownership of the *Charleston Evening Post,* which was acquiring the interest in the *News and Courier* company.

Robert Lathan continued as editor of the *News and Courier* and retained his stock interest until the following April 1927 when he officially transferred his financial participation in the ownership of the *News and Courier.*

During the last several months in 1926 and early 1927, Lathan had been contacted and courted by the publisher of the *Asheville Citizen*, Charles A. Webb. In March 1927 approximately ten letters were shared between Editor Lathan and Publisher Webb. Lathan wrote to Webb that "the new owners were personally his friends, but the *Evening Post* would be dominant."

When the new ownership purchased Lathan's stock in February 1927, Webb and Lathan were able to discuss a date when Lathan would begin working as editor in Asheville. With the planned Carnegie Endowment European trip set for June, Webb and Lathan settled on a beginning date to be April, 1927 so that the Lathan family could be established in western North Carolina before sailing on the trip to Europe.

Farewell Dinner for Editor Lathan by the Citizens of Charleston April, 1927

Robert Lathan was given a farewell dinner by the citizens of Charleston on April 11, 1927, only a few days before he resigned as editor of the Charleston *News and Courier* and moved to Asheville, NC.

The dinner was presided by R. Goodwyn Rhett and addressed by Editor, Thomas R. Waring,, Jr. followed by the response by Lathan. The program included several music selections and spirituals.

Farewell Tribute

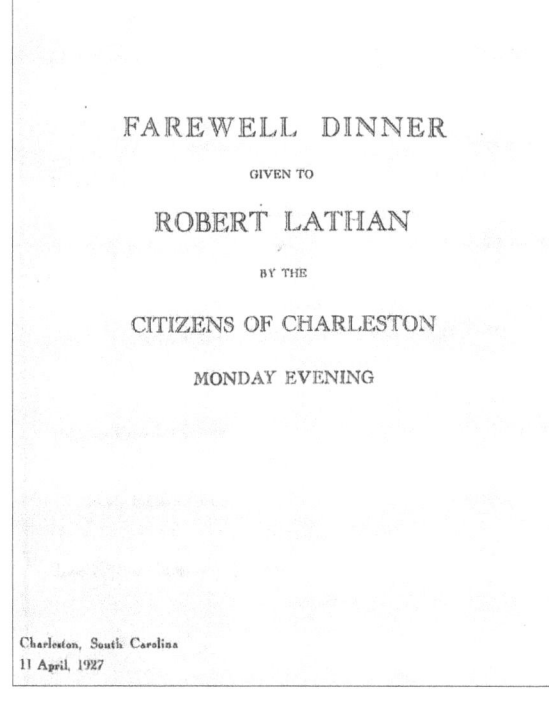

Chapter Five

Gift of Silver Service to Mr. and Mrs Lathan

As a gift from the community, the Lathan's were presented an engraved silver service, which became the most prized possession of Mrs. Lathan.

Robert Lathan had been editor of the *Charleston News and Courier* for seventeen years before moving to Asheville, NC to lead the *Asheville Citizen* as its editor for ten more years.

From 1906 to 1927 Robert Lathan, Jr. went to work in the morning at the building on Broad Street in downtown Charleston and led the staff of the *News and Courier* through changing times, good and bad. In April of 1927 he moved his geographical location of Broad Street building, in Charleston, SC...to a new building in Asheville, NC where once again his powerful words would lead a community.

Chapter Six

Robert Lathan, Jr.
A Discerning Editor

Why should they go on living like this when to change the whole picture they have only to act upon the realization that to really live they must also let live?

Christmas 1931

Chapter Six

Influential Politicians and Senior Military

Through Lathan's tenure and guidance of *The News and Courier* and the *Asheville Citizen* he always ensured that complete coverage of the political environment was provided to all the audiences. As time conditioned him, the words of his close friend, Hobo describe it best as his "patience became mastered."

Still he covered and corresponded with many of the leading politicians on both sides of any issues. Some of the most influential politicians and military persons with whom Editor Lathan interacted both as a struggle and as a positive are recognized in these words.

In an editorial published on Christmas Day in 1931 Lathan wrote of the need for goodwill toward men even when achievement would not be easy.

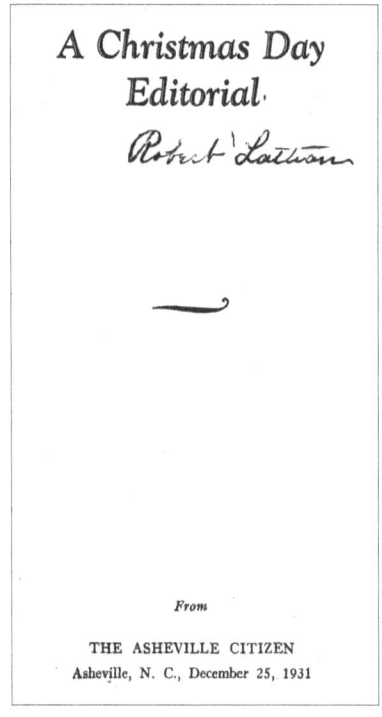

Excerpts are included here. Full text is in reference section. Christmas Day Editorial 1931.

Ah, you say, but that begs the whole question. How can there be good will toward men in a world torn nigh unto death by passion and strife, by jealousies and ambitions, by greed and envy, by hates and fears?

It will not be easy. We grant you that. But neither is it impossible. And the compulsion is absolute. The alternative at the best will be a long continuance of the misery which overtakes mankind. At the worst it will be unspeakable disaster.

We know, of course, how simple it is to sneer at good will as a solvent of the problems that menace the nations. Such sneering has long been common enough. But the world's mood today is a very sober mood. With nation after nation already financially upon the rocks it has had enough and more than enough to make it sober. And the world knows in its heart that there is no reliance to be places upon force alone.

Victors and vanquished in the last great struggle are alike miserable and unhappy now.

How long, we ask you, how long can human beings go on living like this?

Why should they go on living like this when to change the whole picture they have only to act upon the realization that to really live they must also let live?

Power today compels responsibility. Of those who are richest and strongest and greatest, strange to say, the largest measure of service is exacted.

Christmas 1931

Benjamin Ryan Tillman
1847–1918

Benjamin Ryan Tillman was known as "Pitchfork Ben" Tillman. As the democratic governor of South Carolina from 1890-1894, he was a spokesman for poor and rural white population against the ruling white aristocracy. He became the demagogue of the farmer's movement forcing the decline of the influence of the Confederate General Wade Hampton. General Hampton and his party of wealthy "Bourbons" were the conservative planter class who had led South Carolina from Hampton's gubernatorial election in 1876 and senator in 1879 until the early 1890s.

Tillman was born in 1847 on the family plantation "Chester" near Trenton, SC a few miles from Edgefield, SC. His parents with the 5000 acres and 86 slaves were among the largest landowners in the Edgefield District.

Edgefield was known as a violent place, with matters of personal honor potentially ending with a duel or killing. Tillman's father had killed a man. One of Tillman's brothers had died in a duel and another brother who had killed a man yet still served for several terms in Congress.

He was a star student in schools, displaying an excellent vocabulary. In 1864, not yet 17, Tillman withdrew from school and joined the Confederate Army, but became seriously ill with a cranial tumor and abscess which required removal of his left eye. He had not recovered until 1866 after the Civil War.

In 1868 Tillman purchased more land, proving to be an adept farmer. By 1876, he was the largest landowner in Edgefield County. He became a politician and later formed "rifle clubs" to drive African Americans from power. Tillman also participated in the Hamburg Massacre in 1876 when at least seven black militiamen were killed in the incident in Aiken, SC.

In the 1880s, Tillman in an attempt to better the conditions for the farmer, founded the Edgefield Agricultural Club. Later Tillman was promoted as a candidate for governor in 1886 and was called the "Agricultural Moses." Also, he promoted a state college for the education of farmers. Later, Tillman was depicted with a pitchfork in his hand, to show his agricultural roots and his ability to make jabs at his opponents. This was a source of his nickname, "Pitchfork Ben."

In 1886, Tillman met with Thomas G. Clemson, the son-in-law of the late John C. Calhoun to discuss the cost of the new agricultural school. Clemson died in 1888 with a large portion his estate given to the proposed school. Tillman was made one of the seven trustees for life. Clemson College (later University) was authorized by the state legislature in 1888.

In the 1890 when Tillman entered politics for the first time, he was recognized as a great orator and as a leader of the populist movement. Elected as governor in December 1890, his term of service was never without criticism. In February 1891, the first issue of the anti-Tillman newspaper, *The State* was published under the editorial control of NG Gonzales. The Gonzales brothers were opposed to and wrote often, as did the Charleston News and Courier editorials that referred to not only "red neck" policies, but illegal and fraudulent actions.

One of Governor Tillman's early acts was to remove Senator Wade Hampton from office and appoint his campaign manager, John L. Irby to replace him.

Governor Tillman's accomplishments after his two terms included: the creation and endowment of Clemson College, the establishment of the Winthrop College for Women in Rock Hill, SC. and the controversial passage of the Dispensary Laws. This law was considered especially onerous in its potential for fraud as it granted the sale of all alcoholic beverages to the control and revenue of the state.

In 1894, Ben was elected to the US Senate where he served until his death. He helped form a new SC Constitution of 1895, which was to disenfranchise some black people to ensure a continued white majority of voters. As Senator, he opposed the policies of President Grover Cleveland. He became a well-known lecturer, and was in demand as a speaker, especially against his known enemies. In 1902, he was censored while serving in the US Senate for assaulting fellow SC Senator, John L. McLauren in the Senate Chamber. Tillman was quoted also as wanting to stick his pitchfork into President Cleveland.

Tillman's nephew Jim was acquitted of the shooting death of their arch enemy, NG Gonzales, Editor of The State newspaper on the street in midday in Columbia near the State House. Though many witnessed the shooting, the jury found that Tillman had been provoked by the vitriol of the animus covering his political actions.

Buildings on both the campus of Clemson University and Winthrop University are named for Tillman.

Ben Tillman died in Washington while serving as a Senator in 1917, as combative as always. He was brought home to Trenton SC to be buried. His personal friends were his physician Dr. J. W. Babcock and Senator James Byrnes.

Coleman Livingston Blease
1868–1942

Blease was born in Newberry, SC where he practiced law and was in the South Carolina House of Representatives in 1890 as a protégé of Ben Ryan Tillman. Like Tillman, he supported both the white tenant farmers and mill workers.

Coley Blease was elected mayor of Newberry in 1910 and later Governor of South Carolina from 1911 to 1915. While serving he encouraged the practice of lynching and strongly opposed the education of blacks. The newspapers were against him as he praised Jim Tillman for the murder of The State editor, NG Gonzales in 1903.

In 1924, Blease defeated James F. Byrnes for the US Senate in the years when the Ku Klux Klan was at the height of its power, which ruined Byrnes' political hopes that year. Byrnes defeated Blease in his 1930 run for re-election to the Senate.

Major General Johnson Hagood
1873–1948

Major General Johnson Hagood was born in 1873 in Orangeburg, SC and graduated from the US Military Academy in West Point in 1896. General Hagood served in WWI in the artillery in France and commanded army artillery of the Third Army until after the war in 1919 when he returned to the US. He received a Distinguished Service Medal Citation as Chief of Staff of the Services of Supply for his ability for organization.

During his military career, he served as the commander of the 4th Army Corps, headquartered in Atlanta, which included all of the South giving him the opportunity to often visit Charleston.

Major General Hagood was the nephew of Confederate Brigadier General Johnson Hagood (1829-1882), who commanded the troops at Fort Wagner in South Carolina during Colonel Robert Shaw's attack by the all black Massachusetts 54th Infantry. Confederate General Hagood also served as Governor of South Carolina from 1880-1882. The football stadium at the Citadel is named for this General Johnson Hagood (1829-1898).

August 2, 1925 on letterhead from
Army Headquarters,
Second Coast Artillery
District, Fort Totten, New York

My dear Robert Lathan,

I want to thank you for the fine editorial in the News and Courier. I feel that Charleston has given me so much than my due as this promotion which has been due to good luck rather than merit. South Carolina has seen a number of admirals in the Navy, but few generals in the Army as you can see from the enclosed list:

Major Generals from South Carolina in the US Army:

William Moultrie	1782–1783
C. C. Pinckney	1799–1800
Thomas Pinckney	1812–1815
Wade Hampton I	1813–1814
George Izard	1814–1815
Johnson Hagood	1925–

I am fortunate in getting the 4th Corps with headquarters in Atlanta so that the military of South Carolina comes under my command. This will give me a chance to be in Charleston at times and brings to mind that my Uncle General Johnson Hagood commanded the Charleston District for a short time during the Civil War. My new command includes the whole South below Virginia and east of the Mississippi which is a source of pride and pleasure.

Very sincerely yours,

Maj. Gen J. Hagood

Chapter Six

Letters Between Lathan and Senator Benet

CHRISTIE BENET, S. C., CHAIRMAN
JAMES HAMILTON LEWIS, ILL.   FRANK B. KELLOGG, MINN.
PETER G. GERRY, R. I.   IRVINE L. LENROOT, WIS.
E. C. HORTON, CLERK.

United States Senate,
COMMITTEE ON NATIONAL BANKS.

September
Seventh
1918

Mr. Robert Lathan,
News & Courier,
Charleston, S.C.

My dear Mr. Lathan:-

    I expect to go to Columbia Monday night to vote Tuesday and while in Columbia will return to you the Charleston Americans which you kindly loaned me. Included in the lot will be the one that goes back to Mr. Ryttenberg. Will you be good enough to return it to him for me?

    In sending these papers back to you, I feel that you should know that the use of them furnished me with a logical opening for the most effective attack which I was able to launch on Blease. The fact that he still stuck to the American and held it up as the one paper in the state to be followed by the masses in the campaign, enabled me to enter through that gate and link him with many men and facts which were damning.

    I am more than grateful to you for the papers and for the suggestions which you gave me in Charleston and which I got from your editorials from day to day. You have seen my statement and I want you to know that that is exactly the way I feel.

    Before we go into another campaign,- and the sooner the better - I think that a group of us should get together and discuss some constructive program. We have got to offer our people something to turn to if we expect to hold them away from Blease and from other leaders who will arise to lead those who feel that they have a grievance against the Government and against people who have made a success of life. Think this over, and I would like very much to have an opportunity to talk it out with you sometime this fall.

                  Yours sincerely,

CB
HC
                                  Christie Benet

In September 1918, US Senator Christie Benet wrote a letter to Robert Lathan, Editor of the News and Courier, Charleston, SC.

Christie Benet
1879–1951

William Christie Benet, Jr. was a Democratic party politician who briefly represented the state of South Carolina in the US Senate in 1918. He was born in Abbeville, SC and attended the College of Charleston, the University of South Carolina and graduated from the University of Virginia in 1902.

He played college football for the University of Virginia and was an All-South tackle in 1901. He practiced law in Columbia, SC in 1903, solicitor of the 5th circuit in 1908, and Columbia's City Attorney from 1910-1912.

In 1918, he was appointed to the US Senate to fill out the term of Benjamin R. Tillman who died while in office.

One month later, in October 1918, Editor Robert Lathan sent a five page type written letter to Senator Benet apprising Benet about "an attempt which was made just before and just after this country entered war with Germany to acquire control of the News and Courier in the interest of German sympathizers in this country."

Lathan described a visit made to the offices of the News and Courier in March 1917, by a man named George Sirmay, presenting his business card as George Sirmay, Berlin, Germany, working as an agent for a New York publishing house. He requested an interview with Mr. Rudolph Seigling, one of the owners of the newspaper, displaying for him beautifully printed books of German Classics.

At a separate time, Mr. Sirmay returned to report that what he really wanted was to buy the newspaper, subsequently sending a special delivery offer to purchase the stock. He also expressed openly to Mr. Siegling that "it would be a fine business stroke for the News and Courier to change its policy and see things from a German viewpoint." After he left, Editor Lathan and Mr. Siegling, representing the owner's interest, immediately contacted Mr. Waties Waring, the Assistant United States District Attorney.

Later in April 1917 after the US declaration of war, Mr. Siegling received a letter from Mr. Theodore Sutro from New York City, seeking to purchase the newspaper. Sutro had been editor of the German Journal, a Hearst newspaper in NYC and also president of the company.

One week later Mr. Siegling and Editor Lathan were in NYC for a newspaper conference and went to see Sutro, who had learned that Sirmay had been reported to the US Attorney's office in Charleston. The interaction was not illuminating. Editor Lathan stated that the matter was fully before the District Attorney office and had ended the matter for the newspaper.

Lathan stated in his letter to Senator Benet, "Whether anything could be made of them (Sirmay and Sutro) I do not know, but it has always seemed to me a striking thing that immediately on the eve of the declaration of war and immediately following there should have been such an attempt to purchase a paper like the News and Courier by professedly German interests."

James F. Byrnes
1882–1972

James Francis "Jimmy" Byrnes was born on King St. in Charleston, SC. His father died shortly after Byrnes was born. His mother supported the family as a dressmaker. At the age of 14 he left school to work in a law office teaching himself shorthand. He became a court stenographer and reporter in South Carolina from 1900-1908 at the same times as Robert Lathan.

In 1900, he moved from Charleston to Aiken, SC with his mother and grandmother. There he "read for the law" and was admitted to the bar in 1903. He set up a legal office in Aiken and edited a newspaper, the *Journal and Review*, from 1903-1907. In 1906, he married Maude Perkins Busch of Aiken and they had no children. He worked as the solicitor for the Second Circuit of South Carolina from 1908-1910.

In 1910, he began an extraordinary political career. He served first as a US Congressman for fourteen years and then a US Senator 1930-1941, frequently supporting President Franklin D. Roosevelt. Byrnes proved to be a brilliant legislator, working behind the scenes to form coalitions. In the US Senate he was regarded as the most influential South Carolinian since John C. Calhoun.

He had long been friends with FDR and made himself the President's spokesman on the Senate floor, where he guided to passage much of the early New Deal legislation. In 1941, the president appointed Byrnes to the US Supreme Court, but when World War II began, he resigned to become the first Director of Economic Stabilization and the head of the War Mobilization Organization. Roosevelt called Byrnes his "assistant president." Roosevelt took Byrnes to the Yalta Conference in early 1945. Byrnes notes, written in shorthand, composed one of the most complete records of the "Big Three" Yalta meetings. Throughout the years of the war, Byrnes was in almost daily conference with President Roosevelt. A mutual admiration and affection grew between the two leaders. The country thought that the Democratic Convention of 1940 would surely nominate Byrnes as the vice president running mate of FDR. That however did not happen. Instead Harry S. Truman was named Vice President. Byrnes did not sulk, but moved to support Truman.

After FDR's death in 1945, President Harry S. Truman appointed Byrnes, Secretary of State. Truman relied heavily on Byrnes' counsel and it was Byrnes who shared information with the new president on the atomic bomb project. Byrnes also played a major role at the Potsdam Conference, the Paris Peace Conference, and other postwar conferences. In 1946, Byrnes was named TIME man of the year.

At age 68, Byrnes was elected governor of South Carolina serving from 1951 to 1955.

Byrnes died on April 9, 1972 at age 89 and was interred in the churchyard at Trinity Episcopal Church in Columbia, SC.

James F. Byrnes is one of the very few politicians to serve in all three branches of the American federal government while also being active in state government.

Letters from Byrnes to Robert Lathan

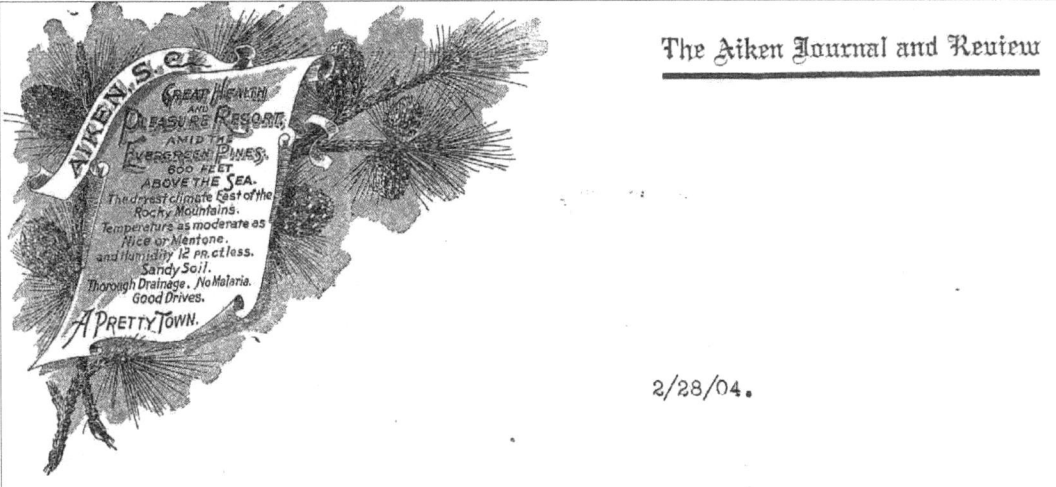

2/28/04.

Dear Lathan:-

I have heard from my friend Pierce as to whom I wrote you and he says that he will be glad to get hold of your job. Now I can personally answer for his qualification, as a stenographer and his character, and would be glad if you would let me know whether you think you can secure the job for him from Purdy. I know that he can "make good" as far as his ability goes, but want to be sure about it before telegraphing him to go to see you.

In case you wish to write him yourself, his address is: Charles L. Pierce, Carlsbad, New Mexico.

When I thought of quitting I intended placing Pierce in my office, but $1500 looks good to me and for the present I am going to hold on. In every way he will fill the position well, and I think Purdy will thank you for getting such a good man. If forced to a competitive examination I believe he can hold his own, and ask that before giving it to anyone else you let me know.

Truly,

J.F. Byrnes

The letters between Byrnes and Lathan display a deep respect and friendship for the individuals and for their opinions on public matters.

Chapter Six

The Journal and Review,
Aiken, S. C.

Monday

Dear Latham;

Of course I am willing to do what I can to help in the good cause though I think I am in a rather bad position just at the — totally — his not only — until next week. Let me know what day you expect to go to Columbia & I will try and meet you. I shall surely be there when the Bar meets. Tell me what you think about that 1500 business.

Byrnes

Some of the letters were typed and some handwritten, but all written in the casual style between friends.

The Aiken Journal and Review

Feb. 14th.

My dear Lathan:-

$25 will ordinarily pay a man's house-rent; buy him cigars or chewing gum in moderation and postage stamps for his wife. Considering this I presume that you feel good about our work during the month of January. That amendment appeared to me to be an imposition and I wrote Covington asking whether he thought best to have the Senate refuse to accept it. His judgment was that it was best to le t the Bill go as it was, so I followed his advice and kept the peace.

Byrnes

Byrnes shares his reasoning against an amendment to be included in a bill.

Chapter Six

Congress of the United States
House of Representatives
Washington, D. C.

Aiken, S. C.,
September 15, 1924.

Hon. Robert Lathan,
    Broad Street,
        Charleston, S. C.

Dear Bob:

I am back at my office this morning and before I attempt to answer my accumulated mail, I want to express to you my sincere appreciation of all that you have done for me during the past few months. My only regret is that you did not have a better horse upon the track. In the past we have defeated Blease because we had united support. The favorite won in the first primary and the defeated Anti-Blease candidates joined in an appeal for united support against Blease. This time the favorite did not win and a sufficient number of the Dial people including some of the newspapers, either supported Blease or were so indifferent as to make possible his election. Other things, of course, contributed, but one has only to look at the returns in Laurens County or in Greenville County to realize the accuracy of my statement.

But the purpose of this letter was not to analyze the result but merely to assure you that I shall never forget your kindness and to express the hope that an opportunity may some day come when I can show my appreciation of your loyal friendship.

Sincerely yours,
James F. Byrnes

As Byrnes assumed more demanding responsibilities in the Congress of the United States he still maintained his friendship with Lathan.

A Discerning Editor

Lathan and Byrnes: Similarities

Robert Lathan and James F. Byrnes were similar in many ways:

	LATHAN	BYRNES
	1881	1882
Birthplace:	York, SC	Charleston, SC
Married:	1904	1906
BOTH:	No Children	
	No College	
	Stenographer	
	Court Recorder	
	Studied Law	Lawyer, Editor
	Editor in Chief	Congressman, Senator
	Orator	Justice of Supreme Court, US Cabinet Member
	Pulitzer Prize Winner	*Time* Man of the Year

Chapter Six

NICHOLLS, WYCHE & BYRNES
ATTORNEYS AND COUNSELORS AT LAW
SPARTANBURG, SOUTH CAROLINA

GEO. W. NICHOLLS
SAM J. NICHOLLS
C. C. WYCHE
JAMES F. BYRNES

April 13, 1927

Mr. Robert Lathan,
Charleston, S. C.

Dear Bob Lathan:

    I regret exceedingly to learn that you are going to leave Charleston, but I want you to know that wherever you go you are going to take with you my good wishes.

    When you reach Asheville your friends from South Carolina will have an opportunity to see you during the summer, and if I am ever in Asheville I am going to invite myself to call upon you.

    With best wishes, I am

Sincerely yours,

James F Byrnes

JAMES F. BYRNES.

JFB-CC

Byrnes responds to the news that Lathan is leaving Charleston to assume new responsibilities in Asheville.

Chapter Seven

Robert Lathan, Jr.
An Editor of
Expansive Horizons

There are some people who object to talk. My own feeling is that while at times it might be annoying, it seldom does harm. It may do good. At all events, it has its uses.

Citizen 1928

Chapter Seven

Letter of Engagement from Charles Webb

ASHEVILLE, N.C.

R.L.#2.   3/1/27

        Answering the next to the last paragraph of your letter, we have no intention whatever of changing our plans and policies for the future development of the paper. The fact is, we are more determined upon an expansion of those plans than ever before. The present depression may delay things but we are contemplating raising our advertising rates, certainly before the 1st of July, which would more than take care of any deficit that has accrued during the last five months, and I feel that we would be perfectly justified in doing so because our circulation has increased since the 1st of last April approximately 3,500, and this circulation is every bit of it absolutely bona fide paid in advance circulation. We are now on the man carrier system, have a fine circulation manager and I believe that he is going to increase this circulation still further.

        Now, it seems to me that the thing for you to do is to take the matter up with Mr. Mitchell at once and explain the situation to him. Tell him fully of the former agreement between us and of our releasing you from that agreement on account of the mix-up with Mr. Rockwell. Then you can give me a definite answer whether or not you would be willing to come at the salary indicated above.

        <u>As to your trip abroad with Dr. Butler, I think that can be satisfactorily arranged. You ought not to miss that opportunity by any means.</u> It is certainly a great compliment for you to be appointed as a member of that party. We would, of course, like to get you firmly established here as soon as possible, as long a time before July 1st as possible, and we would be willing to continue your salary during your absence, paying you the same less what we would have to pay somebody to do your work. I think we could get somebody to fill in during the two months you are gone for probably $60.00 a week. It seems to me that this would be fair. I would like to know, however, how you feel about it.

        I think I have gone into the situation fully, and I feel, just as we have always felt, that you will have a fine opportunity here in Asheville, much finer than you have in Charleston, and that you will have a great opportunity of helping us develop and build up Western North Carolina.

Expanding Horizons
1927–1937

Chief Editor 1927–1937

Asheville Citizen Newspaper building in 1927 when Lathan arrived as Editor

Moving from Charleston to Asheville

Before Robert and Bessie Lathan's departure from Charleston, Lathan and Charles Webb, Publisher of the *Citizen*, had made an agreement that the Lathans would attend the Carnegie Endowment Tour of Europe before officially assuming Lathan's leadership as Editor of the *Asheville Citizen*. Both thought that the trip would be very beneficial to broadening the new editor's horizons and perspective in covering both national and international issues. Their plans of exploring new horizons and listening to new voices would produce tremendous value for all of their readers.

Carnegie Endowment For International Peace

Nicholas Butler

European Conference on International Relations July 16–October 3, 1927

Dr. Nicholas Murray Butler, President of Columbia University and the head of the Carnegie Endowment's section on international education and communication, founded the European branch of the Endowment, with headquarters in Paris. On behalf of the Endowment he invited thirty editors from all parts of the US to spend three months in Europe at Paris, London, Berlin, the Hague, Munich, Prague, and Geneva, in a traveling conference on international relations.

Robert Lathan was one of the thirty editors invited and had accepted to go with this party in the time of his transition from Charleston to Asheville. The sailing was from New York in July with the return to New York in October. Lathan had planned this trip for some time as an extraordinary opportunity and had advised the Endowment of his change to the new editorship in Asheville, NC in the spring of 1927 before the trip.

Nicholas Murray Butler

Nicholas Murray Butler was an educator, university president and an advisor to seven US presidents as well as friend of many statesmen in foreign relations. He had honorary degrees from thirty-seven college and universities. He was an international traveler who crossed the Atlantic at least 100 times. He was called Nicholas "Miraculous" Butler by his good friend Theodore Roosevelt.

In 1882, at age twenty, Butler received his bachelor's degree, in 1883 his master's degree, and in 1884 a doctorate – all from Columbia College. In 1901, he became President of Columbia University, which he retained for forty-four years. Under his presidency, the student body of Columbia University increased from 4000 to 34000.

His association with Carnegie Endowment for International Peace lasted for thirty-five years. He was influential in persuading Andrew Carnegie to establish the Endowment in 1910 with a gift of $10,000,000.

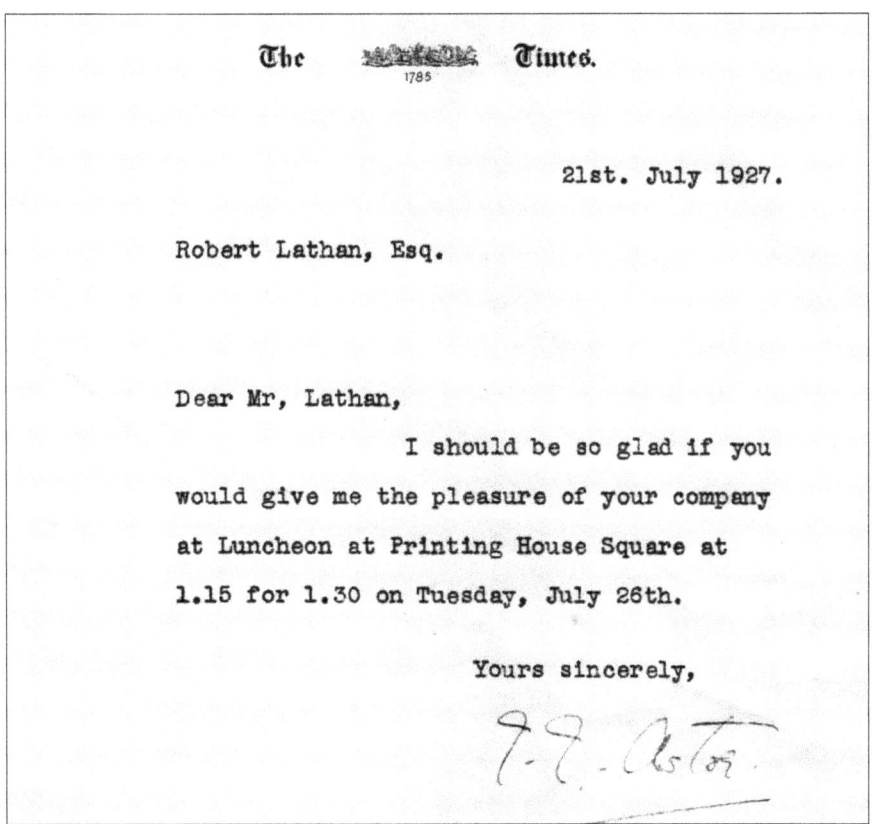

John Jacob Astor

The letters and invitations for Robert Lathan enclosed a small note from "J. J. Astor to Robert Lathan, Esq. to invite him to a luncheon on July 28, 1928 at Printing House Square."

At first there seemed to be a mystery and possible mistake, as "J.J. " or John Jacob Astor died in the tragic sinking of the Titanic in 1912. However, after closely looking at the letterhead of the invitation, "Printing House Square" was a London court and "The Times - 1785" was where the famous newspaper started. The date of July 28 was the time that Editor Lathan was to be in London on the European Carnegie Endowment trip.

Biographical information on John Jacob Astor V (1886-1971) show that he would be the person inviting Lathan to luncheon in Printing House Square. Astor was an American born English newspaper proprietor, politician, sportsman, military officer, and member of the Astor family.

Astor represented Great Britain in the rackets competition in the 1908 summer Olympic Games, winning the gold medal in men's doubles and the bronze medal in men's singles. In World War I, he was wounded twice and rose to the rank of Lt. Colonel.

In 1922, he purchased *The Times* newspaper and remained chairman of the paper until 1959. Under his leadership the newspaper sponsored Edmund Hillary's expedition to climb Mt. Everest. In politics, he served in Parliament from 1922-1945. In 1956, he was anointed Baron Astor of Hever Castle in the county of Kent.

With firsthand experience and knowledge through the recently attended Carnegie international Conference, Lathan brought to the *Asheville Citizen* in-depth discussions of the challenges facing Americans with the new horizons of expanded trade opportunities as well as political battles over the League of Nations. The readers of the columns as well as various community and university groups were the recipients of his opinions.

In an address to the Emory University Citizenship Conference in February 1928, Lathan spoke of many of these challenges.

Excerpts from the speech are included here. Full text is in reference section. Citizen 1928.

I was tremendously impressed a few weeks ago, when I examined the program of the Emory Conference that for this year with the attention given to world politics; for it seems to me in pursing this course Emory has shown a sense of values that is splendidly constructive. I am sure that it has taken courage on the part of those responsible for these Citizenship Conferences to do this. They realize of course, that at the very term "foreign relations," most of us in America are accustomed to close our ears. What concerns have we with international affairs? What can we hope to know about them? Why should we bother with such matters? Why not talk about something worth while, something nearer home, something practical and useful?

You will agree that this is a popular attitude…a member of (a different) audience summed up the opposition as "Let 'em alone." ….Now I am the last person who would set up as an authority on world politics but I know we can not "Let 'em alone" any more than we can let the weather alone. And there is a difference between politics and the weather…in the matter of world politics, unfortunately, the amount that has been done is out of proportion to the talk we have had….intelligent talk, I mean, talk that would have conveyed information and perhaps cleared the air.

And so I am going to make bold to talk to you tonight about America's present world position as I see it. For your reassurance, let me say at once that I shall not attempt to unravel the intricacies of internationalism….Surely it should be the privilege of any of us, even a provincial editor, to "hop around a bit," in spite of the suggestion recently thrown out from high authority that the press would do well in foreign affairs to stick closely to its duty of supporting the Government's policies.

…A questions we need to ask ourselves is… why the delusion of American isolation in world affairs. What nonsense to cling to this wornout theory…It has been some time, in fact, since the United States was a truly self-contained community. It is less so every year.

We have become almost before we know it ourselves the most powerful figure in the family of nations. Out influence has penetrated in one way or another to the far corners of the world.

...Our professions are true when we say we are without covetousness as a people. But how shall we make others believe this?

...Will this continue to be the attitude of the Unites States indefinitely? Personally, I do not think so. My own conviction is strong that the practical force of events will imperatively urge us to throw the weight of our great influence into the scale along with those who are battling through the League (of Nations) ...to keep the peace of the world and promote its welfare.

...As a practical people we are being faced with a question of alternatives and if we can but come to see clearly what these alternatives are I am sure, for my part, that we will not elect to organize only for war and refuse to do our part to organize also for peace.

Emory University 1928

In an address to the South Carolina Press Association almost ten years later, in June of 1937, Lathan emphasized again his opinions of American nationalism and international isolationism.

Excerpts from the speech are included here. Full text is in reference section. South 1937

I am trying in what I am saying to suggest how definitely, how inescapable, South Carolina is tied into the national and international picture. Economically. I do not wish to abuse your hospitality or try your patience: and so, passing over the period of the present depression, I hurry to a conclusion.

...Millions of individuals, thousands of businessmen, realized suddenly that their destinies, were not, as they fondly believed in their own hands.

The fact the consequences of national and international policies might destroy quickly the opportunities of great numbers of people even to make a living was brought home cruelly to every community.

No one was able to question in the banking crisis that banking was in a measure never previously acknowledged a concern of government.

No one was able to question then that the functioning of the economic system of the social system of the nation is a concern of the national government.

Columbia SC 1937

Chapter Seven

Pen and Plate Club

Soon after arriving in Asheville, Lathan found a welcoming group of like minded citizens who practiced the research of history as well as current affairs. His thoughts and convictions were being readily perused by the readers daily in the *Asheville Citizen*. The Pen and Plate Club provided him with both a place to express these views, but also an opportunity to receive opinions through peer discussions.

The Pen and Plate Club in Asheville, NC was founded in 1904, with many of the same literary goals as the Cosmos Club of New York. The original adoptions described it as a "society with few rules and with provision for full and free expressions of opinion and convictions." It was thought that the club "would enable distinguished citizens of literary sophistication to gather for social purposes and friendly discussions." At the time of its founding it was considered that the "time was ripe" for such a gathering. Asheville had become known as a resort, a sanitarium, and a social mecca that attracted professional men from other regions.

Many participants described the Pen and Plate as a "social body with gastronomic tastes, tinctured with literary aspirations, a monthly gathering of congenial and friendly spirts to enjoy good dinners together and listen to a reading on a subject freely presented by the member."

Editor of Expansive Horizons

*Pen and Plate Club Members 25th Anniversary
Robert Lathan is pictured on back row, second from right.*

Chapter Seven

In May of 1928, Lathan presented a "Newcomer" perspective of his new home state of North Carolina to the Pen and Plate Club meeting. The depth of his study into the history of North Carolina from a "why" "how" and "result" provided all of the attendees and the recipients of the written address with a story both enlightening and enjoyable, very much recognizing of Lathan's exceptional talent of transforming historical perspectives into very enjoyable and informative communications.

Excerpts from the speech are included here. Full text is in reference section. Accounting 1928.

In the past thirty years—especially in the past ten years—North Carolina, long known, to quote Governor Bickett, as the "Rip Van Winkle State of the Union," has become the "Wonder State of the South." It has blazed its way to the front in highway construction, in manufacturing, in agriculture, in education, in the Little Theatre movement, conservation of beauty and in various other fields. ...It has been a miracle change. What has worked the miracle? That is the question ever on the lips of visitors from the North. When they see what has happened, they want to know how it happened and why it happened. Their questions can not be answered by pointing to the extraordinary variety and extent of North Carolina's resources....They are still left wondering why North Carolina should have been a pacemaker for the South and why they find a spirit here which apparently does not exist in the same measure elsewhere. And the answer is that all of North Carolina's past history had prepared it for the coming of the kingdom at such a time. That as least is my thesis. Now for the proof!

I begin with the suggestion that of all the States of the Old South, North Carolina was, omitting only Florida, from the earliest Colonial period down to the very recent past, the most parochial. That does not sound like a compliment: indeed, when in 1886, Walter Hines Page said something of the sort in his famous Mummy letter it gave great offense. ..."Not a man has ever lived and worked there who fills twenty-five pages in any history of the United States." People did not like Mr. Page's saying this but what he said was substantially true. And since events of the past thirty years have taken the sting out of the words it may be worthwhile to consider now what was back of the condition which he pictured.

If the plantation system had spread in North Carolina as it did in South Carolina, for example, the story would have been a different one, but North Carolina was spared the blight. The two supreme factors in North Carolina's history down to 1890 were which I have just touched upon with the manner in which the State was settled. If, like all other Seaboard States, North Carolina had been settled from the coast, its character would have been developed upon radically different lines.

In North Carolina the character of the coast was such as to make it dangerous for vessels to land on it and so even the coastal counties were settled mainly by people who drifted down into them from Virginia and who did not try to extend their authority over the middle and upper country....There was no sharp conflict between them and before slavery began to grow... conditions in North Carolina had so shaped themselves that in this state there were always, at every stage, at least two white persons for every Negro. This was a greater blessing than could be appreciated. ...Probably a majority of the North Carolinians owned no slaves.

The conditions under which North Carolina was settled influenced the development of the State in one other way that was vitally important. The fact that the state was settled from the interior, that the development was along agricultural lines and the climate was good in all sections discouraged the growth of cities. There were numerous towns and trading centers; and even as these grew in size through the years, they remained trading and nothing more...There never existed the antagonism between town and country which has been so common in so many states.

...Furthermore, since there was little that the national government could do for them, North Carolinians have had always to look for themselves. It is this confidence that has found marvelous illustration in the great movements of the past three decades.

The first of these movements, public school education, while slow to get underway, but became a veritable crusade.More widely advertised than anything else North Carolina has done has been its roadbuilding program; and it is here that the spirit which characterizes the people of North Carolina and which is a product of all their past experience has found its perfect expression...the necessity of taking North Carolina out of the mud. At length the gasoline tax opened the way for doing this and the state legislature was asked to provide a bond issue.

When one studies North Carolina, either its present or its past, curious contradictions present themselves, or what seems contradictions; but the thing that impresses me most in the state's history is that its people are less interested in the rest of the world than most people and have never been afraid of what might happen in North Carolina.

...the need is for leaders who will make us vision and yearn for things of the spirit as the leaders of the past have stirred North Carolinians to glorious endeavor in the realization of the opportunities in fulfillment of the obligation which those opportunities involve.

Asheville 1928

Speakers on stage at hearing in Washington

Blue Ridge Parkway

Lathan's editorial ability to influence projects and issues, which would have positive effects on the community, were not only by written newspaper words, but also through organizational leadership for the project. Securing of the Blue Ridge Parkway project for the Asheville, North Carolina area clearly demonstrates this quality.

In 1933, the idea of the Blue Ridge Parkway originated when President Franklin Delano Roosevelt became familiar with the newly constructed Skyline Drive in Virginia. US Senator from Virginia, Harry Byrd, suggested to President Roosevelt that the Skyline Drive roadway should be extended to connect to the recently established Great Smoky Mountain National Park. Roosevelt met with the governors of Virginia, North Carolina and Tennessee suggesting that a planning team be created. On November 1933, Interior Secretary Harold Ickes approved the park-to-park highway from the Shenandoah Park in Virginia to the Great Smoky Mountain Park in Tennessee as a public works project.

Ickes conducted a study to determine the best route for the parkway with the recommendation being a leg of the highway from the Blowing Rock, NC area into Tennessee connecting with the Great Smoky Mountain National Park. This initial decision was met with great controversy, especially by the city of Asheville, NC, which was in economical stress at the time of the Great Depression. Asheville leaders joined to lobby against the proposed route in favor of a road that passed through their city. An intense campaign then began in Washington.

In Asheville, a dinner was held at the Biltmore Forest Country Club including Robert Lathan, Editor of the *Asheville Citizen*, and many others from Asheville to plan and schedule a meeting with officials in Washington.

On September 18, 1934, a hearing was held in Washington, DC in the auditorium of the Department of Interior before Secretary Harold Ickes to consider two alternate routes for a section of the new Blue Ridge Parkway, hopefully to be built between Blowing Rock, NC and Asheville, NC. At the hearing the delegates from Tennessee argued for a road westward from Blowing Rock through Roan Mountain and Iron Mountain entering the Smoky Mountain Park at Gatlinburg, Tennessee. North Carolina speakers urged a scenic route past Grandfather Mountain, Mount Mitchell, the Craggy Gardens, Mt. Pisgah, and the Balsams.

A special train was arranged with eighteen Pullman coaches and a club car. The train left Asheville on September 14th and another Pullman from Charlotte attached the train in Greensboro. Around 400 North Carolinians attended the hearing outnumbering the Tennessee delegates two to one. Secretary Ickes was obviously impressed by the earnestness of the North Carolinians speakers and the size of the delegation. Charles Webb, president of the *Citizen Times* company provided ten rooms at the Mayflower Hotel to serve as headquarters of the delegation.

The speakers from North Carolina introduced by Governor J.C.B. Ehringhaus were highway engineer R.G. Browning; Frank Page, the former head of the State Highway Commission; Robert Lathan; NC Senators Josiah Bailey and Robert Rice Reynolds; and NC Congressman Robert Lee Doughton.

September 18, 1934, about 600 delegates attended the hearing. A photograph of the panoramic view of the Department of Interior showed a filled auditorium. The seven speakers were on the stage and Robert Lathan can be seen on the right side with a light-colored suit.

Chapter Seven

Rural communities benefitted by the new road access

Editor Lathan pleaded for full consideration of the economic reason identified with the lives of those who lived back in the coves of the mountains and to stabilize the population of the mountain sections. He pointed to the tourist industry that has been operative in Western North Carolina for more than a century and to the substantial investment in hotels and recreational advantages.

Lathan pointed out that "the parkway will be the main avenue to the Smoky Mountain Park and that the natural result of diverting tourist travel from the established resort of Western North Carolina would be to create damage. We depend on that as our main industry. Please do not divert this stream of travel from us."

Editor Lathan insisted that "subsistence farmers in the coves of the mountains had the most at stake and would gain from jobs in craft making and sales farm products. These people live along these mountains- that is their home. You cannot take them to the road, you must bring the road to them."

Rural communities and its citizens would benefit the most.

The Asheville contingency employed the influential U S Ambassador to Mexico, Josephus Daniels, to lobby on their behalf. Daniels had served as Secretary of the Navy under President Wilson with FDR as his Deputy Secretary. When FDR became President, he appointed Daniels to be Ambassador to Mexico. During the time of the negotiations, Daniels was also publisher of the Raleigh, NC newspaper. Daniels' influence helped to sway the administration to favor the Asheville route.

Three days after the hearing, editor Lathan wrote Interior Secretary Ickes a five-page typewritten letter about his points for North Carolina. He wrote, "No other project has ever meant so much to the community by which the mountain counties could be given the opportunity to share generously in the nation's recovery."

Lathan also communicated with Senator Bailey and in Asheville said that "the work on the Parkway is tremendously appreciated here and all over Western North Carolina. I never go on the street without someone asking me about it."

Senator Bailey wrote Lathan one week after the hearings that "I think the point you made at Washington was the best and the most powerful point made."

In November, Senator Bailey sent a letter to Editor Lathan reporting that Secretary Ickes had made his decision in favor of North Carolina, not only because its superior scenic route, but also that it needed a southeastern entrance to the Smoky Mountain Park since Tennessee also had one entrance on the western side. Ickes had had assurance from President Roosevelt, who said long before the hearing that he was going to see that North Carolina got the Parkway.

The Parkway began in September 1935, but there were years of negotiation and World War II halted construction. The parkway was finally opened in 1987, a completion of a continuous 469 mile route.

The scenic route crests the Southern Appalachian Mountains and winds along mountain ridge tops. The Parkway was conceived as a link between the Shenandoah National Park in Virginia and the Great Smoky Mountain National Park in North Carolina and Tennessee. The idea to build the Parkway resulted from many factors, but one of the probable one being the need to create jobs for the people suffering from the Great Depression and for poor mountain families.

Craggy Gardens Visitor Center

Chapter Seven

Linn Cove Viaduct

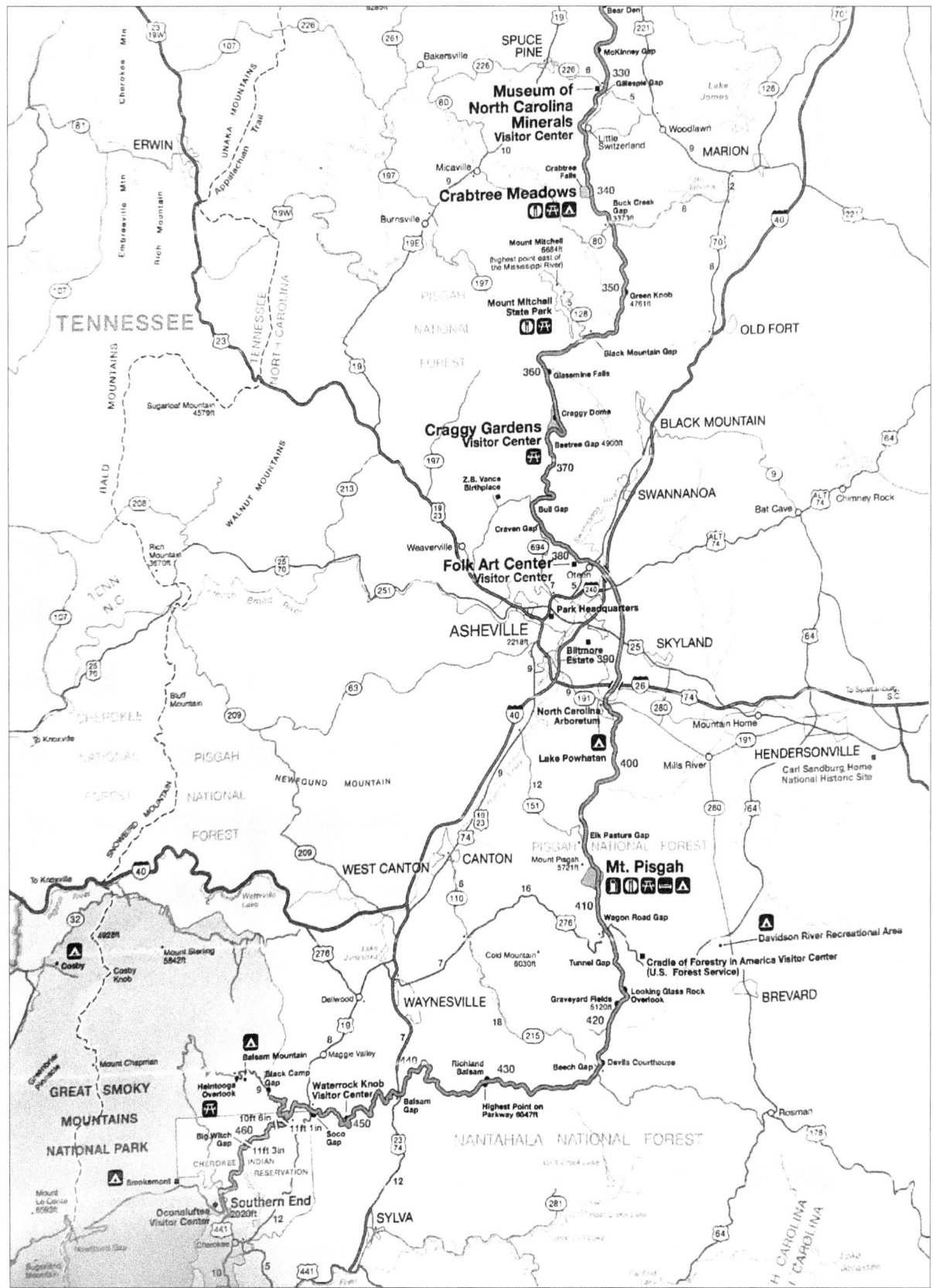

Blue Ridge Parkway Route in North Carolina

Chapter Seven

Peace On Earth Goodwill To Men

Lathan's strong religious heritage of striving for peace amongst individual people and nations was often the subject matter of his editorials for *The Asheville Citizen*. In 1931, in the middle of the Great Depression, he wrote A *Christmas Editorial* describing his opinion of the difficulty to both create peace such as end of WWI in 1918 and maintain it into the Great Depression of 1929 – 1933. The newspaper article was reprinted into a brochure distributed widely in the area.

Focusing on the Biblical scripture of Luke as the Christmas story is repeated to the world each year, Lathan used the verses to describe conditions present in the United States and around the world concluding with the hope of the fulfillment the words.

Excerpts from the publication are included here. Full text is in references section. Christmas 1931.

"Glory to God in the highest, and on earth peace, good will toward men." Deny if you will the divine inspiration of this story. Match it if you can in all literature, sacred or profane.

We look about us today, at the Christmas season, and what do we see?

A world in arms. A world in war. No peace anywhere. Goodwill seemingly a mockery.

Is there any cure? Only one. We have already given it. It was that which was hymned in the ears of the shepherds by the multitude of

the heavenly host. "Glory to God in the highest, and on earth peace, good will toward men."

What is true of nations is true of individuals. Gone is the day when wealth might flaunt itself in the face of sodden poverty. There is no freedom that attached to wealth when distress is general or when discontents prevail.

We are all parts of one whole. In an atmosphere in which this is acknowledged the world can shake off the weights that cumber it, can revive the springs of credit—which is confidence, trust, good will—and regain the equilibrium which it has lost.

It is our attitude toward Christmas which makes the Christmas season what it is; …venturing today to write at such lengths on the direful effects which a wrong attitude among nations and peoples has had..and the urgent necessity for bringing about a right attitude as the only corrective of these evils.

"Glory to God in the highest, and on earth peace, good will toward men."

Editor of Expansive Horizons

Mr. Robinson wrote in the evening for *The Times*.

Mr. Lathan wrote in the morning for *The Citizen*.

Lathan's Daily Columns

While being a much sought after speaker and participant in community events, Editor Lathan wrote and published a daily column in the *Asheville Citizen* newspaper. Described as "vigorous and vivid" the subject matter varied from international news and opinions, AP provided stories, to interesting gossip news from the movie scene. On any one day, the columns under the banner of Robert Lathan, Jr., Editor could contain four or five articles of different subject matter from his very interesting perspective.

Chapter Seven

Examples of Newspaper Columns
Editor, Robert Lathan
September 5, 1937

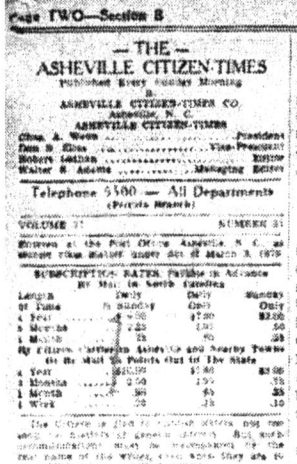

A Palestine Accord
9/5/1937

Moving with ponderous slowness as befits its great dignity the Mandates Commission of the League of Nations has at last made known its opinion in the matter of the partition of Palestine. Geneva, it appears, approves as a test policy the division of the Holy Land, like all Gaul into three parts. It desires, however, that Great Britain retain her mandate during a time of political childhood of the proposed Arab and Jewish states. And the plan also provides the establishment of a permanent British mandate over Jerusalem, Nazareth and other religious shrines.

This partitioning business is in the nature of a major operation and it is certainly to be hoped that the patient survives whether or not the operation is a success from the standpoint of the surgeons. There is no news at this late date covering Great Britain for her opposing positions made to the Arabs and the Jews under pressure of the World War. All of that is water over the dam by now.

Nuremberg Again
9/6/1937

Six hundred thousand Nazis are going to meet in Nuremberg today for the annual congress of the German National Party. There is little doubt that the things said there will outdistance the shot heard around the world. For it is perhaps not too much to say that Germany holds the key to peace in Europe at the moment and Nazi party means Germany.

It has been Der Fuehrer's custom in the past to outline at Nuremberg some of the objectives that he has created for his followers. There he has been accustomed to talk about the riches of the Russian Ural Mountains and the Ukraine and what Germany would accomplish if she had them. There he dwells upon the national self-sufficiency plans and how much dearer cannon should be to all supporters of the fatherland. There he holds forth on the dangers of communism and the sins of the Jews.

The whole affair is termed a National Socialist revival meeting. The gathering might be a matter of indifference, even a joke, to the rest of the world, if it were not such a tragic joke. For thought words that hit the ether from Nuremberg this year may start events in motion on the farthest shores of the globe. Such is the power of good and evil that fate has placed in the hands in the German people.

The world is now tinder for general conflagration. It is to be hoped that mistaken patriotic fervor will supply no sparks.

Paper Money
9/5/1937

According to a story from the Associated Press, A Los Angeles judge gave a fitting demonstration that he did not believe everything that he saw in the movies., not even the size of the pay checks. In the case in question a well known moving picture actress asked for a thousand dollars a month for temporary alimony. and $2500 counsel fees preparing trial against her husband an equally well known screen writer.

The judge cut the alimony fee to $200 a month and allowed $130 counsel fees. He is also quoted as saying, "Back in Pottsdam, PA and Herington KS, people all think that members of the film industry all live in luxurious homes and everything is milk and honey. I have found that that is not the case. An actor is as good as his last film and an author is as good as his last book. Fame is a fleeting thing."

The Movies Come Of Age
9/6/1937

To the little group of pioneers who tirelessly ground out those first flickering films in a Culver City, CA barn hardly more than a quarter-century ago the proposition that the industry they were founding might become a significant social force would have been ludicrous. But such was the power of visual art that what was a toy became an institution—through nothing more than the vitagraph in 1910 wedded to cinematic progress and the sound track.

Technically. It is as simple as all that. Yet so great is the influence of the movies on the mores of Americans, not only mirroring but heralding cultural epochs-that more than one group of thinkers has stopped to consider their implications. Most interesting among them is the Williamston Institute of Human Relations at Williams College, which devoted it research efforts of its assembled savants to the thorough study of the movies as they affect American life.

The consensus seems to be a bill of approval for Hollywood.

So Hollywood, that magic land is coming of age, something more than an age of innocence enforced by the legion of decency, but one in which it finds the imponderables popular and profitable. This is significant, for the magnitude of the cinema audience is the concern of those who see it in far-reaching editorial implications. It is not hard to believe that the American movie audience numbers more persons than are enrolled in every church, public school, college and university in the land, and more people will witness the next feature movie than have seen the plays of Shakespeare in the last 200 years.

Chapter Eight

Robert Lathan, Jr.
The Best Writer for
"A Good Year and
a Goodly Land"

RL 1902

One of the finest things in the history of newspapers is from the earliest times, the men who conducted them have uniformly recognized their responsibilities to the public.

Look 1926

Chapter Eight

𝔚riting 𝔉riendships 𝔄ll 𝔄long the 𝔚ay
1900–1937

Through the four decades of Robert Lathan's newspaper jobs, from researcher to city editor, he collected, nourished and mentored a large newspaper family.

Some of the many of their communications are featured in this chapter.

𝔗he 𝔖tate

𝔑arciso 𝔊ener 𝔊onzales
𝔄ugust 5, 1858–𝔍anuary 15, 1903

"Hoping to give a voice to the conservative wing of the Democratic Party after Ben Tillman's election to the governorship, Gonzales joined with his brother Ambrose to found the State Publishing Company in January 1891, with the financial backing of conservative Democrats." *University of South Carolina Institute for Southern Studies.*

Popularly known as "NG", Gonzales was born in Edingsville, Edisto Island, South Carolina in 1858. He and his brother, Ambrose E. Gonzales, (1857-1926) were the founders of *The State* newspaper in Columbia, SC.

Gonzales was the son of Colonel (CSA) Ambrosia Jose' Gonzales and Harriet Rutledge Elliott. His father was a Colonel in the Confederate Army under the staff of General PGT Beauregard in the Civil War. His father had become famous in Cuba as a Cuban revolutionary leader with Venezuelan General Narciso Lopez, both opposing the oppressive Spanish rule. His mother was the daughter of the wealthy South Carolina rice planter, state senator and writer William Elliott.

After his formal education ended in 1875, at the age of seventeen, NG became a telegraph operator. He worked in railroad depots in Varnville, SC, Savannah, GA and Valdosta, GA. While working as a telegrapher he developed an interest in journalism and state politics. In 1880, he became a reporter for the Greenville, SC *Daily News*. There he also accepted a position as the Columbia, SC correspondent for the Charleston, SC *News and Courier*.

In 1891, NG and his brother Ambrose, founded *The State* newspaper to support a number of progressive causes with editorials that called for an end to lynching, reforms of child labor laws, and women's suffrage. The paper was also frequently critical of the policies of Benjamin R. Tillman (Pitchfork Ben), who had served as Governor of South Carolina from 1890-1894 and US Senator from 1895-1918.

Robert Lathan described NG Gonzales and his brother Ambrose in 1937.

Excerpts are included here. Full speech is in references. South 1937.

It was then coincidentally that liberalism, in any semblance to its modern meaning, had its birth in South Carolina. NG Gonzales fathered it. His brave able and determined fight against child labor alienated some of his best business and personal friends.

They were splendid men. They had done and were doing great work. NG Gonzales appreciated better perhaps than any other man in South Carolina at the time the value of the service they were rendering. But he understood what they did not, that the humanitarianism of the plantation system, however splendid would not suffice in an industrial system.

NG Gonzales was shot on January 15, 1903 by James H. Tillman, the Lt. Governor and nephew of Senator Ben Tillman. Gonzales died four days later.

Tillman had been defeated in his run for governor of South Carolina in 1902. He felt that the vigorous opposition by the editorials of Gonzales in *The State* newspaper had been responsible. Tillman felt the newspaper attacks were not only political but personal. Months later the trial for the killing of Gonzales, Tillman escaped punishment. The jury was considered rigged and highly partisan considering that Tillman shot Gonzales in broad daylight in the presence of many eyewitnesses. The shooting took place in the shadow of the State house on the northeast corner of Main and Gervais Streets. The victim was an unarmed journalist of national reputation while walking on the public street on his way to lunch.

Tillman was acquitted ostensibly on a shaky self-defense theory. In reality the jury believed that Tillman was right in taking justice into his own hands for being denied the election win.

NG Gonzales was survived by his wife Lucie Barron (1870-1936) the daughter of Benjamin P. Barron and Alice Witherspoon, of Manning, SC. She came to Columbia as a child and spent most of her life in the state capital. After her husband's death, Mrs. Barron assumed the role of vice president of *The State* Newspaper and spent much of her time with her Barron siblings. Both NG and Lucie are buried at Elmwood Cemetery in Columbia.

A memorial cenotaph or obelisk for Gonzales was later erected on Senate Street across from the State House in Columbia, purportedly on the route Tillman regularly walked home. The memorial states "A great editor, and eminent citizen, and an honest man NG Gonzales."

Ambrose Elliott Gonzales
1857–1926

1885 *News and Courier*, staff reporter
1891 *The State*, publisher, treasurer, business manager

Ambrose Gonzales, a journalist and businessman was born in 1857 on a plantation in Colleton County, South Carolina. He was a son of Cuban general Ambrosio Jose Gonzales, a colonel in the Confederate Army. Earlier, he had been a Cuban revolutionary leader against the oppressive Spanish rule. His mother Harriet Rutledge Elliott, was the daughter of the wealthy South Carolina rice planter, state senator, and writer, William Elliott.

In 1874, Gonzales became the telegraph operator in Grahamville, SC which led to his involvement in state politics, especially after Wade Hampton III won the gubernatorial race in 1876. Ambrose left the telegraph office in 1879, to manage the family plantation, Oak Lawn, on the Edisto River.

Two years later, he moved to New York City as a telegrapher for Western Union. In 1885, he joined his brother, Narcisco Gener Gonzales on the staff of the Charleston *News and Courier*. NG was a leading reporter and Ambrose became a general agent traveling and reporting all over the state.

Inspired by the rise of Ben Tillman's successful campaign for governor in 1890, Ambrose, Narcisco and their younger brother William, founded *The State* newspaper in 1891, in Columbia as an outspoken anti-Tillman daily newspaper. NG became the editor. Ambrose assumed the titles of publisher, business manager, and treasurer, all of which he retained until his death in 1926.

Gonzales was also well known as a writer of black dialect sketches about the Gullah people of the South Carolina Low Country. Gonzales grew up speaking Gullah with the workers on his family rice plantation. He authored several books of the Gullah writings, including The <u>Black Border</u> in 1922. The second book <u>With AESOP Along the Black Border</u>, in 1924 was signed and presented by the author to Robert Lathan, editor of the Charleston *News and Courier*. Later the 1st Edition was purchased in 2000 by this book's author, S. Robert Lathan, Jr. M.D., the editor's cousin.

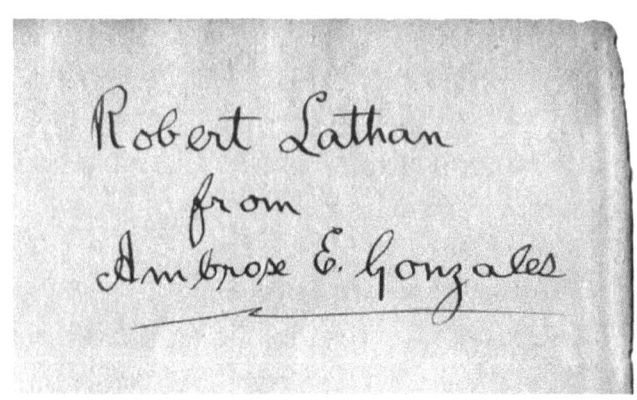

William Elliott Gonzales
1866–1937

1888 *News and Courier*, Columbia bureau assistant to Gonzales
1891 *The State*, telegraph editor, proofreader, writer
1903 *The State*, editor
1926 *The State*, publisher

William Gonzales was born in 1866 in Charleston, SC as the son of Ambrose Gonzales and his wife Harriet Rutledge Elliott. Best known as the editor of *The State* newspaper. He was the youngest of the three Gonzales brothers to lead the publication.

In York, SC, William attended the Kings Mountain Military Academy and later briefly attended The Citadel in Charleston. He began his journalistic career at the salary of $5.00 per week, working as assistant to his brother, NG who was then in charge of the *News and Courier* bureau in Columbia. Later in 1891, as his brothers founded *The State* newspaper William worked as telegraph editor, proofreader, and news editor, writing features and headlines.

NG was William's greatest supporter and mentor, but his death in 1903 left Ambrose to manage *The State* and for William to assume the editorial responsibilities.

"Captain Billy," as he was often called by his friends and admirers, served as did his brothers in the Spanish American War. He was a excellent shot and the champion marksmen of the Carolinas for many years.

William was an early supporter of Woodrow Wilson for President of the United States and worked campaigning for Wilson to win. Later Wilson invited William to become minister to Cuba in 1913 and in 1918 made him Ambassador to Peru.

Following the death of Ambrose in 1926, William returned to Columbia to serve as editor, publisher, and president of *The State* Company. Gonzales also found time to serve his community and the state. He was senior warden of Trinity Episcopal Church. As an excellent hunter and fisherman as well as bridge player and golfer, he could be seen enjoying and promoting many recreational activities throughout the state.

Gonzales was honored by the University of South Carolina with an honorary degree and an honorary member of Phi Beta Kappa. At his death the distinguished South Carolinian was characterized as "a soldier, scholar, editor, churchman, and gentleman."

Chapter Eight

William E. Gonzales, upon the death of his brother, became president and publisher as well as editor, the only person to hold all three titles.

So far as known the only pictures extant which show both William E. and Ambrose E. Gonzales were taken at the home of August Kohn when he gave a luncheon for Woodrow Wilson, then governor of New Jersey, in 1911. The group shown here was excerpted from one of those photographs:

Front row (l to r): J. C. Mace of Marion, Elbert H. Aull of Newberry; Second row (l to r, zigzaging) William E. Gonzales, W. R. Bradley of Columbia; behind Mr. Bradley, Dr. J. J. Watson of Columbia, and, on the end, Ambrose E. Gonzales. Behind W. E. Gonzales, A. Hamilton Seats, city editor of *The State*. Then C. O. Hearon of Spartanburg, and John L. Mimnaugh of Columbia. Back row, (l to r): Robert Lathan and Thomas R. Waring, Sr., of Charleston, J. L. Mims of Edgefield and John J. Earle of Columbia.

The News and Courier

Francis Warrington Dawson
1840–1889

1865 *Richmond Newspaper*
1866 *Charleston Mercury*
1867 *Charleston Daily News*
1873 *News and Courier*, editor

Born in 1840 in London, England as Austin John Reeks, he later changed his name in adulthood. He was born into an educated, upper middle class Catholic family. After graduating from London schools, his father declared bankruptcy forcing great family changes.

Austin took up writing as a career and wrote at least four comedies. From London, he became very enamored with the Southern cause and traveled to the United States in 1861 in support of the Civil War. On arrival, he changed his name to Francis Warrington Dawson.

He served in the Confederate Army, engaging in eleven battles and was wounded three times before being captured. He was later assigned to General James Longstreet's staff and in 1864 was promoted to captain. After the war he became a journalist and worked on newspapers in Richmond, VA. When he moved to Charleston he was employed by the *Charleston Mercury* in 1866. A year later he joined the *Charleston Daily News*. After purchasing the *Courier*, he distributed the first issue of the newly combined *News and Courier* in April 1873.

Dawson published a book in 1880 about his experiences and impressions of his time in the Civil War entitled, <u>Reminiscences of Confederate Service, 1861-1865</u>. In his book he wrote: "After Hagerstown (Maryland), we moved rapidly to South Mountain, where we had a brisk fight and were driven back." Dawson was captured and taken prisoner near Williamsport shortly before the Battle of Antietam. Dawson was later released on parole in October 1862.

An unusual coincidence was that Frank Dawson along with Editor Robert Lathan, Jr.'s uncle Samuel Boston Lathan, were marching the same route from Hagerstown to South Mountain on September 14, 1862. Samuel B. Lathan was wounded in the battle at the top of South Mountain, captured and taken to Baltimore.

The News and Courier became known for speed in news gathering, accuracy, and coverage with correspondents in Washington DC and Columbia. For the next decade Dawson was a powerful voice in the new South promoting the building of cotton mills and diversifying agricultural products including the introduction of tobacco. A devout Catholic, he led a campaign against dueling and lynching.

Through the years, Dawson took many courageous stands. He favored putting blacks on the ballot in Charleston municipal elections. In 1876 he supported the Republican David Chamberlain against Wade Hampton, but supported Hampton when he won the Democratic nomination for Governor. At first Dawson backed "Pitchfork Ben" Tillman, but later rejected him as a demagogue, racist, and opportunist.

Dawson was killed in 1884 by Dr. Thomas McDow after accusing the doctor of dishonorable behavior. McDow was acquitted claiming self defense.

The News and Courier

James Colvin Hemphill
1850–1927

1870 *Abbeville Medium*, publisher
1880 *News and Courier*, Columbia reporter
1882 *News and Courier*, Charleston reporter
1885 *News and Courier*, city editor
1889 *News and Courier*, chief editor
1910 *Richmond Times*, dispatch editor
1911 *Charlotte Observer*, editor
1915 *New York Times*, writer
1919 *Spartanburg Journal*

Christie Benet once referred to the editor of the *News and Courier* as "the unofficial governor of South Carolina." Most observers would assume that all editors would only come from the area of South Carolina referred to as "South of Broad." But for 75 years after the *News and Courier* began, only outsiders had lead the newspaper.

Dawson, Hemphill, Lathan, and Ball were all outsiders, one an Englishman and the other three were up countrymen. Long before his death in 1889, Dawson had picked his successor as James Calvin Hemphill.

Born in 1850 in Due West, SC the "mecca" of the Associated Reformed Presbyterian Church, (ARP). Hemphill was a son of the Reverend W. R. Hemphill, professor of history in Erskine College. After graduating from Erskine in 1870, Hemphill and his brother began their newspaper career when they both migrated to Abbeville, SC, and published the weekly *Abbeville Medium*.

In 1880, Dawson, editor of the *News and Courier* lured Hemphill to replace NG Gonzales at the Columbia bureau, when the latter went to Washington. Gonzales returned in 1882 and Hemphill moved to Charleston. In 1885, Dawson named JC Hemphill as city editor, chosen over Gonzales.

Known as "the Deacon" for his strong Presbyterian association, Hemphill was also referred to as the "Major." The military title was honorary. He was an individualist, almost eccentric, who by 1885 was becoming a legendary leader in Charleston, of which he referred as "the Holy City."

By 1890 at the height of the bitter Tillman political wars, Hemphill was producing strong editorials. Hemphill and the *News and Courier* strongly opposed the Edgefield farmer. Over the years his pen worked nightly on behalf of Charleston progress.

One of his crusades included numerous editorials entitled "Charleston Looks to the Sea." His personal influence with Washington was important to obtain federal aid for deepening the water of the harbor. Along this line he was on the side later of Senator Tillman to get a Navy Yard. Also, he campaigned in behalf of the South Carolina Exposition in 1901 to call the world to the potential of the "Port of Charleston."

He frequently attacked the practice of lynching. Politically his friend was President William Howard Taft who visited Charleston during his presidency.

He moved in 1910 to Richmond, VA to become editor of the *Richmond Times-Dispatch*. A year later he was at the *Charlotte Observer* as editor and later worked on the staff of the *New York Times*. At 69, he returned to South Carolina to edit the Spartanburg Journal. He died in 1927 in Abbeville, SC and was buried in Charleston.

Letters Between Lathan and Hemphill

The News and Courier
CHARLESTON, S. C.

Feb. 3, 1906.

EDITORIAL ROOMS.

Mr. Robert Lathan,
Darlington, S. C.

My Dear Mr Lathan:

    Mr Ball has spoken to me about the correspondence Mr Cooper has had with you about your return to newspaper work. I should like very much to talk to you on the subject and if you could make it convenient to be in Charleston next Wednesday I should like very much to see you. I knew your father very well and had great respect for him. From all I have heard his good qualities have been perpetuated in his son.

    Please let me know whether you can come to Charleston next Wednesday.

Very sincerely yours,

J C Hemphill
Editor The News and Courier.

South Carolina Circuit Court
Third Circuit
Robt. Lathan, Official Stenographer

Darlington, S. C. Feb. 5th, 1906

Major J C Hemphill,
    Charleston SC

My dear Sir:—

    Your letter of the 3rd instant was received on yesterday. I shall come to Charleston Tuesday night, and shall be glad to talk over with you on Wednesday the matter referred to. As I am not acquainted with your office hours, I would suggest that you indicate to Mr Cooper when you would like to have me call. Very respectfully,

Robt. Lathan

Chapter Eight

Communication via Telegraph

> **THE TIMES-DISPATCH**
> RICHMOND, VIRGINIA
>
> March 21, 1911.
>
> Robert Lathan, Esq.,
>   c/o The News & Courier,
>   Charleston, S. C.
>
> My dear Mr. Lathan:-

> **The New York Times**
> Times Square
>
> February 14, 1913.

> **THE WESTERN UNION TELEGRAPH COMPANY.**
> 24,000 OFFICES IN AMERICA.   CABLE SERVICE TO ALL THE WORLD.
>
> ROBERT C. CLOWRY, President and General Manager.
>
> **RECEIVED** at 26 West 31st St., Bet. B'way and 5th Ave.
> TELEPHONE: No. 1217 MADISON SQUARE.
>
> 381Ny Hn 20 Dh
>   Charleston SC 6
> Robert Lathan,
>   Hotel Marquise 5 Ave
> Marcellus ely preached last sermon sunday going to Puyallup washington state. Aint you shamed. Great are the uses of snuffers.
>   J.C.Hemphill.

In February 1910, the daughter of JC Hemphill, Rebecca Hemphill sent a hand written note to thank Lathan for his editorial written to honor Major Hemphill on his retirement from the *News Courier*. She wrote, "what you said editorially is so sincere and so true and so well expressed."

Through the years, Major Hemphill communicated to Lathan by letter and telegraph certain editorial positions that Hemphill was assuming at the *New York Times* and *Philadelphia Public Ledger*, recommendations for individual employees and for important sermons he thought Lathan might enjoy.

> Abbeville, S. South Carolina. April 16, 1927.
>
> My dear Mr Lathan:--I wish you mighty well and congratulate you of having landed in a great town full of good people who will work with you, to make your great mission among them the great success your friends desire.
>
> Please present my most respectful compliments to Mrs Lathan and believe, as ever,
>   Your friend, sincerely,
>   J C Hemphill

Hemphill was one of the first friends and recognized editors to congratulate Lathan on his move to the Asheville Citizen newspaper.

James Henry Rice, Jr.
1868–1935

1895   *Columbia Evening News*, editor
1895   Colonial Records of South Carolina
1896-1898   *The State,* editorial writer
News and Courier, editorial columns
1903   *The Field,* editor
1905   *The South Carolina Field,* editor

Rice was born in 1868 near the town of Ninety-Six, in Abbeville County, SC. He was a prolific writer and renowned conservationist. He distinguished himself as a proponent of wildlife conservation, environmental farming, preservation of wetlands, and the appreciation of the flora and fauna of South Carolina. He was chief game warden of South Carolina and inspector for the US Biological Survey. During his lifetime he was active in the Audubon Society and the American Forestry Association and the Conservation Society of South Carolina.

After graduation from South Carolina College he taught high school students and began a career in journalism and writing. In 1895, be began his journalism career at the *Columbia Evening News*. Later he joined the editorial staff at *the State* and then *The News and Courier*. He and his wife had seven children.

Leading a varied and colorful life, Rice was a marksman, chess tournament champion, environmental lecturer, poet, collector of rare books, and at one time field shooting champion of the world. He was the author of numerous magazine and newspaper articles and two notable books, <u>Glories of the Carolina Coast</u> (1925) and <u>The Aftermath of Glory</u> (1934).

Rice and his family owned and lived full-time at Brick House Plantation in Wiggins, Colleton County, SC documenting in his columns and books the wonders of the Low Country, South Carolina. He died in 1935 at age 66 and is buried in Magnolia Cemetery in Charleston.

Chapter Eight

Letters Between Lathan and Rice

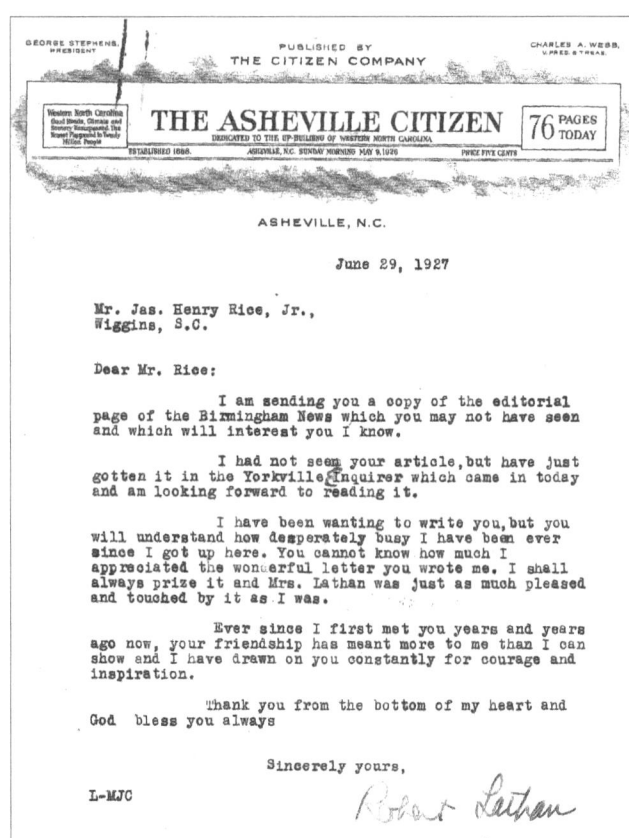

Lathan and Rice met for the first time in the fall of 1900, when Lathan was secretary to NG Gonzales at *The State*. Their friendship meant so much to each other, providing years of inspiration.

Rice responded to Lathan after reading the editorial in the *Birmingham News*. He explained his disappointment at the inactions of a small group of individual politicians who had been unable to carry forward a proposed program of the creation of statues honoring famous South Carolinians. He also reports to Lathan his upcoming travels to the Egg Bank, a seabird rookery, and the chess state championship in Charleston.

```
JAMES HENRY RICE, JR.          BRICK HOUSE PLANTATION
   "Dis Aliter Visum"              CHEE-HA RIVER
                                   WIGGINS, S. C.
                          August,8,1934. (My Father's birthday)
Dear Robert:-

        "Between our acts and our intentions ever
           There is a bridge without a parapet;
           Beneath it flows life's unreturning river".

     For many a month I have hoped to write you. Daily perplexities,
     trials and embarrassments,with persistent  goading from
     neubitis,have held me back.  Carew wrote me of seeing you
     and was charmed with you,naturally. He is a talented boy,
     who has a future, I think.
```

In 1934, just eight months before his death, Rice sent a long typed letter to Lathan in which he explained many of the consuming activities to finish his book, The Aftermath of Glory that was due to the publisher on September 1. He also reported that Mrs. Rice was very ill, and that his own strength has been greatly reduced. Rice gave a very detailed description of the loss of friends and places in the Charleston community. "The Charleston you first knew is as different from Charleston today as London is from Timbuktu…. Old Charleston was an ideal community and had solved the problem of living. The present crowd is always rushing around, sees nothing, hears nothing, knows nothing."

After the death of James Rice, Lathan wrote a very poignant letter to Mrs. Rice.

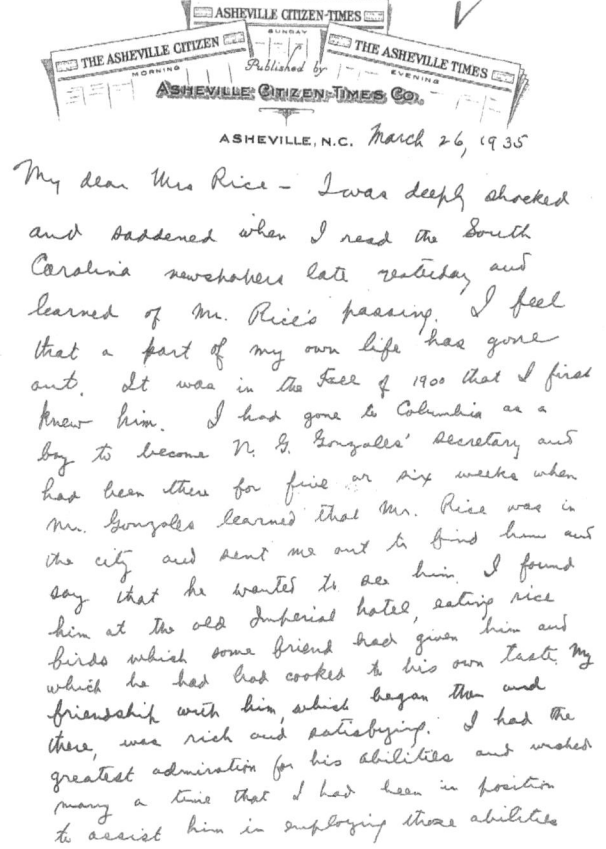

The News and Courier

August Kohn
1868–1930

1888 *Carolinian Newspaper*, editor
1889 *News and Courier*, roving reporter
1891 *News and Courier*, Columbia bureau chief

August Kohn was important for the *Charleston News and Courier* for fifteen years. Editor Frank Dawson gave him his first job as a reporter for the *News and Courier* in January 1889 and was a loyal lieutenant for editor JC Hemphill. He was respected by Hemphill's predecessor Robert Lathan and friends with editor Ball. At one time or another, Kohn was a journalist, businessman, warehouseman, philanthropist, and a leading figure in Columbia, SC society for more than forty years.

Born in Orangeburg, SC, Kohn received his early education there. Lather he attended schools in New York, but after two years he and his brother, Sol were sent to the University of South Carolina where they both graduated with distinction. At school he was active in debating and had a fascination with statistics. He later became the editor -in-chief of the *Carolinian*, the University newspaper.

As a student he was influenced by Narcisco Gonzales who was head of the Columbia bureau of the *News and Courier* and provided him with news items from a student perspective. After graduation, Kohn landed his first job in Charleston at the *News and Courier* as a roving reporter in 1889. He covered everything: hurricanes, elections, governments, developing reliable sources in every county of the state. He also gained a national readership through his work in a New York magazine.

In 1890, when Ben Tillman became Governor of South Carolina, the *News and Courier* took a known opposition that was countered in measure by Tillman. In 1891, NG Gonzales resigned as the Columbia bureau chief of the *News and Courier* to start *The State* newspaper with his brother. Their main focus was exposing the Tillman regime. Kohn then filled the vacancy of Columbia bureau chief of the *News and Courier*. He actively fulfilled his responsibilities around Columbia, visiting the government offices daily covering both the governor and the state legislature.

Kohn was always objective, accurate and unbiased with his own principles of reporting in all of his twenty-five years in charge of the Columbia bureau. His daughter Helen Kohn Henning, an author in her own right, said of her father, "Papa had complete copy and never cut or edited."

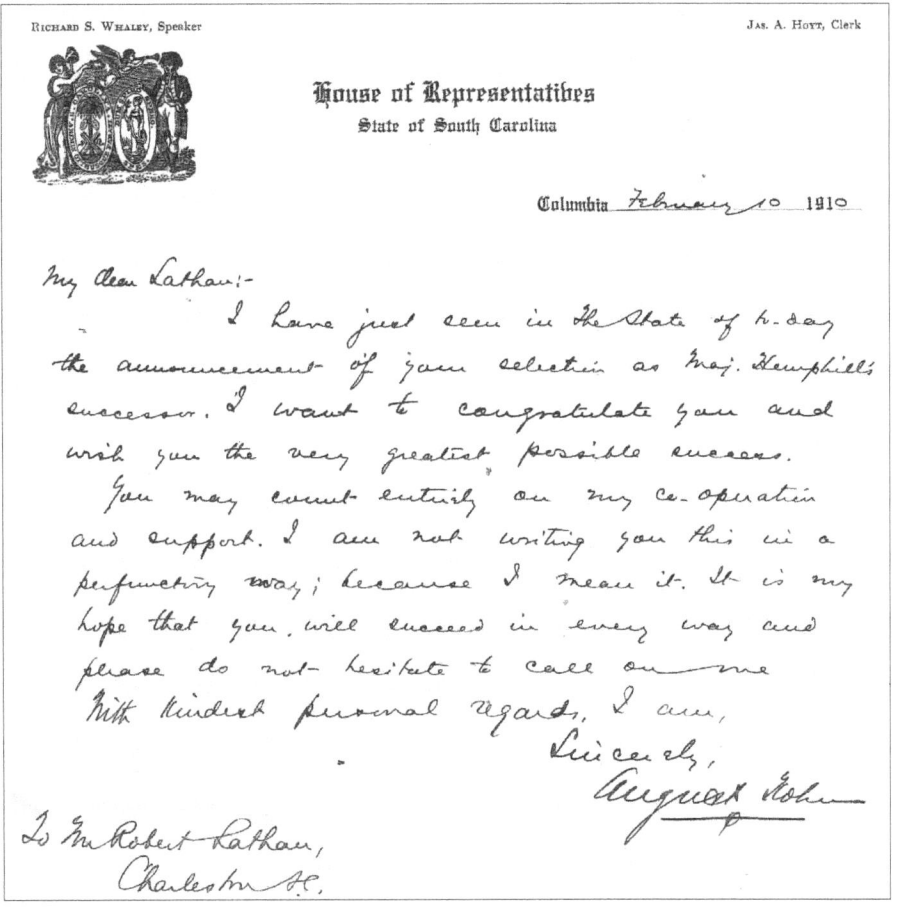

In 1893, Governor Tillman's effort to enforce the disastrous dispensary law, prohibiting the sale of alcohol to only state-run stores, resulted in a riot in Darlington, SC, followed by the governor declaring martial law. Tillman prevented Kohn from filing a report from Darlington. Nevertheless, Kohn rode several miles outside Darlington with a telegraph operator he had hired and tapped into the wires, transmitting his excellent reports to Charleston. He had seen this strategy before, when it was accomplished by Gonzales at *The State* to circumvent attempts at the news being blocked for distribution across the state.

In 1906, Kohn decreased his reporting career to spend more time in his growing business enterprises. He became a successful stock and bond broker. He also became a Trustee at his alma mater, the University of South Carolina, an honor he cherished. He continued his interest in the South Carolina Press Association, serving as Treasure and President.

With his intellectually gifted wife, pride in their Jewish ancestry was displayed in their support of the synagogue in Columbia. Kohn was very proud of his father's extraordinary service as a soldier in the Civil War. He made an eloquent speech to the reunion of the Confederacy "old soldiers."

Kohn was a regular member of the Cosmos Club at Columbia and wrote many papers there. In 1902 and later in 1917, he wrote feature articles on "The Cotton Mills at South Carolina" and in 1910, on the "the Water Powers of South Carolina."

Kohn was supportive of Lathan's newspaper work at both *The State* and *The News and Courier* including Lathan's appointment as successor to Editor James Hemphill.

He was director of banks and insurance companies and founded the Standard Warehouse Company and developed two of Columbia's real estate suburban areas: Wales Garden and Rose Hill. He often served as chairman of fund-raising groups in the support of charitable causes.

Kohn's mansion on Senate Street has been the site of many of the hospitality events afforded to important visitors to South Carolina, including John D. Rockefeller, Woodrow Wilson and Bernard Baruch. His collection of antique furniture and his library were much renowned for their historic collection.

When August Kohn died in 1930, he was honored as an extraordinary citizen of South Carolina. His book collection was donated by his family in 1999 to the University of South Carolina, at Columbia.

<u>August Kohn, Versatile South Carolinian</u> is the title that Helen Kohn Henning gave to the biography of her father. "She described him as an enthusiastic and eminently successful collector of South Caroliniana."

The Kohn-Hennig Library: A Catalog

EX LIBRIS

South Caroliniana Library
University of South Carolina
Columbia, South Carolina

James A. Hoyt, Jr.
1877–1932

1899 *The State*, assistant editor
1904 *The State*, city editor
1906 *News and Courier*, Columbia correspondent

James A Hoyt, Jr. from Greenville, SC, joined *The State* in 1899 at age twenty-two as an assistant to NG Gonzales writing editorials and working with Robert Lathan. After the death of NG Gonzales, Hoyt remained at *The State* and In 1904 moved to be city editor. In 1906 he became the Columbia correspondent for the Charleston *News and Courier* along with August Kohn. He later became editor of the *Columbia Record* and then Speaker of the State House of Representatives in 1915, and later a bank President.

While Lathan was working as a state stenographer with Judge Purdy in Sumter, SC, he continued his work with Hoyt in his role as assistant editor at *The State* and later while Hoyt was working in Columbia with the *News and Courier*.

Letters from Hoyt to Lathan

Hoyt praised Lathan for getting out a very good paper.

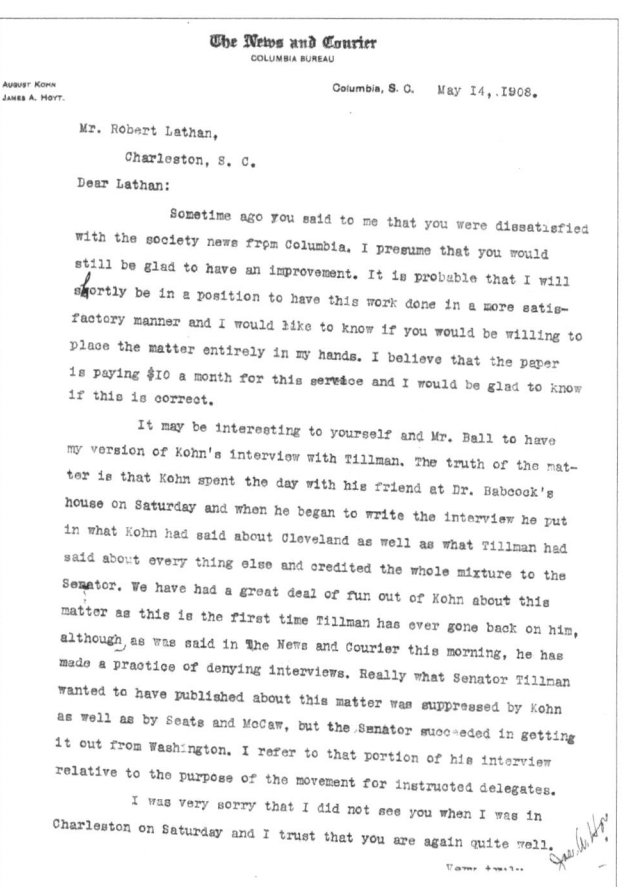

Hoyt wrote to Lathan to give his version of Kohn's interview with Tillman.

Herbert Ravenel Sass
1884-1958

1908 *News and Courier*, reporter
1924 Independent writer
1940 *News and Courier*, wire reporter

Herbert R. Sass was born in Charleston in 1884, the son of the poet George Herbert Sass and Anna Ravenel, the daughter of Dr. and Mrs. St. Julien Ravenel. His grandfather was the creator of submarines for the Confederacy and his grandmother was the author of the classic book Charleston: The Place and the People.

Sass graduated from Charleston High School and the College of Charleston with a BA in 1905 and then MA in 1906. In 1922 he received an honorary Literature Doctorate from the college.

He joined the staff of the *News and Courier* in 1908 under the editor J.C. Hemphill. He served there for over fifteen years as reporter, state news editor, city editor, and assistant editor under editor, Robert Lathan. While working at the newspaper, he wrote a very popular column about his beloved Lowcountry South Carolina area, titled "Woods and Waters."

He left the *News and Courier* in 1924 to become a full-time writer of nature stories. His use of intricate descriptions of birds and animals and their habitats were characteristics of his stories that made them popular nationally. Many were published in the *Saturday Evening Post, Harper's, Atlantic Monthly, Good Housekeeping,* and *National Geographic* magazines.

His collection of magazine articles led to the publishing of several nature books, the first being The Way of the Wild in 1925. Later his writing made a change as he began to publish historical novels beginning with War Drums in 1928. One of his best-known works was a tale of the Civil War titled Look Back to Glory published in 1933.

Sass returned to the *News and Courier* in the 1940's as a wire editor. He continued to write and publish non-fiction books including Outspoken: 150 Years of the News and Courier, in 1953 which also appeared in the sesquicentennial edition of the paper. Its title comes from the slogan of the paper that appeared on its masthead of the editorial page and included features on its history and stories about its legendary editors such as Robert Lathan.

Several of his stories were turned into movies including "Affair at St. Albans" in 1954 which the studio renamed "The Raid" starring Van Heflin, Anne Bancroft, Richard Boone, and Lee Marvin.

Sass was described by Harlan Greene as "Shy, redheaded, tall, lean and gracious.... a passionate naturalist called "Hobo" for his wanderings in the Low Country of South Carolina."

Sass and his wife Marion Hutson lived their life in Charleston. He died in 1958 and was buried in Charleston's St. Phillips Episcopal Cemetery.

Letters from Sass to Lathan

Mr Lathan :

I had to leave early, being due at Fred's at 7. I think the one thing to press for at this session, so far as fresh water game fishes are concerned, is a fishing license law, the license to be either $1.00 or $1.50 (probably $1.00) is better), to be state-wide, and if possible the whole of the proceeds to go to the Game Dept.

I think it would probably be a mistake to try to get a closed season also, because there would be strong objection by many and the whole effort might fall through. Later on we might try for a closed season during the spawning period.

What is most needed is a fund which will make it possible to enforce the laws against illegal fishing, especially trapping, netting and dynamiting. This is what is killing out the fish, and if this can be stopped the fish caught by the anglers with hook and line in legal fashion won't deplete the supply.

The fishing license law is the only way to get the money needed for enforcement of the fishing laws. If the Game Dept then still fails to put an end to trapping, dynamiting, etc., we ought to get a new Game Dept.

H R S

Letter from Sass requesting that "the one thing to press for at this session, so far as fresh water game fishes concerned, is a fishing license law. If the Game Dept then still fails to put an end to trapping, dynamiting, etc we ought to get a new Game Dept."

Chapter Eight

>   23 Legare Street, Charleston, SC.
>   May 3, 1927.
>
> Dear Bob:
>   I'm going to adopt the informal version of your
> "maiden name," as the ~~party is darkey~~ expressed it. Of course
> I've been thinking of you often, though there hasn't been
> much time for thinking. You have probably had so much to do
> that Charleston has not come often into your mind. Yet mem-
> ories of that night at the Francis Marion must have recurred
> from time to time. What a splendid manifestation that was
> of the love and admiration of Charleston, certainly one of
> the most reticent of cities! No man except yourself could
> have brought Mr Barnwell there. It was Kirk's first banquet
> in 26 years and his next, so he says, will be the one
> that is given you when you come back. Certainly there is
> mighty and enduring inspiration for you in the esteem
> which you have built here in perhaps the most exacting
> city of America.
>   Best of luck to you both.
>   As ever. Hobo

Sass reminds Lathan of their friendship and how much he is missed in Charleston.

Thomas R. Waring, Jr.
1907–1993

1927 *News and Courier*
1929 *New York Herald Tribune*
1931 *News and Courier*, city editor
1942 *News and Courier*, managing editor
1951 *News and Courier*, editor
1974 *Evening Post*, editor

Tom Waring, Jr. was a native Charlestonian, the first native to serve as editor of the *News and Courier*. After graduating from the University of the South as valedictorian in 1927, he approached his father for a job on the *Charleston Evening Post* and was turned down, reportedly because Tom Waring, Sr. wanted him to pursue a different career. So Waring, Jr. went to his uncle, W.W. Ball, editor of the *News and Courier* and was hired immediately.

He spent two years as a reporter and another two as a reporter for the *New York Herald Tribune*. He returned to the *News and Courier* as City Editor in 1931 and became managing editor in 1942. Waring became the editor for the *News and Courier* in 1951.

In 1954, The *News and Courier* campaigned to elect Strom Thurmond as a write-in candidate for the US Senate. It was thought that the Democratic party's power brokers would fill the Senate vacancy with the SC State Senator Edgar Brown. The vacancy was created by the sudden death of Senator Burnet Maybank.

Editor Tom Waring, Jr. started the newspaper's editorial on page one, headlined "Let Voters Choose Him" believing a primary election should be held. Brown was head of the "Barnwell Ring" that dominated state politics for a generation.

On election day on November 3, 1954, Thurmond defeated Brown decisively for the US Senate, the first write-in-candidate to be elected Senator in South Carolina.

In 1950s and 1960s Tom Waring, Jr. emerged on the national spotlight as a conservative spokesman against desegregation, especially in public schools. He also was against the rise of communism in the third world. Waring was a supporter of the two-party system in the solid Democratic south. His support for President of the United States for the Republicans Dwight D. Eisenhower and later for Richard Nixon and Barry Goldwater appeared on the newspaper editorial pages.

Arthur M. Wilcox was made editor of the *Charleston Evening Post* in 1968. In 1974, he traded jobs with Thomas R. Waring, Jr, editor of the *News and Courier*. The move enabled Waring to complete his career in the position his father had held for 38 years. Waring remained at the *Evening Post* for three years until he retired in 1977 and later died in 1993.

William Watts Ball, 1868–1952

1895 *Charleston Evening Post*
1904 *News and Courier*
1909-1923 *The State*, managing editor,
1923 Dean of Journalism, University of South Carolina.
1927-1951 *News and Courier,* editor

W. W. Ball was born in 1868 in Laurens County, SC. the son of Beaufort Ball and Eliza Watts. He graduated from South Carolina College in 1887 and received his LLD there in 1889. He was admitted to the SC Bar in 1890, but never practiced law. He was married in 1897 to Fay Witte and had five children.

In 1895, Ball began his journalism career at the *Charleston Evening Post*. While serving as editor, the newspaper opposed Governor Ben Tillman. Ball then worked at newspapers in Greenville, SC, Jacksonville, Fl, and Philadelphia. He returned to Charleston in 1904 as assistant editor of the *News and Courier*. Five years later in 1909, he moved to *The State*. While serving as managing editor from 1913-1923, Ball championed ideals espoused by followers of Wade Hampton at the same time as opposing those of Colman Blease.

In 1923, Ball was appointed Dean of Journalism at the University of South Carolina. At the retirement of Editor Robert Lathan in 1927 he assumed the management responsibility at the *News and Courier*. Ball led the editorial focus there until his retirement in 1951.

During his tenure as editor, he used his position to champion certain programs and oppose others. Ball had a strong political resemblance to former Governor and Senator of South Carolina John C. Calhoun, as both were raised in the upcountry of Laurens County.

Under his editorship, he introduced the front-page editorial column of the *News and Courier,* hoping to strongly influence the readers on important policy and candidate records. He also employed the first photographer in 1936.

Some of Ball's well-documented positions include anti-Prohibition and the Santee-Cooper rural electric project. In 1933, he denounced President Franklin Roosevelt's New Deal as "socialism". Prior to WWII he had demanded a stronger national defense and wrote in support of the military in view of the growing Nazi threat. In the election of 1940, he supported Wendall Wilkie, continuing his dislike of FDR. After the death of FDR, he continued his distrust of President Truman's proposals and supported The States Rights Party led by South Carolinian, Strom Thurmond.. Throughout his life and journalistic work, he was considered a rebel who believed strongly in individualism and fought against excessive government.

In his book, <u>The State That Forgot</u> (1932) Ball declared, "I love liberty…" His biographer John D. Stark said he epitomized "a sort of aristocratic conservatism."

When Ball died in 1952, his obituary recalled that "his personality dominated his office. While he was editor, he spoke as the *News and Courier.* He was <u>The News and Courier."</u>

Letters Between Ball and Lathan

Lathan thanks Ball for his encouragement of the positive effect of the change on the future of the paper referring to the new ownership of the News and Courier.

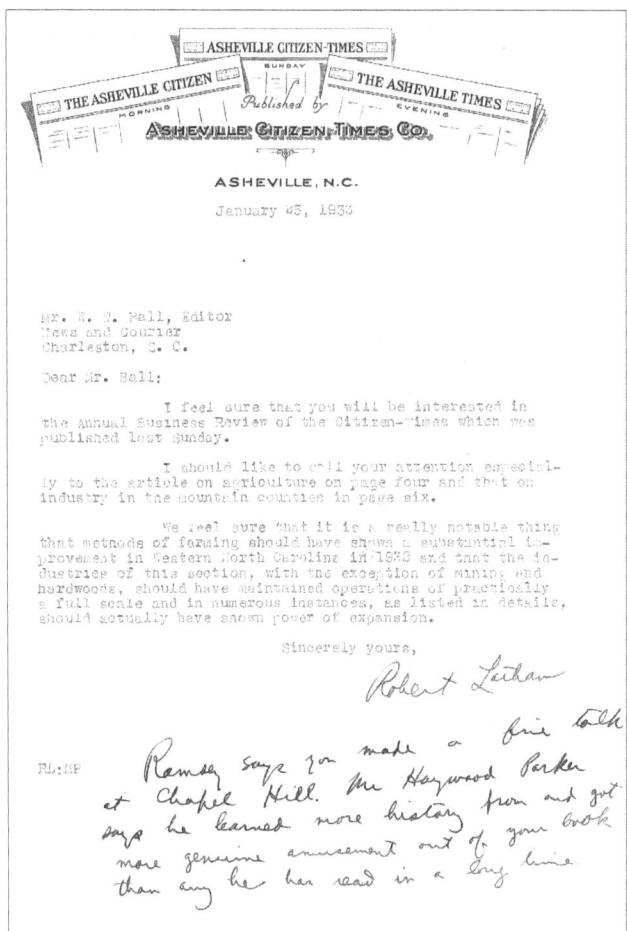

Lathan continues to communicate between editors, sharing official reviews of industry and agriculture in Western North Carolina.

> Llewellyn Park, Orange, N. J.
> 15th Feb, 1910.
>
> Robert Lathan, Esq,
> The News & Courier, Charleston, S. C.
>
> My dear Mr Lathan:-
>
> I am very glad to hear that you have been selected as Editor of the News & Courier. I personally feel convinced that the choice of the Board of Directors was the wisest which could have been made; and the ten years during which I have knocked up against all kinds and conditions of newspaper men have had very little to teach me if I am wrong in the prophecy I make that you have a bright future before you and will conduct the News and Courier successfully and prosperously through whatever may lie ahead for us.
>
> You will be interested to hear that in my conversation with the President at Washington the other day, he showed me the News and Courier on his desk, and said: "Whenever you come in to see me, you will find the latest copy of the News and Courier in that place on my desk. I always read it, because there are few American papers of whose tone I think as highly." I told him that we would do all that was in our power to make it remain worthy of his interest.
>
> With sincere congratulations not only for you but for all concerned in the paper that you should be at its head, I am
>
> Very truly yours,
>
> *Warrington Dawson.*

Warrington Dawson
1878–1962

His father, Francis Warrington Dawson, was founder of *The News and Courier* of Charleston. His mother Sarah Morgan Dawson was a writer best known for her Civil War diary, A Confederate Girl's Diary. She was born and raised in Baton Rouge, LA moving to Charleston when she married. After the death of her husband in 1889, she and her son, Warrington, moved to Paris, where she continued to live until her death in 1909.

Warrington was a historian, editor, novelist, diplomatic chronicler, and reporter. He was also a special assistant to the US Embassy in France. He lived in both Charleston and Versailles, France. Dawson worked with the American Embassy in Paris and the director of French Research for Colonial Williamsburg.

Dawson collected a wealth of original documents pertaining to French participation in the American Revolution including copies of 18th century maps of North America, Williamsburg, VA and positions of the French and American armies in New York and Virginia during the Revolutionary War. His research interests included French manuscripts, early American history, and family genealogy.

Letters From Dawson To Lathan

Robert Lathan's collection of letters comprised numerous correspondence between Lathan and Dawson. Many of the letters regarded proposed and written articles by Dawson for publishing in the News and Courier.

Dawson is suggesting articles that he might write for the News and Courier.

Dawson wrote that his articles had been delayed because of time spent with President Theodore Roosevelt's family.

1 bis, Rue Pardy, Versailles, France,
30th Oct., 1911.

Dear Mr. Jathan:-

I was highly gratified by your letter mentioning the effect produced by my English strike articles and notably the Welsh one being reproduced in part by different papers including the Springfield Republican. That is one of the two things at wich I have aimed with these articles -- first pleasing our own public, of course, but also getting the News and Courier quoted. It has always seemed to me that there was plenty of room in America for articles from abroad unusual either in subject or in handling, but that correspondents followed too closely the established rut. Often it is because their hands are not left free enough; but it also comes from their doing too much newspaper work in too limited a field, so that their vision ceases to be clear.

I am very hard at work now on my negro book; my Paris publisher has advanced the date for its appearance, so that I shall be compelled to stay over here this winter.

I should be obliged to you if you would insert the accompanying review on the Sunday literary page, and send me two extra copies of it -- perhaps you could have them cut out and put in an envelope. I have put my literary signature to it, to distinguish it from my correspondence to the paper.

Yours sincerely,

Warrington Dawson.

I should be interested to know something about Mr Hemphill's move to Charlotte. That was a very subtle editorial note you published.

Good Year and a Goodly Land

Dawson wrote on September 16, 1917 that he had been authorized to visit the American front and had received braces from the American hospital to enable him to walk with less difficulty. He expected to be able to contribute several articles after his trip. He wrote again six days later as he returned from the front.

Dawson reports that his health had seriously deteriorated and was completing his writing duties through dictation.

Chapter Eight

ASHEVILLE, N.C.

November 16, 1931.

Mr. Warrington Dawson,
19 reu de Marechal Joffre,
Versailles,
France.

My dear Mr. Sawson: -

    Mrs. Memminger rang me up early this morning and suggested that she thought you would be interested in reading the enclosed. I would hardly have had the presumption to send it to you otherwise but in the circumstances I am, of course, glad to do so.

    We were very greatly pleased to learn from the Memmingers that your health is so much improved and that your life is moving along so happily. We are always interested in hearing about you and Mrs. Memminger and Christine are, of course, our main source of information.

    It would certainly be good to see you again. I have been most eager, with so much going on, to get back to Europe; but, as you will well understand, the times are not such that any of us here feel that we can afford to get very far away from home.

    With warmest personal regards always, believe me,

Sincerely yours,

Robert Lathan

L:P

Lathan wrote to Dawson from Asheville that he was happy to hear that Dawson's health had improved and that it would be good to see him again.

Octavus Roy Cohen
1891-1959

1910-1912 *Birmingham Ledger, News and Courier, Bayonne Times, Newark Morning Star, Saturday Evening Post*

Octavus Roy Cohen was an early 20th century American author specializing in ethnic comedies. He was a descendant of Portuguese Jews who was born in Charleston, SC. He was educated at the Porter Military Academy, now the Porter-Gaud School. He later graduated from Clemson University. In 1913, and was admitted to the South Carolina Bar, practicing law in Charleston for two years.

Between 1910 and 1912, he worked in the editorial departments of several newspapers. His stories were also published in the *Saturday Evening Post*, many of which were about African Americans. He moved from Birmingham to Harlem, New York and later to Los Angeles in 1929 to pursue a film career. Between 1917 and his death, be published fifty-six books, and many short stories and films.

Letter from Cohen to Lathan

```
OCTAVUS ROY COHEN
3215 SEVENTEENTH AVENUE, SOUTH
BIRMINGHAM, ALABAMA
```

August 29th., 1919

Dear Mr. Lathan:-

    I am afraid that because of the strain under which we were both working during the campaign, I may not have made thoroughly clear to you my deep sense of appreciation of your uniform courtesy and unstinted helpfulness while I was making my earnest (though, for the moment, apparently abortive) effort, through the medium of The Patriot, to assist in bringing about the defeat of Grace. But it all got under the skin with me, and one of the pleasantest recollections of my life will always be my quasi connection with you in that good work. Believe me, I am truly sensible of, and grateful for, the many, many things you did to help and encourage me. Charleston, too, owes you a deep debt of gratitude. Your work was magnificent, and God only knows what would have happened had it not been for your telling presentation of the issues which, in most communities, would have been overwhelmingly decisive.

    Why is it that there has not yet been any definite step toward getting the Writ of Certiorari? I am not criticising, but merely suggesting, that the earlier the matter can be carried over to the courts (without, of course, sacrificing anything of an evidentiary nature)- the better for us.

    With kindest regards to yourself and all of the "boys," I am

Sincerely yours,

Octavus Cohen

Percival Huntington Whaley
1882-1964

1909 *Charleston News and Courier*, editorial writer
1913 *Philadelphia Public Ledger*, reporter
1914-1918 *Philadelphia Evening Ledger*, executive editor
1918-1957 *Whaley Eaton Service*, founding publisher

PH Whaley, with Charleston ancestry, was an editorial writer with the *Charleston News and Courier* in 1909, at the same time that Robert Lathan was working there. He became a reporter for the Philadelphia *Public Ledger* from 1913 to 1914, the first Executive editor of the *Philadelphia Evening Ledger* from 1914–1918. He became the Founding publisher of the Whaley-Eaton (W-E) Service from 1918 to 1957. He was an internationally known business journalist.

His W-E business service was based in Washington, DC, but he also had offices at various times in New York, London, Paris, and Tokyo. His weekly publications the *American Letter* and the *Foreign Letter* were the precursors to the *Kiplinger Letter*.

Whaley published his opinions on politics of the time, especially the financial impact of political decisions on the agrarian interests of the South.

He died in 1964 at his plantation on Edisto Island, SC on land owned by his family since the 1700s.

Letters from Whaley to Lathan

A typed letter on Whaley Eaton Service letterhead was written to Robert Lathan, Editor of the News and Courier, *promoting their London news bureau, which he thought might be very interesting to residents of Charleston*

𝔈𝔡𝔴𝔞𝔯𝔡 𝔗𝔢𝔯𝔯𝔶 𝔥𝔢𝔫𝔡𝔯𝔦𝔢 𝔖𝔥𝔞𝔣𝔣𝔢𝔯
1894-1997

Feature writer of essays published in many publications

E.T.H. Shaffer was a Walterboro, SC businessman and farmer who distinguished himself a historical and economic researcher and writer. He graduated from the College of Charleston in 1902.

In 1922, he wrote "A New South – The Boll Weevil Era," 1997 in *The Atlantic Monthly* and was praised by his friend, J. Waties Waring, an attorney in Charleston. His next essay, the "A New South – The Textile Development" was called the "fairest and most intelligent article.. about this section of the South" by the *Greenville News*. In 1923, his third essay, "The New South—The Negro Migration" was stated by a few prominent South Carolinians "the most sensible writing on the subject that we have read." However, Ambrose Gonzales, editor of *The State*, as well as other editors and groups took issue with many points in the essay. In the next ten years Shaffer contributed several articles to *The State* and the *News and Courier*.

In 1930, the editor of *News and Courier*, W. W. Ball published a Shaffer essay "The People of the Mills in the New South" and wrote at length to discuss it. Other Shaffer essays were communicated to and commented upon by such literary luminaires as H.L. Mencken, Dubose Heyward, John Galsworthy, David Coker, Somerset Maugham, Herbert Ravenal Sass, Alfred F. Smith, William Howard Taft, and T. R. Waring.

Shaffer's boyhood collection contained autographs of Grover Cleveland, Wade Hampton, Benjamin Harrison, William McKinley, and Ben Tillman.

He was a popular speaker as well as able writer. During his lifetime, he published four non-fiction books, two fiction books and many, over 150 informative articles.

Shaffer wrote a beautiful tribute to Lathan's Pulitzer prize editorial.

Walter Lippman
1889-1974

1913   *The New Republic*, founding editor
1921-1929   *World*, writer
1929-1931   *World*, editor
1931-1966   *New York Herald Tribune*, writer, syndicated columnist

Walter Lippmann was an American journalist, author, and political commentator. He was born in New York's upper eastside as the only child of Jewish parents of German origin. At age sixteen he entered Harvard University where he wrote for the *Harvard Crimson*, studied under George Santayana and William James, and was a member of Phi Beta Kappa.

In 1913, Lippmann was one of the founding editors of *The New Republic* magazine.

During World War I he was a Captain in the Army who served in the intelligence section in France. As an advisor to President Woodrow Wilson he assisted in the drafting of Wilson's "Fourteen Point" speech establishing the concept of the League of Nations. Lippmann was sent to Paris by Wilson to cover the negotiations for the Treaty of Versailles in 1919.

In 1920 he published a set of essays entitled "Liberty and the News" which criticized the press for their bias in covering WWI.

From 1921 to 1929, he wrote editorials and became editor of the *World*, moving in 1931 to the *New York Herald Tribune*. The same year his column, "Today and Tomorrow" appeared and was syndicated in more than 250 newspapers in the US and twenty five countries.

Lathan wrote a long article in 1931 describing many of the aspects of Lippman's journalistic career as Lathan experienced it.

Here in our own country hundreds of thousands of people in every part of the United States take their cue on the great public questions of the hour from Walter Lippman's syndicated articles. In the short space pf three years Mr. Lippman has become perhaps the most widely read writer in America on serious questions. His articles deal exclusively with questions of that kind. His appeal is to serious-minded persons, to persons who in unprecedentedly interesting and critical times are eager for information, for an objective statement of the facts of the various problems of the day as they arise, for an interpretation of these facts which invites confidence because of the belief of the reader that the interpreter is honest and competent.

Lippmann was awarded a special Pulitzer Prize for journalism in 1958 citing "the wisdom, perception and high sense of responsibility with which he has commented for many years on national and international affairs." In 1962, he was awarded the annual Pulitzer Prize for International Reporting citing "his 1961 interview with Soviet Premier Khrushchev, as illustrative of Lippmann's long and distinguished contribution to American journalism."

During his lifetime, Lippmann wrote over twenty books. His Public Opinion (1922) has been considered "the founding book of modern journalism"and was reprinted in 1956 and 1962. In his book Cold War

(1947) Lippmann's development of the term "cold War" was established as a much used phrase for years.

In 1967, Lippmann retired from writing his syndicated column. He died in New York City in 1974.

Letters Between Lathan and Lippmann

In 2007 the Princeton University Press described his essays as follows:

Liberty and the News is Walter Lippman's classic account of how the press threatens democracy whenever it has an agenda other than the free flow of ideas. Arguing that there is a necessary connection between liberty and truth, Lippman excoriates the press, claiming that it exists primarily for its own purposes and agendas and only incidentally to promote the honest interplay of facts and ideas. In response, Lippman sought to imagine a better way of cultivating the news.

Chapter Eight

Lathan sent a three page typed letter explaining to Lippman his thoughts about the decision process to leave Charleston and the News and Courier for a different life working in a younger community of Asheville, NC at the Asheville Citizen.

Lippmann sent a response letter to Lathan on The World letterhead wishing him well in Asheville.

Chapter Nine

Robert Lathan, Jr.
A Gentleman in
the Highest and
Best Sense

So much in life is beyond our control.
So much seems to be governed by
blind chance. But our attitudes toward
life are what we make them.
And life is shaped by the attitude
we take regarding it.

Christmas 1931

Chapter Nine

When Editor Lathan died suddenly in September 1937, an adoring family and an admiring public across the South and the nation were left in shock. Lathan's earlier words of "life beyond our control" truly touched many hearts.

Looking back at his lifetime of letters, some read of recommendations to his person by referring to him as a "gentleman of character and good habits" and that "he is an accomplished gentleman of high moral character of more than ordinary mental talents and ability."

The comments on his editorials many times included descriptions such as, "so true," "so sincere," and "so well expressed."

Other letters gave gratitude for his thoughtfulness and kindness in his contributions to the citizens of his community, his states and the South.

For the individuals and institutions that knew Robert Lathan, the words of *The Lantern* newspaper, from Chester, SC written in November 1908, predicted thirty years in advance his positive impact "with entire satisfaction."

THE LANTERN.
November, 1908

City Editor Lathan.

Mr. Robert Lathan has been appointed city editor of The News and Courier to succeed Mr. George Hoyt Smith who was for many years connected with this newspaper. Mr. Lathan is especially fitted for this important position, and, in our opinion, is one of the most promising of the younger newspaper men of the South. He comes by his gift of writing good, strong English naturally, his father, the Rev. Dr. Lathan, having achieved distinction in literary as well as the the theological field.

For a considerable time private secretary of Mr. N. G. Gonzales, the lamented editor of the Columbia State, afterwards official stenographer of the Third Judicial Circuit, and for the last three years the very capable state news editor of The News and Courier he has proved his trustworthiness in a way that has commanded the appreciation of his associates and the intelligent public which the newspaper serves. The News and Courier is very fortunate in having attached to its working force a man of the high character and the liberal gifts of Mr. Lathan. He will fill his new position, we are sure, with entire satisfaction to this community.

Headstone Inscription

Mrs. Lathan received a letter from her sister-in-law, Emma Lathan Martin of Calhoun Falls, SC thanking her for photographs of Robert that had been sent to her.

Mrs. Martin also described the markings on Robert Lathan, Jr.'s headstone very appropriately.

"I like the inscription on the stone. It is very appropriate. Not one of us would cancel half a line, nor wash out any word, of what his finger wrote." Emma

Chapter Nine

Friend Hobo and Bessie Communicate

> 23 Legare St, Charleston, S.C.
> Jan 14, 1939.
>
> Dear Mrs Lathan;
>
> I have written something which is short, very simple, and which has no new thought in it. But it seems to me that what you have to say upon this occasion is necessarily a simple and obvious thing and that you have no purpose except to express your and Robert's satisfaction in an achievement which was dear to his heart. The older I grow the more I admire simplicity in writing and speaking; and his directness was one of the qualities that especially distinguished his own thinking and writing.
>
> It was, as it always is, a great joy to see you. We all hope that you will come often, for so many happy and helpful memories come with you.
>
> Marion sends her love – and you always have mine.
>
> As ever Hobo

Widow, Mrs. Bessie Lathan moved back to her family hometown of Darlington, SC after the loss of her beloved husband. There she gave service to local organizations and traveled to visit friends from the newspaper days.

In 1939 she was requested to address an occasion in remembrance of her husband. Her discussions with close friend "HOBO" (Herbert Ravenal Sass) show their shared feelings about Robert Lathan.

Mrs. Lathan Speaks to Young People

In 1956, Mrs. Lathan was asked by The *News and Courier* to speak on the subject of entering journalism as a profession

BELIEVES NEWSPAPER WORK OFFERS CHALLENGE
Mrs. Lathan With Picture Of Her Late Husband

Young People Are Urged To Consider Journalism

By ELDRIDGE THOMPSON
News and Courier Roving Reporter

DARLINGTON.

The widow of a once famous newspaper editor believes youngsters should give serious consideration to the field of journalism.

"There is no profession that affords a young man or woman a greater challenge than journalism," Mrs. Robert Lathan, widow of the man who served as editor of The News and Courier for 17 years, said today.

"It is a field that badly needs men and women dedicated to unselfish service to humanity. I realize that journalism requires many hours of work beyond the regular eight-hour day. I know, from first-hand experience, that a newspaperman's time belongs to the public he seeks to serve. But there are many wonderful rewards."

Mrs. Lathan, who traveled with her late husband to almost every state and Europe during his illustrious career, now lives with her sister, Miss Ella May Early, in the house in which she was born and later married.

"I find real joy in recalling the wonderful experiences I had as a newspaperman's wife," Mrs. Lathan said. "I met so many fine, understanding people. I came to realize the importance of a good newspaper and to appreciate its services to the people who read it each day."

Lathan was editor of The News and Courier from 1910 until 1927 when he resigned to become editor of the Asheville, N. C., Citizen. While Editor of The News and Courier, Lathan wrote a Pulitzer prize-winning editorial. At the time he was named head of The News and Courier he was the newspaper's youngest editor and became one of its outstanding editorial writers.

"I wouldn't call my husband a fire-eating editor," Mrs. Lathan said. "But he was a determined man. What he believed to be right and just he was ready to defend with all his might. He was dedicated to the pen and to the people of the state."

Mrs. Lathan said during her husband's editorship at Charleston she spent many hours at the newspaper office.

"I was never an adviser. I was a silent partner, there to offer encouragement whenever Robert needed it."

Until a few years ago, Mrs. Lathan continued to visit the hundreds of friends she and her husband made in Charleston, Columbia, Asheville, New York and many other cities in the United States.

"Now I keep in contact with them by mail. They are still just as true and wonderful to me as when Robert was living. I would not have missed the great experiences I had as a newspaperman's wife for anything. I believe it is one of the finest fields a young man or woman can enter. I recommend it to those who seek to be of service to their fellowman and to their country."

In Mrs. Lathan's home here in Darlington are many trophies, awards and gifts that remind her of her newspaper days. One of her most prized possessions is a silver service presented her husband by the citizens of Charleston after he resigned as editor of The News and Courier.

Chapter Nine

Family Communications

Mrs. Lathan continued to enjoy visits with friends in her home in Darlington, even as she began to restrict her own travels.

In October of 1968, Mrs. Callie Mims Lathan, widow of S. Robert Lathan and mother of S. Robert Lathan, Jr. M.D., the author of this biography, renewed her family acquaintance with Bessie Lathan.

Mrs. S. Robert Lathan (Callie) traveled to the home of Bessie Lathan in Darlington, SC which was only twelve miles from Callie's early home in Timmonsville, SC. Her letter follows.

Dear Mrs. Lathan,
It is always a rare pleasure to meet and to know Bob's relatives and especially when they are so lovely. I had heard so many things about your charm, etc. and now I see that it is all true.
I enjoyed the visit with you and your sweet sister so much, and I wish that I could see you more often. I shall come to see you when I am in Darlington again if it is convenient to you. Bob, my son was so delighted that I had seen you. He wishes that he could meet you. He is very interested in the Lathan family and especially your part of it since he has the same name. Bob and his wife Millie are flying to Washington, DC tomorrow where he will attend the International Congress of Chest Diseases.
Give my love to your lovely sister.
Love to you,
Callie Mims Lathan
October 3, 1968, Chester, South Carolina

This letter is a part of collection of Bessie Lathan letters in the archives.

172

Bessie's Death

In 1972, Bessie Early Lathan died in Darlington and was buried in Grove Hill Cemetary next to her husband.

Hall of Fame Induction Article

14-A   Columbia, South Carolina, Saturday, Feb. 24, 1979

Robert Lathan Enters Press Hall Of Fame

Robert Lathan, Jr. Enters the Press Hall of Fame

More than a half century ago, a South Carolina newspaper editor brought distinction to himself, his paper the *News and Courier*, and his state by winning the nationally coveted Pulitzer Prize for the best editorial of the year (1924).

Last night, at the 1979 annual banquet of the S.C. Press Association, the late Robert Lathan won contemporary acclaim by being inducted into the organization's Hall of Fame.

This morning, *The State* not only joins in the deserved praise accorded Mr. Lathan but reprints his prize-winning editorial, "The Plight of the South." At the same time, we succumb to the inescapable temptation to link today's South with that of Mr. Lathan, wondering all the while how he would have reacted to conditions of the moment.

Hall of Fame Tribute Continues

First of all, we submit that the title of a regional assessment today would more appropriately be "the promise" rather the "the plight" of the South.

To be sure, much of what Mr. Lathan perceived in 1924 is apparent in 1979. No one can deny that now, as then, political tides at home and abroad are turbulent and unpredictable. Nor can one challenge his contention that the South's political situation is "precarious."

True, the South occupies the White House in the person of Jimmy Carter of Georgia, but the development hardly warrants the conclusion that the South enjoys national leadership in the sense envisioned by Mr. Lathan. Indeed, as was true under the Presidency of Lyndon Johnson of Texas, there is evidence that the South often suffers from the President's understandable wish to avoid charges of regional favoritism.

Then too, the generally conservative leadership exercised in Congress by committee chairman from the South has waned with their retirement from the scene. At the same time, however, the South has benefitted by its emergence from the one party politics that for so long kept Dixie in the bag for the Democrats. Republican competition, often successful, has brought a new political dimension to the South and given added incentive for all parties to court the region's voters.

Still another political consideration which has changed the South's "plight" to "promise" is its steady growth in population, chiefly through in-migration from more Northern areas. Today, for the first time in modern history, more Americans reside in the South and West – the so-called Sun Belt –than the rest of the nation. And that translates into political influence with each reapportionment of the U.S. House of Representatives.

But the South's greatest asset at the moment is it deserved reputation as a land of economic opportunity where mild climate, bountiful water and other natural resources, expanding markets (and per capita income), rising educational levels and a manifest willingness to work all combine to attract business and industry not only from throughout the United States but from abroad.

Yet, for all these changes for the better, there is still pertinence in Robert Lathan's concluding questions:

"Who is to speak for the South? How many of her citizens are prepared to help formulate her replies?"

Letter of Recommendation for first teaching position in 1897

To Whom it May Concern:—

"This is to certify that I have known Mr. Robert Lathan since his childhood. That he is a gentleman of character and good habits. That he is well educated both from a literary and business standpoint.

That in my opinion he will perform faithfully and creditably any he may undertake; and the person or persons employing him will have no reason to regret their selection.

Respectfully
W. W. Pooley,
Auditor Abbeville Co.

Mr. W.W. Pooley wrote in 1897 that no person or persons would regret employing Lathan. Throughout the life of Robert Lathan, Jr. his actions ensured that he honored Mr. Pooley's prediction.

Robert Lathan, Jr.'s Life and His Own Words Inspired Journalists and Communities to Voice Answers in Support of Lathan's Beloved South

For Robert Lathan, Jr.'s answer to the question of "speaking for the South," the reader only needs to accept the premier editor's admonition in 1937 to all journalists.

With steadfast confidence, therefore, in you and in your heritage, I call upon you now not to be content with knowing how to read the sky. With being able to say when a cloud rises in the West, "There cometh a shower," or when the South wind blows "There will be heat." But with all diligence, you make it your supreme endeavor to "discern this time."

The ability to do this today, when all is said and done, is undoubtedly the supreme need of every patriotic journalist in America.

South 1937

And for the wide ranging community that Robert Lathan served for almost forty years, John Temple Graves of the *Birmingham News* described Robert Lathan very clearly as the man who could certainly speak for the South.

"A trained and loyal newspaper man, a master of his editorial art, a brace and fair participants in the problems and hopes of his land, a liberal whose philosophy never failed him. Robert Lathan was that rare something more that goes by the name of Gentleman."

References

LIBRARY AND ARCHIVAL SOURCES

The South Carolina Historical Society
Charleston, SC
Molly I. Silliman, Librarian

Darlington County Historical Commission
Darlington, SC
Brian Gandy, Director
Ann Chapman, Assistant Director

Caroliniana Library
Columbia, SC
Henry Fulmer, Director
Todd Hoppock, Administrative Assistant
Edward Blessing, Head of User Services

Wilson Library Special Collections
University of North Carolina Library
Chapel Hill, NC
Robert Anthony, Curator

Historical Center of York County
Wanda Fowler
York, SC

Erskine College Archives
McCain Library
Due West, SC
Edith Brawley

Pack Memorial Library
Buncombe County Special Collections
Asheville, NC
Kathy Hill

Charleston Public Library
South Carolina Room
Malcolm Hale

CONTRIBUTING INDIVIDUALS

Hampton Morris, Atlanta
John Rivers, Charleston

BOOK SOURCES

Barnwell, Tim, *Blue Ridge Parkway Vistas*; Asheville, NC: Numinous Editions Bookstore, 2014.

Dawson, Francis W., *Reminiscences of Confederate Service, 1861-1865*; Charleston, SC: The News and Courier Book Presses, 1882. Reprinted 1980.

Edgar, Walter, *South Carolina Encyclopedia*; Columbia, SC: University of South Carolina Press, 2006.

Gonzales, Ambrose, *With Aesop Along the Black Border*; Columbia, SC. The State Company,1924.

Henning, Helen Kohn, *Great South Carolinians of a Later Date, Volume 11* Chapel Hill, NC: University of North Carolina Press, 1949.

Latimer, S.L. Jr., *The Story of the State and the Gonzales Brothers*; Columbia, SC: The State Printing Company, 1970.

Pierce, Robert A., *Palmettos and Oaks, Centennial History of the State*, The State Record Company, Columbia, SC, 1991.

Rowe, Charles R., *Pages of History, 200 years of the Post and Courier*; Charleston, SC: Evening Post Publishing, 2003.

Sass, Herbert Ravenel, *Outspoken-150 Years of News and Courier*; Columbia, SC: University of South Carolina Press, 1953.

Underwood, James L., *Deadly Censorship*; Columbia, SC: University of South Carolina Press, 2013.

Speeches

A LOOK INTO THE FUTURE, Newspaper Institute, North Carolina Press Association Chapel Hill, NC, January 14, 1926 (Look, 1926)

THE CITIZEN LOOKS ABROAD, Emory University, Citizenship Conference, Atlanta, GA, February 15, 1928 (Citizen, 1928)

ACCOUNTING FOR NORTH CAROLINA, THE IMPRESSIONS OF A NEWCOMER, Asheville, NC, May 7, 1928 (Accounting, 1928)

A CHRISTMAS DAY EDITORIAL, Peace on Earth, Good Will Toward Men, *The Asheville Citizen*, Asheville, NC, December 25, 1931 (Christmas, 1931)

SOUTH CAROLINA, PAST AND PRESENT, South Carolina Press Association, Columbia SC, January, 1938 (South,1938)

A Look Into The Future
(Look 1926)

Newspaper Institute
North Carolina Press Association
Chapel Hill, NC
January 14, 1926

Mr. J. B. Atkins, who had just been made editor of the *Spectator*, said in his "Life" of Sir William Howard Russell that Delano was a great editor "because he was always open to new ideas." The quality is one that has distinguished nearly every man and nearly every newspaper of outstanding fame. It may be that some newspaper lacking this characteristic has won distinction, but I doubt it. In our time, Lord Northcliffe's amazing success was built almost entirely upon the fact that when England, due to the extension of education, was passing through a period not unlike that now in the making with us, he grasped what was happening and created a type of journalism which just met the appetite of the multitude of new readers who had been brought into being, reaching them through the most effective of all channels, the eye.

Innumerable examples along the same line might be given. Let me take just one, and I choose it because the newspaper in the question, the *Springfield Republican*, has in our time been conservative to the point of staidness. Yet in the years when the third Samuel Bowles was building it into a great newspaper "the constant freshness of the *Republican* was one of the most marked qualities and strongest charms." Of Mr. Bowles his biographer said: "He was so ready for a change of method that it put him in a degree outside of the sympathies of the mass of men who like to move in channels and ruts. His judgement of political situations was somewhat warped by his own impulse toward novelty."

The history of newspapers proves over and over that for the journalist the ability to sense changes while they are yet in the making is a priceless possession. But Mr. Atkins, having made the remark just quoted about Delano, goes on to add, that the tendency of all newspapers is to become conservative and stereotyped. The subsequent history of the *Times* and of the *Republican*—to go no further—bears him out. "It has often happened," says Mr. Atkins, "that the only way of changing trifling and unessential customs in the production of a newspaper has been to change the editor." If the criticism is a just one, and I believe that it is, then it follows that of all institution's newspapers should be constantly on guard lest they fall into a groove to the neglect of opportunities that are golden. And if this is true of newspapers of the South at the present time. How then are the sweeping changes that are taking place in the South affecting the newspapers of this section? Is the press of the South adjusting itself adequately to the new conditions? What is its present status and what is the outlook for the future?

The timeliness of these questions is obvious, for the South enters this month upon the second decade of what, we can now safely assert, is in most respects already the most remarkable period it has known. Let us think back for just a moment to January 1916.

For a year and a half, the World War had been raging, but we were not yet involved and while the President was writing some pretty stiff notes to the Kaiser, war with Mexico seemed much more imminent that war with Germany.

Out own entrance into the maelstrom was yet more than a year distant. The South had emerged from the panic into which it was plunged when the outbreak of the war, coming just as a new crop of cotton was ready for market, sent the price to six cents and resulted in all sorts of hysterical outbursts such as the "Buy a Bale" movement, when King Cotton paraded Broadway as a mendicant. In January of 1916 the price of cotton had gone back to eleven cents. It was to touch twenty before the year was out—and with its rise began the South's new era. I am not suggesting of course that the rise in the price of cotton brought about this new era. It was, nevertheless, one of the important contributing factors, for the cotton crops of 1916 and 1917 were the first in at least three decades that sold for a real profit above the cost of production, and in those years, also, the South found a ready market for all that it produces at prices that meant prosperity not for a few but for many.

It is not my purpose to review the ten years that began in 1916. There are just one or two points that I want to make. The first is that until 1916 the South in many respects had long been almost static. The history of the South from the Revolution until 1916 can be suggested broadly in a few sentences. First, in the years immediately following the Revolution, was the period of settlement when white immigrants of the best type poured into the region and began to build a civilization which would have been a happy blending of agricultural and industrial activities. But the invention of the cotton gin, creating, in conjunction with the inventions of Arkwright, in England, a demand for cotton that speedily resulted in breaking down of the barriers erected against the growth of slavery, brought about the spread of the plantation system, and proved a chief factor in driving thousands and tens of thousands of whites across the mountains and on toward the ever receding western frontier. From all this country about us here and from all the Piedmont region they went in a stream so constant that sometimes for months together the covered wagons that carried them through the mountain passes never lost sight one of another; in such numbers that when the first shot was fired on Fort Sumter two out of every five native born white South Carolinians were living in other States. The great problem of the South for fifty years before the War Between the States had been to adjust itself to slavery. Nearly every other matter was subordinated to that.

So, we come to the War of the Confederacy, when the South wrote large an undying story of valor and devotion, and to the Reconstruction period that followed when its men and its women kept the faith and upheld the ideals in which they had been nurtured with a courage that were proof against every hardship and every danger and every temptation. And the South in that period proved that it had brains as well as bravery. Within ten years it was again exercising real power in national affairs while twenty years after Appomattox the influence of the South, under Grover Cleveland, was once more dominant in Washington. There was a record that can hardly be matched in history. But there were some questions which the South had not learned to solve. As slavery had cast its shadow over the whole destiny of the South in the years before 1860, so in the period that followed its ending, the South's best thought had to be devoted for years following to working out a new modus vivendi. The political phases of this problem the

South solved after a fashion in due course. But in 1916 it had not yet discovered how to build roads without money, and it neither had the money nor knew where to get it. It had not learned how to make education accessible to all its population and was still apologizing for widespread illiteracy. Financially and economically its people continued to be in bondage to New York. Their crops were grown with money borrows there, and the growers had small voice in saying when or how they would sell or fixing the price of their products. The same thing was true, though possible not in the same degree of its industries. Most important of all, perhaps, the South had no transportation systems and the freight rates fixed for it in the North were an almost impassible barrier to growth.

It is obvious when we stop to think that the changes the past ten years have made, striking as they have been, have in fact merely paved the way for further changes that in the very nature of things must be infinitely more striking. We have seen, and nowhere so notably as here in North Carolina, what good roads can do for communities, but we have yet to see what can do for a section. We must wait for that until the whole South is fully linked up with paved highways as parts of North Carolina are linked up now. We have found out how to provide schoolhouses and school teachers enough for every child and college for those who want to go to college, but the effects of this educational broadcasting are yet to be manifested. An amazing amount of outside money has sought investment here but if we are justified in our hopes this is only a beginning. What will it mean when all of our people are educated, to least have as much schooling as they are capable of taking? When agriculture has fully recovered from its troubles, most of which are accidental and temporary, and is again fully prosperous? When we are no longer drained of our young men and young women as has been the case for nearly all our past history and instead new white population begins to pour in on the whole South as it has already poured in on Florida? All of us believe that these things are going to happen. What will be their effects?

This is too pregnant a question for me to attempt an answer to it here. I can, however, venture a few suggestions as to what these changes that are taking place in the South mean to the press of the South. No matter what the future holds, already we are committed to changes that have moved so swiftly and cut so deep, that as yet few of us appreciate the magnitude of the transformation that the South has experienced. Even these of us who like to think that we are still young but who are old enough to have gotten our bearings a decade and a half or two decades ago find ourselves challenged almost weekly by something which we were quite sure could never happen in our world. I know that I was shocked only last week when a story came out showing that the population of the South Carolina State Penitentiary at Columbia included more whites than blacks. Only a few weeks before I had read in the *Greensboro Daily News* that at one term of court in Greensboro seventeen young men pleaded guilty to larceny. Judges in both Carolinas have been saying from the bench that whereas a generation ago it was almost an unheard of thing for a white man to be accused of stealing there is now hardly a term of court without such a case. Who in 1916 would have thought that with an era of unprecedented development in progress, with universally better schools and better roads, would some such jarring notes as these? What prophet of doom in January ten years ago would have dared to hint that any man or woman then living would live to see the day when it was the accepted thing on the part of great numbers of young girls, of respectable families, to drink the vilest corn liquor from hip flasks at public dances. And what pray, would have been the fate of one so bold as to have foretold that before the decade was out one of the oldest and finest and proudest Southern cities, far famed for its mellow charm and dignity, would be advertised on two continents by a dance banned by the police in many cities, frowned on by college faculties, and feared by apartment house owners as more dangerous than an earthquake?

Verily, verily, friends and brethren, in more ways than one, the Grand Old South "aint's what she used to be!"

What I am trying to indicate is that difficult as were some of the problems with which the newspapers were called upon to deal ten years ago, they were simple compared with those that confront us at the present time. The opportunities of the press in the South have been enlarged many times over but the obligations which the press is called upon to meet have been enlarged likewise. Until ten years ago most of the questions which we had to handle were of long standing and we were all reasonably familiar with them. Today we do not even know the facts of the problems upon whose solution so much depends. We are still groping our way in meeting the innumerable new questions which are arising before us in manners and morals and economies and taxation and development and government. How are we equipped to offer leadership in dealing with these matters? Are the newspapers of the South competently manned for the extraordinary work ahead of them in these extraordinary times?

All of us here present know that they are not and here amongst ourselves it may be well for our souls, well for our newspapers, well certainly for the public, that we should make the confession and consider candidly its implications.

Since 1916 the newspapers of the South, generally speaking, have shared amazingly in the South's new growth. In many instances, it is true, the country weeklies have suffered severely, but on the whole the newspapers of the South have prospered during this period as never before. Scores of them have known for the first time what it was to make money. Some of them have become rich. They have doubled and trebled and quadrupled in size. In not a few respects they are wonderfully improved. They offer their readers vastly more reading matter, first class sports pages, telegraphic news from every quarter of the globe, the best comic strips the market affords. But as yet they have not qualified for the new leadership that is required of them and in this respect, they are vastly inferior to the newspapers of the South fifty years ago.

I am not saying this by way of criticism, understand, but I am stating a plain fact as plainly and as strongly as I can. What has happened has been this. Until ten years ago the newspapers of the South were seldom money makers. In the average newspaper establishment the editorial end out weighed the business management. The newspaper was a public institution and took itself quite seriously as such. With the changes that have taken place in the South the newspapers as business organizations found themselves for the first time in many cities confronted with the opportunity to make money. That was all right, and more than all right. It was fine that it should have come about, but it is not a fact that in the zeal to improve the new opportunities a very large number of newspaper owners have shifted their major interest to the business end at the expense of the editorial end? I want them to shift this interest back. I want them to bear in mind, as Adolph Ochs has done with the *Times*, for example, that there is a vast difference between spending money on the reading matter of a newspaper and giving thought and study to how that money shall be spent.

It is true, of course, as I have already suggested, that there is hardly a daily newspaper in the South that has not made notable improvements of some kinds, that has not enlarged its telegraphic service, that does not give two or three times the space to baseball and football and basketball and to other sports that it gave in 1916, that does not print at least two or three comic strips and a great many other features. And all these things are excellent. They all go to make a good newspaper. These is probably more interest in sports than in any other one department of the news and it would be extremely foolish, therefore , if the newspapers did not try to have the very best sporting pages they can afford. But the danger is that the publisher when he has done these things and when they have been duly and loudly applauded, bringing new popularity and increased circulation, may conclude that he has done all that is necessary to make a good newspaper. He could not make a mistake fraught with more serious possibilities for the public he serves.

For the newspaper is not an organ of entertainment. It is not primarily a money-making establishment, though it ought to make money. It is a serious institution with serious public duties and responsibilities. It is important in the fulfillment of these responsibilities that it should bring to the readers, the best national news and the best foreign news available, for these are many of us in the South who know that we are a part of the great world and that what happens in Europe and to Europe is of real concern to us. It is a service to our readers to give them the fullest possible news of world affairs and it is a further service to give them the opinions of world statesmen and world publicists. But are the newspapers of the South fitting themselves to perform a like service as to serious affairs nearer at hand?

I wish that I could believe that they were. I have not seen many evidences that point in that direction. The news that goes on the sporting pages is written by experts, by men who know the games about which they write, who are intensely interested in those games and who follow every move relating to them with keen and informed minds. Of how many other news departments of the average Southern newspaper is that true? Can any of you name a newspaper which today makes a systematic effort to give its readers really informed news of schools, of colleges, of the courts, of the farms, of the factories? How many reporters can you name who could write a story about such matters that would have any special value? How many first class reporters do you know of any kind outside of sports? I mean men who will measure up to the best men in their community, who will be as competent as reporters, as competently equipped for their work, as the best lawyers in the community and the best doctors in the community. Why is it that most of the reporters that you see on the average Southern newspaper are boys? It is because reporting has not been recognized as a career. I want to see it recognized as a career. It is a career. It offers in the South right at this moment opportunities of public service quite as great as those opening to any lawyer, any doctor, as any preacher of businessman.

The men can be had. All of us see them come from time to time. Most of the time we see them go. Why do they go? Because they are not paid enough. That is the plain truth bluntly put. In the years that followed the War between the States there were dozens of Southern newspapers and made great reputations. They deserved those reputations because they were manned with exceedingly able staffs. Young men who could write sought employment, were trained for their work, and stayed with the newspapers that employed them after they had gained maturity and force. They stayed of course in many instances because there were no other openings for them unless they went North, and they did not want to go North. Today there are other openings, and the most promising young men take them because they come o feel that journalism, on its editorial side, is a "blind alley." But they would not leave if they were given a fair compensation and had an assured career. They would stay and become a source of great power and prestige to the newspapers they served and of the great good in their communities. They would bring to the newspapers enormously increased leadership. We hear not a little about the decline of newspaper leadership, but it does not decline where it is really exerted. Make it competent and people will welcome it gladly as they have always welcomed it.

For the first time in years the newspapers of the South are coming to be in position to build for themselves organizations on the editorial side which will enable them to do things for their communities and for their section which in the past they were not in a position to perform. We talk a great deal about the South, about the sentiment of the South, about the South as a section. But who today speaks for the South? Is there any longer a public opinion in this section? If so, who make it? The newspapers used to keep in closest touch with all the other important papers, and the exchanges were read. They are read no longer. The readers of the average southern city will probably learn from the front page dispatches of a big fire or a murder or something of that sort in another southern state, but they have small chance of finding out what their fellow citizens in that state are doing in the way of solving their problems, how their point of view is changing, if at all, in manners or morals or politics or religion. There is rarely a picture of anything happening south of the Mason & Dixon's line. The cartoons which give them a plant upon public affairs more powerful perhaps than any written word are nearly all made by Northern or Western artists. And so it goes. Is this to continue and become more and more accentuated? I hope not. It will be tremendously unfortunate for the South if it does. I hope that as they prosper increasingly more and more Southern newspapers will see this; that they will accept their obligation and rise to their opportunity.

One of the finest things in the history of

newspapers, it seems to me, is the fact that from the earliest times the men who conducted newspapers have uniformly recognized their responsibilities to the public. They did in many notable cases where they were only accidentally in charge of what we call the editorial conduct of the newspapers with which they were connected. The history of the press is full of instances where job printers, who were issuing newspapers only as a by product of their printing plants, found themselves involved in situations where great public rights were at stake, and they maintained those rights, be it said to their glory, in the face of every danger to their property and to their persons. Newspapers in those early days, when they did so much to establish human rights, did not have behind them the splendid traditions which are ours today. Those traditions are our pride and spur us on when as now we have before us the largest opportunity and the noblest challenge that the press of the South has faced.

Chapel Hill, 1926

The Citizen Looks Abroad
(Citizen 1928)

Emory University
Citizenship Conference
Atlanta, GA
February 15, 1928

Perhaps I should say at once that my subject tonight is not entirely of my own choosing. Mark you, I do not say this by way of apology; but saying it brings me, nevertheless, at once to the heart of the thought which I wish to enlarge upon. That thought is this: That while most of us in America shrink from discussing world problems, and yet there is no question which today so imperatively calls for consideration as the problem of America's changed position in the world at large.

I was tremendously impressed a few weeks ago, when I examined the program of the Emory Conference for last year and that for this year, with the attention given to world politics; for it seems to me that in pursuing this course Emory has shown a sense of values that is splendidly constructive. I am sure that it has taken courage on the part of those responsible for these Citizenship Conferences to do this. They realize, of course, that at the very term "foreign relations" most of us in America are accustomed to close our ears. What concern have we with international affairs? What can we hope to know about them? Why should we bother with such matters? Why not talk about something worthwhile, something nearer home, something practical and useful?

You will agree, I am sure, that this is the popular attitude. Only a few weeks ago I was at a meeting where an American who has spent years in the study of world politics was the speaker. In the discussion that followed his address, a member of the audience summed up his opposition to America's entering the League of Nations. "I don't know anything about European politics," he said, "and I don't believe anybody else in this country does. So what I say is "Let 'em alone."

Unless I am greatly mistaken that was pretty fair representation of the point of view of a large proportion of the anti-leaguers. It brought to my mind the deacon's prayer, which Doctor Poteet of Wake Forest quotes: "Lord, I thank thee that I am ignorant. I pray thee to make me ignorunter."

Now, I am the last person who would set as an authority on World politics but I know that we can not "Let "em alone" any more that we can let the weather alone. And there is this difference between politics and the weather: Everybody, as Mark Twain said, is always talking about the weather, but nobody ever does anything; whereas, in the matter of world politics, unfortunately, the amount that has been done is out of all proportion to the talk we have had—intelligent talk, I mean, talk that would have conveyed information and perhaps have cleared the air.

There are some people who object to talk. My own feeling is that while at times it may be annoying, it seldom does harm. It may do good. At all events, it has its uses. You remember the story of the old maid who went to confessions. She confessed that fifteen years before she had let a man kiss her. "Well, my child," said the good old priest, "I am sure that the Heavenly Father has forgiven you long ago and you need trouble yourself about it no more." "Yes," said she, "but I like to talk about it."

And so, I am going to make bold to talk to you tonight about America's present world position, as I see it. For your reassurance, let me say at once that I shall not attempt to unravel the intricacies of internationalism. I am not so ambitious as all that. Perhaps you have heard the story of the man with the hare lip who went to his bootlegger.

"I want," he said, "another bottle of the Kangaroo Liquor."

"I am sorry," said the bootlegger, "but I haven't got any more Kangaroo liquor. I can let you have a bottle of Old Crow."

"No," said the customer, "I don't want to fly. I just want to hop around a bit."

Surely it should be the privilege of any of us, even a provincial editor to "hop around a bit," in spite of the suggestion recently thrown out from high authority that the press would do well in foreign affairs to stick closely to its duty of supporting the Government's policies, the difficulty, or curse being for the press to know what the government's foreign polices actually are.

The fact is that except for the Monroe Doctrine, we have no foreign policy other than a program of negation—no foreign policy, that is to say, which represents the thought and conscience of America, no foreign policy that resolutely faces the future and seeks to mould and shape it.

Here is a situation beside which all the other problems of our time shrivel. If we have not begun to understand this and to appreciate its import, we have been blind indeed to the developments of the past decade.

The supreme problem of the world today is that which faced it when, in November ten years ago, the cannon ceased to roar. The problem then, the problem now, was whether the civilized nations of the world would be able to organize for peace or whether they would, as always in the past, organize anew for war. Ten years ago, of course, the world was utterly sick of war--- so sick that most of us believed that generations would have to pass before the nations could be dragged into another conflict. That is still our hope, but it would be fatuous to cherish it and remain oblivious to the obvious trend of the times. The lessons of Armageddon are fading in the public mind and the old psychology is more and more reasserting itself.

The two questions which we heed to ask ourselves are, first, why this is true and, second, what does it forecast. It is true for a number of reasons, upon a few of which I should like to touch briefly. In the first place there is no greater delusion than that which has been fostered in America so diligently—the delusion of American isolation in world affairs. What nonsense it is to cling to this worn-out theory. In its day it was sound enough, but that day has passed. The whole fabric of American life rests upon a different basis. It has been some time, in fact, since the United States was a truly self-contained community. It is less so with every year that passes.

The funded debt of European nations to the Unites States, growing out of the World War, amounts to more than eleven billion dollars but that is only a beginning. During the past ten years foreign investments of the people of the United States have been mounting with an amazing rapidity. At the present time they are estimated to exceed twenty billion dollars. Can people with so much money at stake in other lands be indifferent to what goes on in those lands? Of course not. Peace in Europe is a matter of vital concern to the millions of American investors whose money, directly or indirectly, has been farmed out there.

During this period, moreover, the course of events has made us increasingly dependent upon foreign markets. There are certain raw materials which we must have from abroad—rubber, for example; and we must be able to find a growing outlet for our products in other countries. How can we do this unless these countries emerge from their present poverty and recover their prosperity? And how can they get on their feet and stay on their feet unless they have peace and assurances of peace?

The whole trend of events in the United States is away from agriculture and toward industry. It is the industrial development of the South that is creating new values in this section to the extent of millions of dollars daily. A few weeks ago I heard speaker tell of having been in Atlanta at the time of the exposition there. That was in 1894 or 1895. He was wandering through the exhibits and stopped to look at one of the worlds great paintings, which had been loaned to the exposition. Two women were looking at it also. " Isn't it beautiful! Isn't it beautiful!" said one. "Yes" said the other, "but I am almost sorry they brought it here. It seems pitiful to show us these treasures and fill our hearts with longing for them when we of the South can never own any of them." The South thirty years ago was a poverty-ridden region. Today it is growing miraculously in wealth and in power. Because this increase in wealth has been most apparent in the years since the World War, many people have the idea that the World War was in some way responsible, at least in part, for the change. The very contrary is true. Two things chiefly brought about the change. One the development of the great hydro-electric power resources of the region, and even more than this, the passage of the Federal Reserve law which for the first time rendered available the credit resources of the South. If it had not been for the World War, the South would have been further along in prosperity that it is. Its industrial development would have gone forward, its agriculture would not have been so gravely demoralized.

But the point I am making is that is that the South, like the rest of the nation, is becoming more and more a manufacturing center; it can understand, as it could not have understood a generation or so ago, the implications of this development. It can appreciate, it must appreciate, that isolation for a manufacturing people is an impossibility. For a time a manufacturing people can find prosperity through the expansion of their own markets at home; but they reach a point, as we have already reached it is this country, where this prosperity can be sustained and enlarged only if additional markets are built up abroad.

This America can do and is doing. We are doing it ably and competently. We have built up some fine machinery for the purpose. Our Commerce Department has been functioning most capably in this direction. The Federal Reserve Board, as Secretary Mellon said at Charlotte the other day, is probably rendering its most useful service at the present time, in helping to stabilize the finances of some of the countries with which we must do business. Day by day, week by week, month by month, year by year, we are reaching out and out into other lands, becoming more and more a world figure and a world power; but the astounding thing it that, with all this, we still decline, as a nation, to accept any share of responsibility in the effort to organize the world against war when, as I have tried to suggest, we can as little afford war, probably, as any nation on earth.

What is the consequence? So far as we are concerned, the consequence is that the background of the work which has been done for world peace in the past eight years by the League of Nations we see today the formidable beginnings of a new movement looking to the organization of the world for war. Of course, it is denied, vehemently denied, that this is the purpose of the movement. It is the effect none the less. My protest it that so far as America is concerned the movement, on its present lines, is as futile as it is dangerous. Take the Naval Bill now before Congress, for example. Estimates as to the cost of the implied program run all the way from three quarters of a billion to billions of dollars. The program, as endorsed by the President, is in fact, only a paper program. There is no assurances as to how many ships would be built under it but on its face it is no doubt about America's being able to find the money for such a navy; there is no question about America's willingness to maintain a navy adequate to the national needs. But what kind of navy would be adequate to the national needs? Here a broad field of discussion is opened up and it is this field which is yet to be explored. If what America requires is assurance of an uninterrupted commerce with world at large, we can not secure that through a naval program alone. The total foreign trade of America at the present time approximates nine billion dollars a year. Only one third of this trade is carried in American ships. We have at this time fewer than five hundred vessels flying the American flag in over-seas trade. They are operating, nearly all of them at a loss. In 1927, the shipyards of this country launched vessels totaling 180,000 tons and the rest of the world 2,105,000 tons. I quote the *Wall Street Journal,* which in this matter should be good authority. Plainly, the United States, to go it alone, must do much more than restore a fighting navy.

I am not arguing against a navy; I am pointing out that a navy alone can not afford us a guarantee of peace. I am pointing out that if we determine as a national policy to place our reliance in armaments alone it is time now for us to take account of where this policy is likely to lead us. What attitude will it place us in before the other nations? What obligations will it impose upon us in the protection of our own interest?

We have become almost before we know it ourselves the most powerful figure in the family of nations. Our influence has penetrated in one way or another to the far corners of the world. Still protesting our insularity, the rest of the world sees us as rising steadily to an imperialism that makes itself felt everywhere. You and I may know that our professions are true when we say that we are without covetousness as a people. But how shall we make others believe this? How shall we give proof of our disinterestedness that will quiet envy and dissipate fear?

This is our problem as a nation. Its importance can not be exaggerated, as I see it; and if that be true then surely it is unfortunate that until now the American people have hardly put their minds to this problem at all. We had, it is true, a great campaign over the League of Nations. It was a campaign compounded from beginning to end of political prejudices. The League of Nations has yet to be considered by the American people in its merits and unless they are ready to give it this consideration, then we shall indeed do well to consider whether the people who are urging us to arm and to arm thoroughly are not giving us the soundest possible advice.

It is not my purpose tonight to urge America's entrance into the League of Nations. It presents but one phase of the broad problem which I am attempting to postulate. It is in order that I should touch briefly upon it and upon its record. The League has just celebrated its eight birthday. That is a very short time as events are marked in world affairs. It has been long enough to let all men of open mind see that in the League we have an organization different from anything of the kind every contemplated before. For centuries, it is true, there had been talk of a parliament of nations but, in the past, it had never been believed that such a parliament could be more than an occasional assembly of statesmen to consider political problems. Practical men admitted the desirability of such a parliament but the obstacles to its functioning seemed insuperable. That was still their attitude when the present League came into being. It was, of course, the creation of Woodrow Wilson. For it in his own country he was damned, and his party swept to overwhelming defeat. The bitterness of that campaign has died out, but such was the atmosphere left in its wake that no outstanding leader has yet ventured to take up the fight anew. Yet, in theses eight years, the League has been making history. It has moved to such account that in this country sneers against it have ceased; and that at least is progress. In Europe and in the world at large it has achieved a position which America, as yet hardly appreciates.

When the campaign against the League was made in the United States the attacks upon it found ready sympathy in many countries of Europe. It is true, I think, that most of the responsible statesmen in Europe did not want the league in the beginning. When America repudiated it many of them would have been glad to join in the repudiation. They could not do so because President Wilson had made it a part of the Treaty of Versailles. They felt rather bitterly at first that such a thing should have been left on their hands. They treated it with scant respect. In spite of them it began to function; its power and its usefulness became evident until today the delegations sent to the League by the various nations are composed not of idealists but of the leading statesmen of the member nations and rivalry for a place on the Council on the part of the smaller nations is exceedingly keen. No student of affairs in Europe questions anymore that the League is a going concern and that it is enormously powerful.

Why is it so powerful? Not, surely, because of any inherent force to carry out its will. That it lacks. That it probably will never have. It is powerful for three reasons. The first is because in one crisis after another it has proved its value. In every year since its establishment the peace of the world has been threatened in some quarter of Europe and in every such instance it has been the League which averted that threat. It was probably in the Greco-Bulgarian dispute of 1925 that its usefulness was made most conspicuously clear. But for the League in that crisis there would almost certainly have been war in the Balkan; and from that storm center war, once started, can sweep far and fast. The settlement effected only a few months ago between Poland and Lithuania was another striking illustration of the League's good influence for peace.

Now has this influence been brought about? The answer is that the League has compelled a calm consideration of vexed issues such as was never before possible between hostile nations. The League has compelled periodic international conferences at which the foremost statesmen of Europe sit together for days at a time and hear all sides of these issues. Let no one jeer that not always are these issues composed. In many instances this is all but impossible. There are many sore spots in Europe some of which only time can cure, if indeed they can be cured. The Council of the League can take action only by a unanimous vote. The same thing is true of the League Assembly. I do not think that many Americans understand this. It is the answer to the argument that if the Unites States were a member of the League it might find itself bond to some decision obnoxious to its people. It could not be so bound except by the vote of its own representatives. The provision requiring unanimity is a protection to every nation belonging to the League; but of course, this provision is a limitation upon the League's power which at times is insuperable. The influence of the League has been exerted in growing measure in spite of the limitation because its influence is bottomed upon public opinion as developed through the periodic conferences during which there is the opportunity to get at truth and to see all sides of problems in dispute.

The League, too, owes its increasing prestige in part to a fast growing appreciation of the constructive activities of the various commissions created and functioning under it auspices. Besides the statesmen who compose the Council and the Assembly hundreds of leaders from all parts of the world are co-operating in these various commissions in dealing with world problems, such as the control of the infectious diseases, the control of the traffic in dangerous drugs, the control of traffic in women and children, the codification of international law, the regulation of the traffic in arms, the dissemination of learning, and the solution of economic difficulties. At many of these conferences the United States has been represented and in many of them its representatives have taken a foremost part. Only at actual membership in the League does our Government today draw the line.

Will this continue to be the attitude of the United States indefinitely? Personally, I do not think so. My own conviction is strong that the practical force of events will imperatively urge us to throw the weight of our great influence into the scale along with those who are battling through the League to keep the peace of the world and promote its welfare. We are too sane a people not to recognize in due course that the League has become the most important machinery that exists for world peace, not to realize that with our support it can and will maintain world peace even against the dangers which threaten from the far north of Europe and from the south.

Our greatest mistake as a people has been to think of Europe as a unit. What we are beginning to realize is that there are various forces struggling there, that is this struggle we would do much to turn the decision the right way and that it is to our interest to do this.

I might say that it is our duty as well but to say that would be to put the discussion at one upon another plans one upon which America has so far refused to let it be put.

Let us not quarrel now with that decision. We can afford not to do so. As a practical people we are being faced with a question of alternatives and if we can but come to see clearly what these alternatives are, I am sure, for my own part, that we will not elect to organize only for war and refuse to do our part to organize also for peace.

refuse to do our part to organize also for peace.

Accounting for North Carolina
(Accounting 1928)

The Impressions of a Newcomer
Paper Read Before The Pen and
Plate Club of Asheville
May 7, 1928

In the past thirty years, especially in the past ten years, North Carolina, long known to quote Governor Bickett as the "Rip Van Winkle State of the Union," has become the Wonder State of the South. It has blazed its way to the front in highway construction, in manufacturing, in agriculture, in education, in the Little Theatre movement, in conservation of beauty and in various other fields. Its leadership has found national and even international recognition. Will Rogers, who has been everywhere and seen everything, says that there is no State like North Carolina--"They got everything!" Arthur Brisbane tells his readers to "Watch North Carolina!" Irvin Cobb says, "all the state needs is a good press agent."

It has been a miracle change. What has worked the miracle? That is the question ever on the lips of visitors, especially visitors from the North. When they see what has happened, they want to know how it happened and why it happened. Their questions cannot be answered by pointing to the extraordinary variety and extent of North Carolina's resources, by expatiating on the climate, by explaining that our birth rate is high and our death rate is low, that the cost of living is cheap compared with some other parts of the country, by pointing to the vast stores of energy which have been released for productive activity through our hydro-electric developments. They are still left wondering why North Carolina should have been the pacemaker for the South and why they find a spirit here which apparently does not exist in the same measure elsewhere. And the answer is that all of North Carolina's past history had prepared it for coming to the kingdom at such a time as this. That, at least, is my thesis. Now, for the proof!

I begin with the suggestion that of all the States of the Old South North Carolina was, omitting only Florida, from the earliest Colonial period down to the very recent past, the most parochial. That does not sound like a compliment: indeed, when in 1886, Walter Hines Page said something of the sort in his famous Mummy letter that gave great offense. "There is not," wrote Page, "a man whose residence is in the state who is recognized by the world as an authority on anything. Since time began, no man or no woman who lived there has ever written a book that has taken a place in the permanent literature of the country. Not a man has ever lived and worked there who fills twenty-five pages in any history of the United States. Not a scientific discovery has been made and worked out and kept its home in North Carolina that has ever become famous for the good it did the world." People did not like Mr. Page's saying this, but what he said was substantially true. And since events of the past thirty years have taken the sting out of his words it may be worthwhile to consider now what was back of the condition which he pictured.

Why was it that North Carolina was so reluctant to enter the Federal Union, the last but one of the States to accept the Constitution? Why was it that North Carolina, during the period when the other Southern States were ablaze with leaders, took so inconspicuous a part in the great discussion of national problems? Why did the state send to Washington no Henry Clay, no John C. Calhoun, no Alexander Stephens, no Robert Toombs, no Jefferson Davis, no William H. Crawford, no Robert Y. Hayes? Why in a day of great orators, did she produce no orator like William Lowndes Yancey or Sergeant Prentiss or Howell Cobb or George McDuffie? Why in a period of great pulpit orators did she have no preachers whose representatives compare with the relations of James H. Thornwell or Moses Hoge or John Broadus or B.M. Palmer or Bishop Capers or Bishop Wightman or Dr. Girardeau? Why had she no post like Sidney Lanier or Henry Timrod or James R. Randall or Theodore O'Hara or Paul Hamilton Hayne or Father Ryan? Why no humorist, racy of the soil, like George Washington Harris who wrote <u>Sut Lovingood</u> or Dr. George W. Bagby of Virginia or William J. Thompson who wrote <u>Major Jones Courtship</u>, or Judge Longstreet who wrote <u>Georgia Scenes.</u>

Mr. Page in the letter from which I have quoted offered an explanation, but I do not think that it is the true one. "Most of the most active and useful and energetic men born in North Carolina have gone away, he said. "They are in Louisiana, Texas, Illinois, Washington, New York, Pennsylvania, Massachusetts----every one of them doing himself credit and making a place for himself against the fiercest competition among strangers. So it has always been---the greatest men that were ever born in the State, the Presidents we boasts about and a large number of those whose names are on tablets in Memorial Hall at Chapel Hill, went away from their homes for free air and better chances." Go away, they certainly did in droves. Three claimed by North Carolina as having been born here achieved the Presidency from Tennessee ---Andrew Jackson, James K. Polk, and Andrew Johnson. Thomas H. Benton of Missouri, another North Carolina ex-patriate, made himself one of the great figures in the Senate. Among the citizens of North Carolina who had migrated before 1849 there were thirty-seven who represented other States in the Federal Congress. A dozen native North Carolinians were elected to Congress from Tennessee and ten native North Carolinians represented Alabama.

The fact that when North Carolinians went to other states they rose speedily to leadership, not only in those States but in the Nation, would seem to show that only in those States but in the Nation, would seem to show that the causes, whatever they were, that kept men in this State from exercising such leadership to the same degree had nothing to do with the stock of the people. Abraham Lincoln sprang from identically the same stock that could have been found in thousands of North Carolina homes. Would he have ever been a national figure if he had lived in North Carolina? Would Andrew Jackson, would Andrew Johnson, would old Joe Cannon? No. Then, what was it that these men found in other States which North Carolina lacked? The answer, I think, is conflict. There was an absence here of great issues agitating the people to the degree that obtained elsewhere. North Carolina had not the stake that some of the other Southern States had in the great controversies that marked our history before the Civil War. These controversies did not make the stir here that they made elsewhere and so North Carolinians were quite content to live under the philosophy of Nathaniel Macon, long their patron saint. "Always pay as you go" and "never build your house where you can hear your neighbor's dog bark," preached Macon. All he wanted for his private behalf, we are told, was to be let alone. For the broader horizon of the State he asked the same, that her sisters should not interfere with her and especially with her "peculiar institution." It may be suggested that this was the philosophy of the South, but in North Carolina it was accentuated to a marked degree. The people of this State had no ambition to run the country. They asked only that the country not try to run them.

If the plantation system had spread in North Carolina as it did in South Carolina, for example, they story would have been a very different one but North Carolina was spared this blight. There is not one thing for which North Carolinians of today have greater cause to be thankful. I am confident that it is not too much to say that if slavery had overrun North Carolina as it did in South Carolina the miracle of progress which we have witnesses since 1890 could never have happened. The two supreme factors in North Carolina's history down to 1890 were which I have just touched upon with the manner in which the State was settled. If, like all the other Seaboard States, North Carolina had been settled from the coast its character would have been developed upon radically different lines. The example of South Carolina proves that. In South Carolina the English and Huguenots on the coast merged into a ruling class with sought to maintain its power over the entire province and State even after the population of the upper territory, made up largely of Scottish-Irish who had come down from Pennsylvania, had become numerically greater. The two elements approached almost every question from a different angle and the situation early produced a conflict which has been an outstanding feature in the State's history—so much so that when some years ago a student of these matters wished to write the history of sectionalism in America he was able to find every element entering into the struggle within the confines of the Palmetto State. This struggle produced strong men—men who made themselves national figures; but it produced, too, bitter feeling which has cost the state heavily again and again, down to this day.

In North Carolina, on the other hand, the character of the coast was such as to make it dangerous for vessels to land on it and so even the coastal counties were settled mainly by people who drifted down into them from Virginia and who did not try to extend their authority over the middle and upper country. The rest of the State was colonized in a large measure by Scottish-Irish who came here in great numbers from Pennsylvania and by Pennsylvania Dutch and the Moravians. These various elements were fairly homogenous. These was no sharp conflict between them and before slavery began to grow by leaps and bounds, following the inventions of Whitner and Arkwright in the closing years of the eighteenth century, conditions in North Carolina had so shaped themselves that in this state there were always, at every stage, at least two white persons for every Negro.

This was a greater blessing that could then be appreciated. It is true that North Carolina during the first half of the nineteenth century had a considerable migration but it was decidedly smaller than that of South Carolina, where the Negroes came to be in the majority and whence two fifths of the native-born white population, unable to meet the economic competition which the plantation system created, were forced before Fort Sumter was fired upon.

Thus slavery was never the burning issue in North Carolina that was in some of the other Southern States. Probably a majority of the North Carolinians owned no slaves. Furthermore, since the slave population was comparatively small, they did not stand in the same fear of the abolition of slavery which was felt by non-slave-owning whites in sections where the slave population was large. On the other hand, it is important to note that while North Carolina was not tremendously concerned to preserve slavery neither was it subject, like Tennessee, to internal strife over the question of its attitude in the controversy over slavery and secession. When at last secession became imminent North Carolina frowned upon the movement. Her people refused to leave the Union, They did not want to secede. They did so only when President Lincoln's call for troops left them no other choice than to secede or take up arms against the South.

When they did cast their lot with the Confederacy, they did it wholeheartedly. No other State gave more generously either of its men or its resources. With a voting population of 115,000 North Carolina put 127,000 men into service under the Star and Bars. True, she produced no outstanding general, unless you want to except Braxton Bragg; but she bore her part in the struggle gloriously and then, when the war was over, so far as she was concerned, it was over. She was not left, like Virginia in a State of widowhood; she was not left, like Tennessee and Kentucky, with an aftermath of bitterness among her people; she was not left, like South Carolina, with the whole scheme of her existence uprooted, and confronted with a train of class problems deeply coloring the politics of the State and making unescapable for class consciousness, strife and division. Indeed, it may not be too much to say that the abolition of slavery came for North Carolina fortunately and at a fortunate time; before the system had gone so far here as to become a source of blight such as it proved elsewhere; in time to release North Carolina from its handicaps and dangers and set its people free to develop their resources at the earliest favorable opportunity.

The conditions under which North Carolina was settled influenced the development of the State in one other way that was vitally important. If the settlement had been from the coast or at the head of navigation of some river. The fact that the state was settled from the interior, that the development was on agricultural lines and the climate was good in all sections discouraged the growth of cities. There were numerous towns, trading centers; and even as these grew in the size through the years, they remained trading and nothing more. Not one of them occupied a position of commanding importance. Thus, there never existed that antagonism between town and country which has been common in so many states. When the rise of manufacturing at last gave a sudden and marked impetus to the growth of an urban population, it happened fortunately that this growth distributed itself in a number of centers, giving the State not one huge city half a dozen chief cities of approximately the same size and smaller cities by the score. All of these places drew their new population from the surrounding territory; the interest of the cities in their back country was keen and the interest of the back country in the cities was keen. There has been an absence jealousy of a hurtful character either between country and cities or between cities.

If I have succeeded at all in what I am attempting to do, I have now given you three substantial reasons why North Carolina more and more acquired a distinctive character of its own. Most of us have a habit of generalizing too broadly in our thinking. We speak loosely of the far West, as if all the people who lived on the Pacific could be lumped. We visualize the Corn Belt and forget that different parts of the Corn Belt have their different problems. We talk about the North as a unit and Northerners talk about the South as unit. The truth is that while the South has much in common there is also much that differentiated North Carolina from other Southern States is that it has been and still remains more self-contained than any of them, coupled with the fact that the whole course of its development has been such as to bind its people together instead of separating them into groups or factions. There has never been any class of the population which was dominant. All of the public affairs have been managed consistently upon a give-and-take principle, as illustrated in the arrangement under which a governor is chosen now from the East, now from the West. Furthermore, since there was little that the national Government could do for them, North Carolinians have had always to look for themselves. This has made its impress on their character. With the Scotch influence prevailing they could hardly have been other than thrifty; but the conditions under which they have worked out their problems did something more for them than that. What it did preeminently was to give them a confidence in themselves and in their leaders that has been in marked contrast to the situation which has prevailed in many other Southern States. It is this confidence that has found marvelous illustration in the great movements of the past three decades.

Eager souls, like Walter Page, were impatient over the slowness with which the first of these movements, that having to do with public-school education, got under way; but when the voices of McIver and Aycock were once heard the movement from which they pleaded became in fact a veritable crusade. Only now are its fruits becoming fully apparent. A few figures will indicate its progress. Let us take the total high-school enrollment in the State was 7,144. Last year the growth in high-school enrollment was 7,653 and the number of graduates 10, 587. There are 81,000 white children in the high schools of the State at the present time and more than 10,000 Negro children. In the past five years North Carolina has put $35,000,000 into new school buildings and the State is spending $32,000,000 a year on public school today as against $1,000,000 in 1900.

More widely advertised than anything else North Carolina has done has been its great roadbuilding program; and it is here that the spirit which characterizes the people of North Carolina and which is a product of all their past experience has found its perfect expression. The highway program, as the country knows it, dates from 1921 but it was in fact a decade or more in the making. As Aycock and McIver had preached the public schools, so Governor Craig, Governor Bickett and Governor Morrison preached the necessity of taking North Carolina out of the mud. At length the gasoline tax opened the way for doing this and seven years ago the Legislature was asked to provide a bond issue of $50,000,000 to start the work. Know well this striking fact: When the measure was brought to a vote only seventeen votes were cast against it. At the next session an additional bond issue of $15,000,000 was asked for. Only eleven votes were cast against it. In the 1925 session a further bond issue of $20,000,000 was sought. This time only seven votes were cast against it. Last year the request was for a bond issue of $31,850,000 and this time the unanimous. You cannot match this record, search where you will; and you cannot match it because you can not find another State where the people share to the same extent that faith in themselves which gave North Carolina assurance that their money would not be diverted from the purpose for which they were voting it and that they could look to the future to vindicate them in what they were doing. It has not been lack of appreciation of the benefits inherent in the program followed in North Carolina which kept other states from adopting it. I know that in several of these other states it has been factional politics which has made the body of the people unwilling to embark upon so expansive a venture.

Of course, North Carolina's progress in highways, in schools and in other public enterprises could not have been achieved except for the State's phenomenal growth in wealth and in productive power. It would be extremely interesting to trace in detail the steps by which North Carolina has learned to utilize its varied and extensive resources. Most of the public works have been financed, it is true, to a large extent through bond issues; in other words, it is true, to a large extent through bond issues; in other words, the State's advance has been made possible largely through its discovery of the sources of credit. In 1890 the per-capita debt of North Carolina amounted, United States and all its governmental subdivisions, to but $6.87 and as late as 1912 this figure stood at $4.88. The total debt of the State and of its subdivisions in 1902 was but $15,348,000---less than that of the city of Asheville at present. The total debt in 1926, the State and all its civil divisions, had climbed to $392,725,000 or $137.50 per capita. The total debts of all the States and of their civil divisions in 1902 was $1,865,035,000 and had climbed by 1926 to $12,798,691,300 or $109.30 per capita. Justifying North Carolina's course in the extensive borrowing thus indicated it is enough to point out that in 1900 its investment in manufacturing establishments was $68,000,000 whereas today this investment is estimated at more than a billion and a quarter dollars. Its six hundred cotton, woolen, cordage, silk and knitting mills now have a total annual output approximating $400,000,000. Its furniture factories in 1919 turned out products valued at $9,355,000. Last year they turned out products valued at $50,000,000. It seventeen tobacco factories manufacture tobacco products valued at $251,000,000. Its forest products are worth more than $100,000,000 a year. Its mineral products, just beginning to be developed, are valued at $11,000,000. Its total manufactured products are worth over a billion dollars a year and its agricultural in 1927 totaled $453, 605,000. It may be, as Governor McLean and others suggest, that the time has come when the State should be careful about issuing more bonds but its growth in wealth has more than kept pace with its public expenditures to date. There are real values back of the bonds it has issued and we have only begun to draw upon our resources. Where it was once difficult to find capital it is easy now to do this; and, in an age where hydro-electric power has come more and more to tell the tale, North Carolina ranks fifth in the United States in water-power development and second in the South in the output of power.

So far as material prosperity goes, it is entirely reasonable, therefore, to look for a continued expansion reaching from the mountains to the sea. Our fisheries and inland streams are capable of yielding richer and richer revenues. The balance between agriculture and manufacturing has not yet been upset, new crops are being developed, by comparison with other States the value of the cotton crop has hardly been affected by the coming of the boll weevil, due to North Carolina's geographic position, and the market for the tobacco crop is still being enlarged. We shall soon have a trained citizenship, so far as the school can provide that training---something no State in the South has ever had until now. Establishment of the Great Smoky Mountain National Park is about to be realize the dream of the decade. What more could anyone want?

The profitable use of all these blessings; that we may see their influence not alone in the realm of the material but everywhere. Our place in the picture or progress has not been based on materialism alone, but there is danger nevertheless that the material may overshadow other and yet more shing opportunities. We have had, for example, in some of our colleges, struggling though they were, centers of culture whose fame has reached beyond the borders of the State solely because they had made themselves dynamos of truth. This has been notably true of Chapel Hill and true as well of Wake Forest. There we see that after all the personal equation is of chief importance. North Carolina wants more men like Dr. William Louis Poteat. It can feel a due pride in the great establishment, which is being built up at Duke University, but it is imperative that it discern also the threat which an establishment of such wealth presents. The creation of such a foundation offers danger as well as opportunity. It may quicken, but at the same time it may chill.

When one studies North Carolina, either its present or is past, curious contradictions present themselves, or what seems like contradictions; but the thing that impresses me most in the State's history is that its people, less interested in the rest of the world than most people, have never been afraid of what might happen in North Carolina. They let the free Negroes vote until 1835, and there were more than 22,000 of them—and the franchise was taken away by a narrow margin. They removed, after a full discussion, the disability on Catholics holding office, and this at a time when prejudice on the subject was yet deep in England. They refused to shackle their colleges when the effort to do this was made a year or two ago. They are not afraid now to educate the whole body of people, black as well as white, although this is undoubtably going to raise up problems which before a great while will be very real. They will not be afraid, I hope, these next few years to take to hear the truth that unless they do much more than they have yet done and set up for themselves new objectives all that they have achieved and are achieving will be without wholesome meaning or purpose in the larger sense. The very rapidity with which North Carolina is advancing along material lines should put its people on guard lest they come to place an undue emphasis permanently upon the materials, to point only to the fact that they are spending millions on education and fail to see how grotesque it is to remain content with bookless homes and almost bookless schools—one book for each pupil. Unquestionably, we have laid and are laying here the foundations for a culture which can broaden and sweeten the lives of all the State's citizenship and whose influence reach far. But the need is, or so it seems to me, that shall arise leaders who shall make us vision and yearn for things of the spirit as the leaders of whom I have spoken stirred North Carolinians of the past three decades to glorious endeavor in the realization of the opportunities which were open to them in fulfillment of the obligation which those opportunities involved

෩෨

A Christmas Day Editorial
(Christmas 1931)

Peace On Earth, Good Will Toward Men

The Asheville Citizen
Asheville, NC
December 25, 1931

There was no room for them in the inn. So the carpenter and his espoused wife, who had come up to the city of David to be taxed, had taken up their lodgings in the stable; and there Mary, when she had brought forth her first born son, wrapped him in swaddling clothes, and laid him in a manager.

And there in the same country shepherds abiding in the field, keeping watch over their flocks by night.

And, lo, the angel of the Lord came upon, and the glory of the Lord shone round about them: and they were sore afraid.

And the angel said unto them, Fear not: for, behold, I bring you good tidings of great joy, which shall be to all people.

For unto you is born this day in the city of David a Savior, which is Christ the Lord.

And this shall be a sign unto you; ye shall find the babe wrapped in swaddling clothes, lying in a manger.

And suddenly there was with the angel a multitude of the heavenly host praising God, and saying,

Glory to God in the highest, and on earth peace, good will toward men.

"Glory to God in the highest, and on earth peace, good will toward men."

Deny if you will the divine inspiration of this story. Match it if you can in all literature, sacred or profane.

A modern philosopher, searching devastatingly for some key to the meaning of history, and admonishes his readers at the last that "It is hopeless to ask the purpose of humanity and its existence—as hopeless to ask the purpose of Sirius, the Milky Way, or the comets."

"We must cease," he says, "to regard humanity from the point of view of eternity. It dwindles else before our eyes to an almost invisible speck, without performance, significance, or aim, the contemplation of which leaves us utterly humiliated, broken and dispirited."

"But," he asks finally, "is there one out of all the ideals to which the noblest and ablest of men have aspired which can stand the cold examination of knowledge?" And he answers: "only one—the ideal of goodness and of selfless love. To add no inevitable touch of cruelty to the inexorable evils with which nature scourges man, but, within limits of their strength, to lessen the sum of human suffering—this is the ideal towards which the most perfect men our species has known have aspired, which they have felt to be noble and high enough to inspire and recompense them. It is an ideal that is still far from being realized. It may suffice us for a long time to come. It can yet make life worth living to many, and those the best among us."

The book in which a Russian student and writer embodied these sentiments was published in this country early in 1914. And then came the war of wars!

"Glory to God in the highest, and on earth peace, good will toward men."

Peace on earth, good will toward men.

We look about us today, at the Christmas season, and what do we see?

A world in arms. A world in war. No peace anywhere. Good will seemingly a mockery.

A world in arms. Impoverished, but armed to the teeth. Bankrupt, yet spending billions on military establishments. So weighted down with debt from the last great conflict that its credit has been destroyed and the whole machinery of civilization thrown out of gear, yet still feverishly intent upon the perfection of its agencies of destruction in preparation for other possible wars.

Schools may close for lack of funds, but we must have guns. Factories may shut down because no one has the money to buy their output, but the building of warships must go on. Farm produce may rot in the fields, for want of buyers, while millions go hungry, but the armies and navies of the nation must be maintained.

Security, we are told, is imperative. We must have security.

Security from what?

From attack by some potential enemy? Look about you. Look first at our own country. Have we been saved from attack? Here we live in a land free of invasion this long time past by any armed and hostile force. It is a land of plenty. But millions of its people today are without means to buy the things that are so abundant, the things they so eagerly want, the things which in too many instances they need to support life itself.

Security for what?

Have our fighting men been able to secure the worker in his job, the rich man in the value of his stocks and bonds and lands, old age in its comforts, youth in its pleasures?

No. Invisible forces more destructive than any army have wrought havoc on every hand. All the soldiers and sailors in the world—millions of them—and all the guns and warships and fighting machines, though their cost has run into the billions, have been futile to stop this havoc.

We would not scoff at the gallant men who serve in our armies and navies. We honor and respect them. But today their helplessness to protect us, their helplessness to protect any nation, is apparent.

For there are wars and wars. Thirteen years have passed since the guns ceased to sound upon the Western Front. But the war itself has not ceased. It still goes on. Its hates still survive. Its fears still flourish. Its costs still mount. Its sufferings still grow. Its ruin still spreads.

There is not now a part of the habitable globe, armed or unarmed, that has escaped its dreadful consequences.

Security!

The banker's vault may be proof against the assaults of the burglar trying in vain to blast through their masonry and steel but of what avail is that when the values which those vaults incase vanish into nothingness?

Security!

The worker at the lathe may have sought it through training hand and eye until the product of his skill became his pride, his own support and that of those he loves. But what security is there for him when dust gathers upon the machine at which he was wont to earn his daily bread?

Security?

The farmer's acres may be broad and fertile, they may be far beyond the reach of any seen enemy, and the farmer's industry may match his knowledge of the times and seasons and methods which govern a wise husbandry—but heartsickness will still be his portion when the harvest comes and there is no market for the fruits of his labors.

Students of such matters tell us that here

in our own state of North Carolina there are between fifteen thousand and twenty thousand tenant families who will not be needed next year on the lands upon which they have been living and to which alone they can look for subsistence. What is to become of them they do not know, no one knows.

Where is their security!

In Alabama, it is authoritatively stated, the farm labor supply is estimated to be double the requirements of 1932. Where is the security for those whom no work is in sight? How are they and their families going to live? Can armies and navies help answer that?

Such illustrations might be multiplied indefinitely; might be extended to take in every State and most communities; and the word comes from other lands that by comparison we in this country are blest!

The whole world is sick, desperately sick, sick in every part. But is it sick beyond remedy? Is there any cure?

Only one. We have already given it. It was that which was hymned in the ears of the shepherds by the multitude of the heavenly hot.

"Glory to God in the highest, and on earth peace, good will toward men."

Ah, you say, but that begs the whole question. How can there be good will toward men in a world torn nigh unto death by passion and strife, by jealousies and ambitions, by greed and envy, by hates and fears?

It will not be easy. We grant you that. But neither is it impossible. And the compulsion is absolute. The alternative at the best will be a long continuance of the misery which overtakes mankind. At the worst it will be unspeakable disaster.

We know, of course, how simple it is to sneer at good will as a solvent of the problems that menace the nations. Such sneering has long been common enough. But the world's mood today is a very sober mood. With nation after nation already financially upon the rocks it has had enough and more than enough to make it sober. And the world knows in its heart that there is no reliance to be places upon force alone.

Victors and vanquished in the last great struggle are alike miserable and unhappy now.

How long, we ask you, how long can human beings go on living like this?

Why should they go on living like this when to change the whole picture they have only to act upon the realization that to really live they must also let live?

There was a time, we are told, when a conquering nation could bestride the earth, or such part of as was then known, like a Colossus.

That time has passed. Civilization today is infinitely complex. Power today compels responsibility. Of those who are richest and strongest and greatest, strange to say, the largest measure of service is exacted.

The glory of the victor as it was chanted in the ancient sagas has become a myth. The nation now that would be chief among its neighbors must become the servant of them all.

The law is inexorable. It is unescapable.

Those who thus serve may fix their hire if they will. But beneath the trappings of their armaments they will wear the yoke of servitude. And if they fix that hire unjustly their anxieties will be constant. Their griefs will be continuing. Their people will eat their hearts out in their longing for peace.

What is true of nations is true of individuals.

Gone is the day when wealth might flaunt itself in safety in the face of sodden poverty. There is no freedom that attached to wealth when distress is general or when discontents prevail.

The doctrine of private property is implanted deep in human nature; ineradicably so, we think. But its rights are sacred only as those who would assert and maintain them are ready to acknowledge that implicit in this doctrine is the right of others to live.

Cain's question, "Am I my brother's keeper?" must ever be answered "Yes."

When millions of able-bodied men and women ask for work and can not find it there is no security for them, there is not security for anyone.

Peace on earth there can never be while this condition continues. Its correction is imperative.

But how? By correcting the dislocations which have produced it. That does not lie in the power of any individual, or of any group of individuals. It does not lie in the power of any nation. It does lie in the power of the nations. It does lie in the power of the people of each nation to create the will that it shall be done.

Good will toward men.

It has been the want of such a will that has been and that still is at root of all our troubles.

An intense, selfish, narrow, bitter nationalism is today intolerable and as preposterous in the world as it now exists as an intense, narrow selfish, grinding plutocracy has become in any nation.

We have had over the past thirteen years an orgy of nationalism of this type. It has brought us to despair.

It cannot go on. The days when a robber chieftain might barricade himself in his castle and sally forth to prey upon his neighbors are over. The days when a nation can wax fat upon the spoils of its own strength is over.

We are all parts of one whole. In an atmosphere in which this is acknowledged the world can shake off the weights that cumber it, can revive the springs of credit, which is confidence, trust, good will, and regain the equilibrium which it has lost. The machinery of civilization will then fall back into place. The fear that is stamping itself upon the hearts of men will lift. There will be work for him who labor and a fair return for those who render honest service.

Thus, thus only, can contentment and good feeling be restored or, if you will, created, and made to walk the earth.

This is no dreamy idealism that we are talking. It is the sternest of all the stern realities in the world today. And if hope for the future burns in our heart, as it does, it is because of the multiplying evidences that more and more the leadership in almost every nation is awakening to the verities, and seeking to adjust its attitude to these verities.

It is this matter of attitudes which is so vital and determining.

So much in life is beyond our control. So much seems to be governed by blind chance. But our attitudes toward life are what we make them. And life is shaped by the attitude we take regarding it

It is our attitude toward Christmas which makes the Christmas season what it is; and it is because of the continuing manifestations of the influence of this season upon our thoughts and emotions that we are venturing today to write at such length on the direful effects which a wrong attitude among nations and peoples has had upon every land and every people and of the urgent necessity for bringing about a right attitude among the nations and peoples as the only corrective of these evils.

If we can but do that increasingly over the coming critical year, weighted with so much that is momentous to the welfare of mankind, we shall have done all that is in the power of men to make next Christmas and the Christmases that follow happier and happier for the children of men.

We are not talking idealism today but we point now at the last to the ideal which the Russian skeptic whose words we have quoted declared to be that towards which "the noblest men our species has known have aspired, which they have tried to realize, which they have felt to be noble and high enough to inspire and recompense them." The ideal which he envisaged was the ideal which the multitude of the heavenly host proclaimed to the shepherds as they watched their flocks on the Galilean hills.

The man who said that refused to regard humanity from the point of view of eternity; but even so he felt that there was no other ideal worth the seeking except that which embodied in the words we have made from the refrain of this article—"on earth peace, good will toward men." There is no other: and when we seek it, whatever our discouragements, we have only to remember that we do not strive unaided. The mightiest of invisible forces work with us. We serve with the angels of the Christmastide. Their glorious music will refresh our spirits when they droop; and there is healing in their wings.

"Glory to God in the highest, and on earth peace, good will toward men."

South Carolina, Past and Present
(South 1937)

South Carolina Press Association
Columbia, SC
January, 1937

I wish, Mr. President, that I could make each of you realize the pleasure it gives me to be here with you today.

My very earliest and certainly my most continuous recollections are bound up with the newspapers of South Carolina.

I could not have been more than four or five years of age when I went with my father to the office of the *Yorkville Enquirer* and saw old Capt. Lewis M. Crist puttering about the place in his shirt sleeves. I remember him distinctly.

First Abbeville Trip

The one thing that stands out in my memory of my first trip to Abbeville is eating dinner in the editorial office of the *Press and Banner* with my father and Mr. Hugh Wilson. If I had the ability to draw a picture it would be of him now coming across the square with his close cropped reddish beard and high silk hat.

I has just turned 19 when one of my duties under N. G. Gonzales was that of clipping for him anything I saw in the state papers that I thought would interest him.

How much of my life I have spent with those papers in the years that have followed I would hesitate, Mr. President, to figure out. Certainly, a very great part of it.

It is not strange, therefore, that when I think of South Carolina it is primarily of its newspapers and of the men and women who have made and who are making those newspapers. It is not strange that the invitation with which you have honored me is one which I value in the highest degree.

There is another reason why I am honored by this opportunity to address you. No one, I think, could have a livelier appreciation than I of the service which the press of South Carolina has rendered in the past; or of the character of the men and women who have distinguished it.

Personal Recollection

The temptation is strong to talk about some of these men personally. I should particularly like to say something about August Kohn, whose efforts helped mightily in the upbuilding of this state and of this institution whose guests we are; about Thomas R. Waring, who illustrated so conspicuously the graces of life; about many others.

My pleasure today in looking into the faces that I see is tempered by my sorrow for the faces that I miss; faces that are absent not only here but from this earthly scene.

Death in the decade that has passed since it was my privilege to serve you as president has taken a shining toll.

> For some we loved, the loveliest and the best
> The Rolling Time hath from his vintage pressed
> Have drunk their cup a round or two before
> And one by one crept silently to rest.

The work that has been done in the past by the leaders of the press in South Carolina, and especially the work done in critical days by men like NG Gonzales, Ambrose Gonzales, J.C. Hemphill, Francis Warrington Dawson, Carlyle McKinley, Alfred B. Williams and a host of others—to go no farther back nor come yet nearer the present—is the rich heritage of you who are making the press of South Carolina today.

You cannot hope to eclipse their courage, their integrity, their brilliance, their vigor, their usefulness. It would not be possible to wish for South Carolina anything better than that you shall carry on, as I have confidence that you will, in the spirit which they exemplified.

Purpose of a Newspaper

There are today those who maintain that a newspaper is merely a merchandiser of news, or of news plus entertainment. You and I know that this is not true.

We know what more than once the press of South Carolina has done for South Carolina. We know that the press can be and should be a powerful instrumentality of public service; that its supreme responsibility is to fix public attention upon the things that are vital; to maintain and promote standards that will conserve the public weal; to arouse the public conscience to its obligation; to serve as sentinels against dangers and as heralds of opportunities; to help guide the public intelligence to sound decisions; to hearten the spirits of the people when they droop.

Repeatedly the press of the South Carolina has done all of these things. That is the great tradition which belongs to the press of South Carolina today. And my message to you is that your times and your problems, your opportunities and your responsibilities are more challenging than any the press of South Carolina has been called upon to face in the past.

Ours, Mr. President, and I trust you will allow me to put it thus, ours is a state with a distinctive record and a distinctive personality. There are features of its record which have not encouraged us to boasting. But to a degree which only a few other states can rival South Carolinians, for generation however bitterly they may have differed, have had one thing in common—the intensity, the fierceness, I may say, of their affection for South Carolina.

"I wish," said a newspaper man from another state, after a listening to a South Carolinian talk. "I wish that I could feel about Michigan as you feel about South Carolina." But he did not have back of him what the South Carolinian had, for Michigan is not South Carolina. Few states indeed, have back of them a record which inspires the kind of feeling which the life and traditions of South Carolina have inspired.

"Love South Carolina"

William Henry Trescot, whose superb inscription to the Confederate dead glorifies the little monument to them that stands on the State House grounds out yonder, voiced what I have in mind in his magnificent eulogy of General Stephen Elliott.

The men and the women who made the civilization of which Stephen Elliott was a product had, said Trescot, a simple creed. "It could be stated in three words –Love South Carolina—A statesman," he continued, "might call it narrow. A philosopher might call it weak. But it was broad enough to cover them in life. It was strong enough to sustain them in death."

"What generation of South Carolinians has there been of which this could not have been said? What South Carolinian is there who has not felt about South Carolina as Burns felt about Scotland when he exclaimed—

"Ev'n then a wish (I mind its power), A wish that to my latest hour,
Shall strongly heave my breast,
That I poor auld Scotland's sake
Some useful plan or book could make
Or Sing a song at least."

Today, however, there are South Carolinians who fear—as do many in other states—that their state is losing its identity. They feel that it is being degraded in its powers and privileges; that the loyalties of its people are being fixed elsewhere; that the liberties for which South Carolinians fought in the American Revolution have been utterly invalidated; that the principles for which the blood of thousands of South Carolinians stained to a deeper hue to red hillside of Virginia in the 60s have been brought humiliatingly to a final contempt.

Are Changes Evil?

If this be true, Mr. President, then is there cause indeed that we should rend our garments, cover us with sackcloth and ashes, give ourselves over to lamentation and despair. But is it true? Are all the changes that have happened as evil as they are sometimes made to seem? May we not still borrow a line from Kipling—

"If England was what England seems,
And not the England of our dreams,
But only putty, brass and paint,
How quick we'd chuck her-but she ain't."

Do not, however, misunderstand me. If there is one thing which, in what I am saying, I wish to make clearer than anything else it is that the changes upon which we are embarked are fraught with perils as well as with hopes.

It will take more than wise leadership to bring the hopes that have been aroused to fulfillment.

The heaviest obligation that can rest upon any American journalist today is that of guarding, to the fullest extent of his abilities, against the dangers which unquestionably are involved in so profound an alteration of conditions as they had existed, even though those conditions had in many ways been vicious, even though the need of alteration was imperative.

No other state is the union, Mr. President, was so unfitted as this, temperamentally, historically, traditionally, for the sweep into an intensive nationalism which America has experienced.

The foundations upon which South Carolina was to build were established far back in the Colonial period. It was then that the colonists, led by Charleston, and almost unaided by England held for England, against the Spaniard, against the Indian, against all comers, not the territory which is not South Carolina alone but pretty much the entire Southeast.

Spirit of Formation

The sacrifices which they made, the courage and intelligence which they displayed, distinguished our early history. They used up both their public and private credit. They risked and gave their lives. They exhibited a boldness of spirit which was beyond which was beyond praise.

It was in that spirit that South Carolina was formed. Later, when on the coast wealth increased swiftly, and when in the upper sections the sturdy settlers, the Scotch-Irish and others, moved in, the tradition of stout independence, of militant individualism, was fixed. The struggles of the first half of the 19th century accentuated this tradition.

Nor did Appomattox destroy it. It might have done so, for the decision whose fruits were now eating was determined. But in the cruel aftermath of Reconstruction the faith of the fathers was not merely kept alive. It became more than a doctrine. We made it a religion.

The world tides ran against us. We did not even sense this, most of us; nor did the people of the United States, for they were still living, though most of them less militantly than ourselves, in the heritage of a fierce pioneer economy.

Great Britain, ever our mentor though we had severed our political ties with her, moved forward, all through the 19th century, from one adjustment to another, all aimed at the preservation of the democratic principles through more intelligent exercises of democratic functions to meet new times and new conditions.

Less critically placed, with a continent still to conquer, with the pressure upon us socially and economically far less acute, we in America continued to hold to the formulas and practices which had been, we fondly believed, tested and proved by time and experience.

There has been a great deal of shouting during the past year, Mr. President, about the alleged betrayal of the sacred teachings of the Democratic party in this country, about America's departure from the democratic principle.

As to the Democratic Principle

I am not interested here in the discussion of the fortunes of the Democratic party. But as regards the democratic principle in America the truth is that the departure from it occurred long ago.

How South Carolina fitted in with the operation of that principle might make a curious study.

What as understood in this country is the democratic principle? Is it embodied in the slogan "Equal rights for all and special privileges for none?"

We have lustily proclaimed our allegiance to that slogan. We proclaimed it even in the days of slavery. We proclaimed it throughout the long period when, for generation after generation, tens of thousands of white boys and girls grew to manhood and womanhood without having enjoyed the privilege of learning even to read and write.

I am not seeking to exalt the democratic principle. What we once had in South Carolina may have been vastly better. But many of those who clamor about this principle now are indulging in mere verbal pyrotechnics.

What we had in South Carolina in what many look back to as this state's golden age—and it was a golden age—was an agricultural oligarchy. What we came to have in the United states in the years that followed the downfall of the Confederacy was a financial and industrial oligarchy.

South Carolina suffered crushingly under that tyranny—for it was a tyranny. The pivotal thing that happened in 1865 was not that the wealth of the South was in great part obliterated. It was that our wealth, largely destroyed with our economic and social system thrown into the utmost confusion, the wealth of the nation was left largely unimpaired, relatively greatly enhanced.

Years Before Sixties

Between 1840 and 1860 the wealth of the South doubled twice. It took 44 years after 1860 for it to double again. In that period the wealth of the nation was increased seven times; the wealth of parts of the nation increased perhaps seven times seven.

Look back in your minds and you will see that it was not until after the turn of the century that the picture in the South, and particularly in South Carolina, began to change.

We had had the rise of cotton mills before that. The part which the able leaders produced in South Carolina had in bringing about that rise is an epic. But the profits of cotton manufacturing, such as they were, went elsewhere in good measure. Manufacturing wages in South Carolina in 1904 were $14,000,000; in 1909 they were but $20,000,000.

With the cornering of cotton by Sully and Hayne and Brown there followed a definite lift in the price of cotton and a definite lift in land prices.

I do not say that what the New Orleans speculators did brought this about. But their action had a psychological effect on the South; and at any rate cotton prices, which from 1891 until 1900 had touched 10 cents only once, then momentarily, the farmer in most years getting 5, 6, and 7 cents, rose sharply after 1904, holding their gains until 1914 , when for a few months, with shipping demoralized, they sagged.

We were living in those years in a static civilization, had come to accept it as the best that could be expected, came, indeed, many of us to like it. The energies of the public discussion were used up in a fights over the liquor question and things like that. The period, for all its poverty, its discomforts, its hardships, was mentally a rather comfortable period.

We were used to the physical discomforts. It was pleasant to sit back and damn the Yankees and Wall Street and the government.

State's Definite Change

I think I can definitely date the change. In the autumn of 1902, about the time of the State Fair, NG Gonzales wrote an editorial reviewing the improvement the year had recorded in South Carolina economically. I wrote the head for the article and his praise of the head the next day warmed my heart and fixed it in my mind. The heading was: "A Good Year and a Goodly Land."

It was then coincidentally that liberalism, in any semblance to its modern meaning, had its birth in South Carolina, NG Gonzales fathered it. His brave, able, determined fight against child labor alienated some of his best business and personal friends.

They were splendid men. They had done and were doing a great work. And NG Gonzales appreciated, better perhaps than any other man in South Carolina at that time, the value of the service they were rendering. But he understood, what they did not, that the humanitarianism of the plantation system, however splendid, would not suffice in an industrial system.

His insistent demand for a definite legislative check upon the exploitation of the labor of children in the cotton mills shocked the industrialists and disturbed all who were affiliated with them in interest. They believed in all honesty that their rights as employers were being invaded, that what Mr. Gonzales was preaching was pernicious Socialism-Paternalism was the word then used- and that the prosperity of industry in South Carolina was about to be undermined.

Mind and Conscience Improve

The mind and the conscience of South Carolina have come up markedly since 1903 when the first child labor law was enacted.

It was not until the century was 12 years old that the democratic principle found a leader in America the nation would accept; and this leader won his way to power then only because the opposition split, more than half of those who had been identified with the forces of privilege being appalled by lengths to which the privileged had gone in their pillaging.

The leader who then entered the White House had spent some part of his boyhood in this community. It was before your association, I think that he first delivered here in Columbia, his challenge to the financial autocrats whose serfs the people of America had become. It was that challenge, translated into legislation in the Federal Reserve Act, which opened the springs of credit to the people of the nation.

Woodrow Wilson's Reforms

What the great and wise reforms sponsored by Woodrow Wilson would have achieved for South Carolina and America must be left to conjecture; for his service as president was over, before he had been two years in the White House, the World War came.

In that war when eventually we were swept into it, the soldiers from South Carolina added a new luster to the escutcheon of their state. They won far more congressional medals of honor in proportion to population than did the soldiers from any other state. Their record on the fields of France filled all their fellow South Carolinians to bursting with pride. It thrills us yet.

And in that was South Carolina for the first time since 1860 tasted a prosperity in which the entire state shared generously. There was nothing that was not salable. The price of cotton and the price of tobacco rose to dizzying heights. Manufacturing plants ran night and day. Many families which had never owned an automobile or a horse and buggy bought as many as three or four automobiles, one for the husband, one for the wife, and one for the children. Negroes had their front teeth plugged with gold. Almost every county seat boasted a crop of men who were rated, not as millionaires, but as being worth a hundred thousand or more.

It was not to last. Few of us even sensed then what was really happening; that it was the war purchases of the Allies, financed first by their own credit until that was exhausted and then our generous loans, that sent prices skyrocketing.

Post War Slump

We were dazed when the slump came at the end of the war; did not understand that such a slump was inevitable, when the money we had loaned the Allies had been used up; watched helplessly in the cruel deflation of 1920 and 1921 as the imaginary values we had pit upon our lands and other possessions shot bottomwards and banks toppled over until in some countries not a bank was left.

The experience we went through then should have taught us the profound truth that whatever our spirit, whatever our history, whatever our traditions, we are today, economically, socially, only part of a larger whole; our fortunes, our very bread and butter, determined not by our own energies alone but far more largely by what is done in the nation and in the world at large.

We did not learn this lesson. Before the decade was out the price of cotton had risen again and we could not see that this had come about principally because of the huge loans which were being made to other countries, particularly Germany, from the United States and Great Britain.

Our loans abroad, private loans these were, but turning into billions, stopped and the price of cotton went down again. We floundered, did not perceive the relationship between cause and effect, were not prepared for the financial crash when it came, did not foresee the collapse of Germany and of post-war "peace" structure which had been erected in Europe to keep Germany in leash.

Woodrow Wilson's Warning

Why this last at least was not obvious to South Carolinians, of all people, is a mystery. With their own memories of Reconstruction, or filled with t recollection of the tales their mothers and fathers had told them, they should have understood, whether others did so or not, what was due to happen to the Treaty of Versailles; further, dependent as South Carolina was on cotton as a money crop, South Carolinians, one would think, should have appreciated that the pauperization of Germany meant robbing us of a market which, before 1914, was second only to Great Britain-and a close second—in its purchases of American cotton.

Woodrow Wilson in one of his last messages to Congress in one of the ablest state papers ever written, pointed out with amazing clarity the changes that had occurred in America's world position, and with even amazing foresight urged only the policies that would have served our interests in the light of all that had happened. His message fell on deaf ears.

In National Prayer

I am trying in what I am saying to suggest how definitely, how inescapable, South Carolina is tied into the national and international picture economically. I do not wish to abuse your hospitality or try your patience; and so, passing over the period of the present depression, I hurry to a conclusion.

Of the grinding depression that followed the bursting in 1929 of the bubble of a spurious prosperity I shall say only this. It demonstrated conclusively that the American system, in which Americans had been taught to take blinding pride, was in fact dangerously imperfect in its Constitution,

Millions of individuals, thousands of businessmen, realized suddenly that their destinies, were not, as they had fondly believed, in their own hands.

The fact the consequences of national and international policies might destroy quickly the opportunities of great numbers of people even to make a living was brought home cruelly to every community.

No one was able to question in the banking crisis that banking was in a measure never previously acknowledged a concern of government.

No one was able to question then that the functioning of the economic system of the social system of the nation is a concern of the national government.

Turn to Washington

The instinct which in 1932 and 1933 caused every part of the nation, and every element of the population, to turn to Washington for guidance as well as for succor was irrepressible.

That grave dangers are involved in the swift and sweeping centralization of power that has followed I have already freely acknowledged. The dangers take varied forms. It is extremely doubtful if Washington can lay down rules and regulations that will work equally well in all parts of a country as vast as ours and as complex in its civilization as ours.

There is appalling hazard that "in wrong hands" the vast new machinery which has been built up might, as the leader in its construction himself has warned, be used to the great injury of many people and whole areas.

The possibility that the morale of large sections of our population may be sapped by the unwise distribution of relief is not to be minimized.

On the other hand, Mr. President, in addition to all the other factors making for centralization upon which I have hurriedly touched, there had been two other supremely important developments. One was that in the year in which Woodrow Wilson became President the federal income tax amendment was ratified. That gave the government at Washington powers which the states individually could no longer even approximate.

It was the federal income tax which made possible the gigantic financing of the World War. It was the ability of Uncle Sam to reach out his long arm over state lines and expand his credit by tapping the sources of wealth wherever they existed that in the crisis of depression rendered irresistible the pressure for federal aid, many communities and many states being for immediate and all practical purposes practically bankrupt.

All Countries Nationalistic

The other development was that, launched in and by the World War, and given steadily increasing impetus by the economic conditions that followed, and especially so by the passage of the Hoover-Grundy prohibitive tariff law, every other important country in the world became more and more intensely nationalistic.

The pressure of this situation became for us the pressure of a vise.

We were faced when we looked abroad by highly organized nations in every direction.

By Soviet Russia, dynamic tyrannical, its people as well as its leaders consumed by the feverish ambition to carve out for themselves a planned civilization.

By Italy, ruled by a brilliant dictator, as dynamic as Soviet Russia, scheming desperately for a place in the sun.

By Japan, led by daring adventurers, seizing her opportunity to overlord the Orient.

By Germany, galvanized by despair into despotism of savage determination.

By France, animated to the core by a stubborn and bitter and relentless fatalism and fear.

By Great Britain, heavily weighted by debt, and foundations of her wealth sapped, forced reluctantly to turn here back upon the policies which had been instrumental in the creatin of what wealth, forced to the acceptance of a managed economy.

Sustained as we were by no great ambition or purpose or hope, except the hope of better times and of again being able to make money, how could we, I ask you, have stood the strain of this situation under a continued policy of drift? The demand that went up for a vigorous, aggressive, determined leadership from Washington, for the assertion by the federal government of all its latent powers, was insistent. It was nation-wide.

Duty Upon Citizenry

That is how we have arrived at the position in which we find ourselves today. Blind resentment of what has happened will serve no useful purpose. Blind satisfaction with what has been accomplished will be criminal folly. The new order has laid its definite responsibilities upon the entire citizenship regardless of what they think of it.

It is a tragedy that in the face of the existing situation organized conservation in the United States has almost completely collapsed. The country urgently needs a strong well organized, competently led and competently directed conservative party.

Such a party could not prosper in America today unless its leadership were alive to realities, unless it were a leadership which like that of the Conservative party of England in the days of Disraeli and the other great Conservative leaders could prove itself capable of rising brilliantly to the occasion.

It is comparably disturbing on the other hand, gravely disturbing that the faith of those who have accepted the new order is centered so positively, not in any program that has been proposed, but in a single leader. The question of what would happen to the new order without the inspiration of the man who is now President will not down. It challenges you especially.

It challenges you because in spite of the improvement that has been achieved in South Carolina the gains do not yet guarantee a continued prosperity. The textile industry is flourishing and the $5,000,000 kraft paper enterprise at Charleston and the $8,000,000 like enterprise at Georgetown are developments rich with promise. Retail sales in South Carolina showed an increase of about $60,000,000 in 1935 over 1933 and while the figures are not yet available, we can be sure that there was a gratifying further increase in 1936.

But the productive income of manufactures in South Carolina is less than 1 percent that of the nation. The cash receipts from the sale of all the principal farm products of the state in 1936 was less than the cotton crop alone used to bring. The spendable income per capita of South Carolina is less than a third that of New York and even below that of most of the states of the South.

Duty of Newspapers

To maintain the prosperity of the newspapers of South Carolina, and to increase that prosperity, it is imperative that the newspapers work, as I know, of course, that they have done and will do, to buttress and better the earning power of the people of South Carolina-all elements of the population.

The increment of wealth in South Carolina was very rapid in the coastal region at one time, but that was long ago. The increment of wealth in this state from productive income has been very slow in the past three quarters of a century; and the drain upon that increment has been heavy, wholly apart from government and taxes and the new public services that have been created. It may be permitted to wonder whether the money sent out of the state annually in recent years to Michigan and to the oil fields of Texas has not exceeded the net profits from all activities within the state.

There is talk now of a plan under which the evils of farm tenancy can be checked and perhaps in large measure eliminated. You and I know that this is an urgent need. We know that the most serious thing that has happened in South Carolina in the past 50 years has been the decline in the dignity and prosperity of country life. Hard pressed as the farmers of this state were in the 80s and 90s, low as were the prices they got, rural life then, and life in the small towns, had qualities which dignified it; and these qualities have in good part been lost.

Is it not possible to repair much of the damage that has been done? The reparation cannot be accomplished from Washington alone. It can be achieved only if men like yourselves, men who know your countryside and its people, guide the reparation. It will take longer time to get things on a better basis than it did for the havoc that has been wrought to make itself as sadly apparent. No get-well-quick remedy will succeed. It might make things worse.

On Social Security

So as to social security. It is established that this is a field in which government both the national government and the state government must operate in future. But the whole proposition is bewildering in its complexity. If the hopes that have been aroused are not to be cruelly disappointed, then men like yourselves must put your minds upon this situation. Must help whip whatever is one into practical shape. And what is true in this matter is true in almost every other matter-specially relief.

The obligations of this time are peculiarly great on you. South Carolina is no made state. From the first it has been more than a mere organization. From this little commonwealth streams of influence have poured forth for at least two centuries. You are the heirs of a past which will not let you rest.

With steadfast confidence, therefore, in you and your heritage, I call upon you now, not to be content with knowing how to read the sky, with being able to say when a cloud rises in the West, "There cometh a shower." Or when the south wind blows, "There will be heat." But with all diligence, that you make it your supreme endeavor to "discern this time."

The ability to do this is today, when all is said and done, and undoubtedly, the supreme need of every patriotic journalist in America.

Columbia 1937